IMAGES
of America

AUBURN

On the Cover: Japanese American laborers made up a significant portion of the agricultural workforce in Auburn in the first half of the 1900s. Discriminatory land laws made it impossible for these workers to purchase their own land, so many families of Japanese descent leased farmland or worked as laborers on other residents' farms. These workers, representing four different families, are harvesting strawberries around 1917. (Courtesy of the White River Valley Museum.)

IMAGES
of America

AUBURN

Hilary Pittenger

ARCADIA
PUBLISHING

ISBN 978-1-4671-3111-7

Published by Arcadia Publishing
Charleston, South Carolina

Printed in the United States of America

Library of Congress Control Number: 2013945121

For all general information, please contact Arcadia Publishing:
Telephone 843-853-2070
Fax 843-853-0044
E-mail sales@arcadiapublishing.com
For customer service and orders:
Toll-Free 1-888-313-2665

Visit us on the Internet at www.arcadiapublishing.com

Dedicated to my parents, Mark and Maureen—
my first and best history teachers

Contents

ACKNOWLEDGMENTS

A truly astronomical amount of thanks is owed to the White River Valley Museum, its staff, and its volunteers for the contributions they have made to the preservation of the history of Auburn. Without their extensive photographic collection, this book would not be possible. Special thanks go to museum director Patricia Cosgrove for encouraging me in this project and to volunteer David Payn for his many long hours of work scanning and cataloging the museum's photographic collection in order to make it available for browsing online. I have had the pleasure of working with these people and this collection in various capacities for eight years, and I have never ceased to be astonished at the amount of knowledge and experience contained in this community and this institution.

Unless otherwise noted, all of the images appearing in this book are courtesy of the collection of the White River Valley Museum.

Thanks go to my editor, Rebecca Coffey, and to local historians Josephine Emmons Vine, Mildred Tanner Andrews, Roberta Morley, and Stan Flewelling. Without their pioneering work researching and preserving the stories of Auburn, most of the facets of Auburn's history would shine less brightly. Dr. Michelle Marshman, my most influential history professor, is significantly to blame for my pursuit of history as a profession and for my introduction to the White River Valley Museum and so deserves an equally significant amount of thanks for making this book possible.

Finally, thanks must go to my family and my church for supporting me, my friends for bearing with me, and my husband, Lane Leathers, for making me many dinners while I was busy writing. I could not operate in this world without any of you, much less write a book. Thank you from the bottom of my very grateful heart.

INTRODUCTION

On the surface, Auburn has a history very similar to other small cities in the Pacific Northwest: although already inhabited by Native Americans, white immigrants from Europe and the East Coast began settling in the region in the 1850s. Land was timbered, farmed, and ultimately built upon by subsequent waves of immigrants from every corner of the world. Wagon roads and railroads were built and then replaced by paved roads and highways. People had families, ran businesses, and formed organizations for the betterment of their community. It is the details of each of these stages and how the city has persevered through both the fat and lean times that make Auburn unique among other cities in the southern Puget Sound region.

The geography and natural resources surrounding Auburn had a profound impact on the development of the city. Auburn is situated on the floor of a large river valley that was shaped by two meandering rivers: the White and the Green. The White River, originating from glaciers on Mount Rainier, flows northwest until it reaches Auburn, while the Green River flows west from the Cascade Mountains. A third river, the Stuck, flowed through the southern portion of the river valley and fed into the Puyallup River to the south. All three rivers were highly susceptible to seasonal flooding and often changed their courses due to the buildup of debris from previous flooding.

The White River spent most of its life flowing through the center of the river valley to join up with the Green River, which, in turn, fed into the Duwamish Watershed in Seattle. A catastrophic flood in 1906 caused the White River to break over the barrier between itself and the Stuck River, completely overtaking the Stuck's channel and drying up the northern riverbed where the White had formerly connected to the Green River. This is the same river arrangement that can be found in the valley today. The rivers and ecosystems they fed provided a rich set of resources for the Native Americans who lived in the valley for thousands of years. Salmon made massive annual migrations up the rivers, providing one of the main dietary staples for humans in the valley and returning nutrients to the forests surrounding the river systems. Dense old-growth forests comprised largely of western red cedar, western hemlock, and Douglas fir trees provided shade and protection for dozens of species of edible berries, fern shoots, and game, including deer, elk, and fowl. Edible roots and bulbs, especially camas, were harvested from prairie-like grassland clearings, which were usually purposefully created by humans to ensure a regular supply of these sun-loving plants. The ocean was never far away, and shellfish were harvested annually throughout the Puget Sound region.

Now known as the Muckleshoot Indian Tribe, the original inhabitants of the White and Green River Valleys were Whulshootseed-speaking members of a larger cultural group called the Southern Coast Salish. Unlike some Native American groups from other regions of North America, the Coast Salish did not identify themselves as a unified cultural group with starkly defined tribal, clan, and family groups. Instead, they identified themselves with extended family groups who lived and traveled together. Families lived seminomadic lives, moving between seasonal settlements that were returned to year after year. Settlements were usually along rivers and other navigable waterways since the primary mode of transportation through the wooded valley was by canoe.

The forests provided other resources as well, namely cedar wood and bark. The trunks, branches, and bark of the western red cedar were all utilized, providing planks for the building of longhouses, logs for carving canoes, withes for making baskets and pieces of art, and strips of soft bark for making clothing. Cedar's natural resistance to water, rot, and insect damage made it an ideal material for each of these purposes.

The first nonnative visitors to the White and Green River Valleys were British fur trappers following beavers and other valuable pelt animals upriver. Native people and the trappers were friendly with each other, and the few forts and trading posts established in the area were open to white trappers and native traders alike.

When the Oregon Territory, which included modern-day Washington State, came under the jurisdiction of the United States in 1848, the US Army began to move into the region and build encampments. The fort that oversaw the White River Valley region was Fort Steilacoom, built in 1849. The US government, unlike the British fur traders, had an explicit policy of encouraging the settlement of white immigrants in an effort to push native peoples off of their lands. This caused a great deal of friction between whites and natives, and violent clashes became the norm in the early 1850s. These skirmishes culminated in a conflict now known as the Puget Sound Treaty Wars, or simply the Puget Sound War, in 1856.

An event often cited as the beginning of the conflict took place in the White River Valley. In October 1855, nine white settlers were killed by a group of Native Americans. No record of any native deaths was kept. Aside from the political and racial ramifications of this violent encounter, the skirmish was seen as especially heinous due to the death of white children. A native man named Wiletchtid (nicknamed "Indian Tom" by the settlers) rescued three children after the fighting was over and smuggled them by canoe to relatives living in Seattle. A fourth child was held hostage for six months before being released to his family. This was quickly labeled the White River Massacre, and the story was retold and romanticized for generations after the event.

Because the native peoples of the White and Green River Valleys were not a bureaucratically united group with a single name or leader who could speak for them, they were lumped together under the assigned name Muckleshoot and made a single tribe when treaties were written in the 1850s designating reservations for native peoples. The reservation system, along with the US Homestead Act of 1862, paved the way for significant, unopposed white settlement in the White and Green River Valleys.

New settlers were not as pleased with the natural bounty of the valley's forests as native peoples were. Settlers struggled to clear tracts of land to create farms. Native shrubs that had evolved to take advantage of every small bit of sunlight available grew out of control in these new clearings, frustrating farmers, who viewed them as nuisance weeds that choked out struggling crops. Rainfall only encouraged more growth of these native plants. Most early farms in the region had a stark appearance, with a log cabin or timber house positioned in the center of a very flat, completely deforested section of land planted with food crops or pastures for livestock.

White settlers in the area first named their village White River, after the river that served as their main mode of transportation. When a town was first platted in 1886, it was not named White River but Slaughter, after Lt. William Slaughter, an officer slain in the Puget Sound Treaty Wars. Slaughter, for obvious reasons, was not a name that inspired pleasant images for a generation of settlers raised on stories of the White River Massacre. For this reason, it was often mistakenly assumed that Slaughter was named after the massacre itself, rather than for a soldier's surname. The name was retained when the town was incorporated in 1891, but it was changed to Auburn in 1893 in an effort to sound more scenic and business-friendly.

Geography and resources continued to impact Auburn's development as the 20th century approached. The flat river valley was an ideal path for railroads, and it would eventually play host to four different railway lines. Coal in the foothills of the Cascade Mountains was a powerful draw for railroads and other businesses, and the coal-mining industry fueled the settlement and development of much of the surrounding southern Puget Sound area. Clay deposits from the river valleys fueled a significant ceramics and terra-cotta industry. A temperate climate and plentiful rainfall made Auburn a productive agricultural region, first with hops and later with dairying, berries, lettuce, and beans.

Agriculture led to immigration, as peoples from around the globe came to Auburn to work as laborers, railroad workers, and eventually, to own farms themselves. The most prominent ethnic groups to settle in Auburn were from Ireland, Scandinavia, Italy, Japan, and the Philippines, but smaller communities from Greece, Bulgaria, and countless other regions also made their mark on the city. In almost every case, previous settlers expressed a racial or religious prejudice against new groups of immigrants, only to see the tensions fade within a generation as residents lived, worked, attended school, and generally built a community together.

The following chapters will show glimpses of the people, places, and events that shaped the city of Auburn from its earliest settlement through the beginning of the 21st century. Unfortunately, the nature of historic photography causes some incidental bias in the information presented. Photographs in the 1800s were difficult to take and required specialized equipment and training to process. Working-class people and people of color were often not photographed at all or only photographed as part of a labor force rather than as individuals. This can make it appear as though upper-class white people were the sole inhabitants of early Auburn, but nothing could be further from the truth. Where possible, notations have been made in the captions to give a more accurate description of the racial and economic realities of historic Auburn.

Photographs in the 1900s, though more prolific thanks to the invention of the portable hobby camera, suffer from similar deficiencies in the diversity of their human subjects. People of color in Auburn tended to be part of working-class families who were more transient due to the nature of their professions. This means that when and if photographs were taken of members of these families, the photographs tended to travel with their families when they moved away from Auburn, rather than staying with families who could pass them on to libraries and historical repositories. Photographs can tell a powerful story, but it must be remembered that they are only one slice of the historical record and must be taken in the context of other fields of research. A selected bibliography of resources used in researching this publication can be found at the back of this book, and they are a good starting place for any researcher hoping to dive into the history of the Auburn area.

Modern Auburn has been shaped by forces ranging from the geological to the political. Let this book take you on a tour of familiar names and places that may have a surprising history.

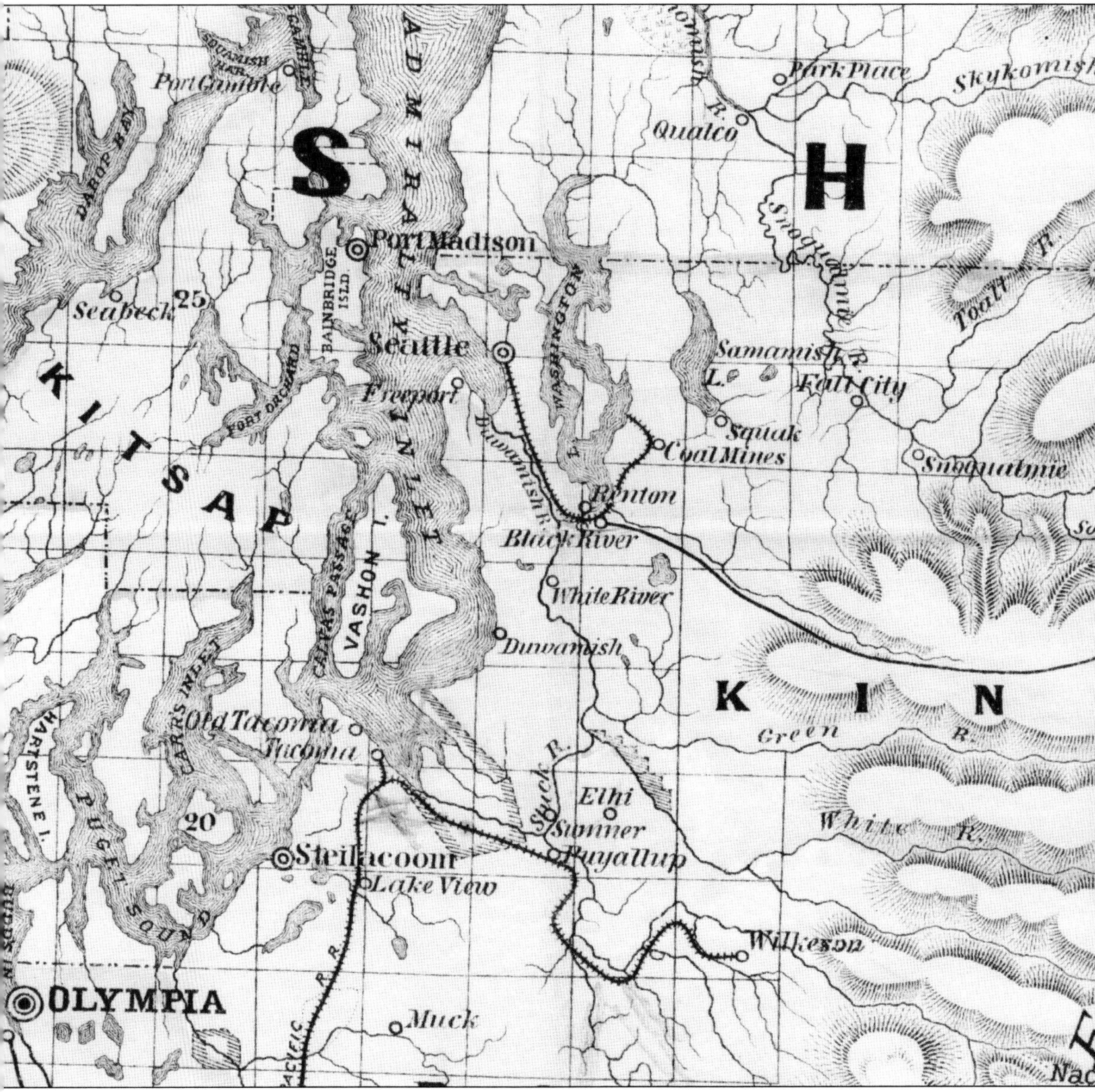

The settlement of White River on this 1878 map marks the spot where Auburn would later be located. Cities on this map are located along waterways, because canoes and steamboats were the most reliable form of transportation around Puget Sound during this time. The White, Green, and Stuck Rivers can be seen in the bottom half of the map, flowing west and north toward the Puget Sound.

One

Ilalko and White River 1850–1885

The area now called Auburn was first inhabited by Native Americans. These first peoples belonged to a group called the Southern Coast Salish, who led a seminomadic life, traveling across the southern Puget Sound region to seasonally fish, hunt elk and deer, and gather berries and shellfish. Extended families had permanent winter homes, berry fields, and fishing spots that they returned to year after year. One of these fishing spots was on the Green River, on the southern border of the present-day city of Auburn. This spot was named Ilalko, and it was the first name given to a settlement in the area.

When immigrants from Europe and the East Coast began to settle in the area in the 1850s, they renamed the region White River after one of the two rivers that ran through the valley. The White River Valley was the first agricultural area to be settled by Europeans in Washington Territory; prior to that, most immigrants lived in port towns like Tacoma, fur trading posts like Fort Nisqually, or farms farther south in the Willamette Valley of Oregon.

Early encounters between white newcomers and Native American residents were sometimes difficult and even violent. The new settlers, promised land by the US government, wanted to set up systems of land ownership like they were used to in their previous homes. The native residents were frustrated that these new immigrants were claiming land for themselves and cutting off native people's access to their traditional campsites, fishing locations, spiritual sites, and other vital natural resources.

The conflict between these two groups escalated, culminating in the Puget Sound Treaty Wars in 1855–1856. Civilians and soldiers on both sides were harmed or killed, and the native peoples, who had once traveled freely in small bands between the Puget Sound and the Cascade Mountains, were forced onto a reservation and collectively renamed the Muckleshoot Tribe, a word meaning "prairie" in their native language, Whulshootseed. White settlers continued pouring into White River, lured by the promise of "free" land and hoping to escape the strife of the brewing Civil War.

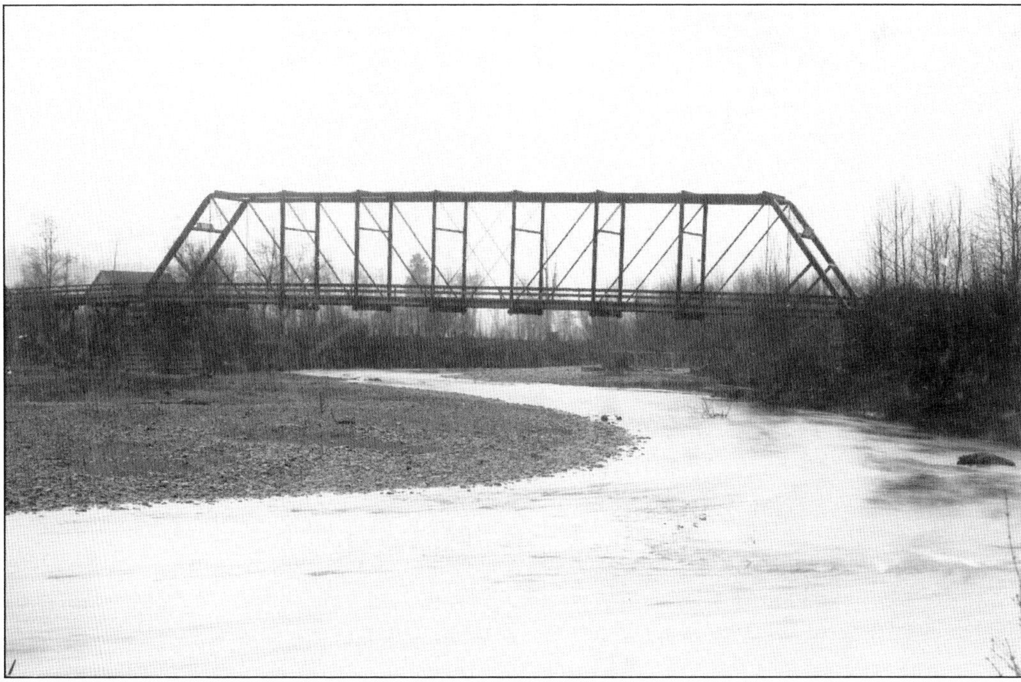

The White River once ran through the center of Auburn. This photograph from around 1900 shows the White River Bridge going over the river. Today, this bridge crossing is the intersection of Main Street and Auburn Way, the latter of which follows the curving path of the now-dry riverbed.

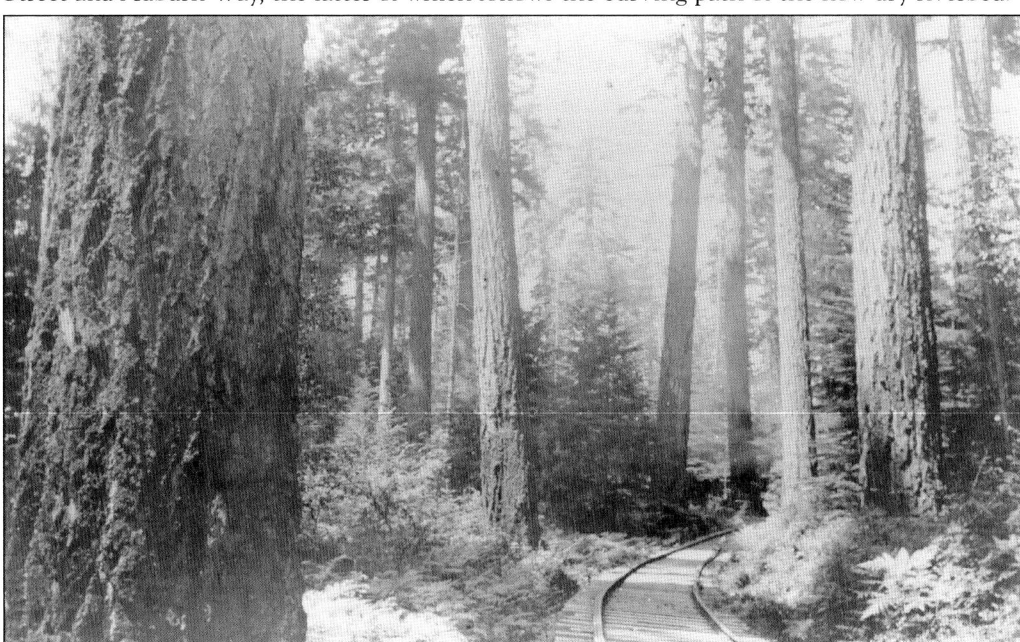

Tall forests of red cedar, Douglas fir, and big leaf maples covered the river valley before white settlers arrived. Huckleberries, salmonberries, and many other varieties of berries grew in the shade of the trees. Sunny clearings in the forest allowed bulb flowers like lilies and camas to spread. Camas root was an important part of the diet of native peoples in the area.

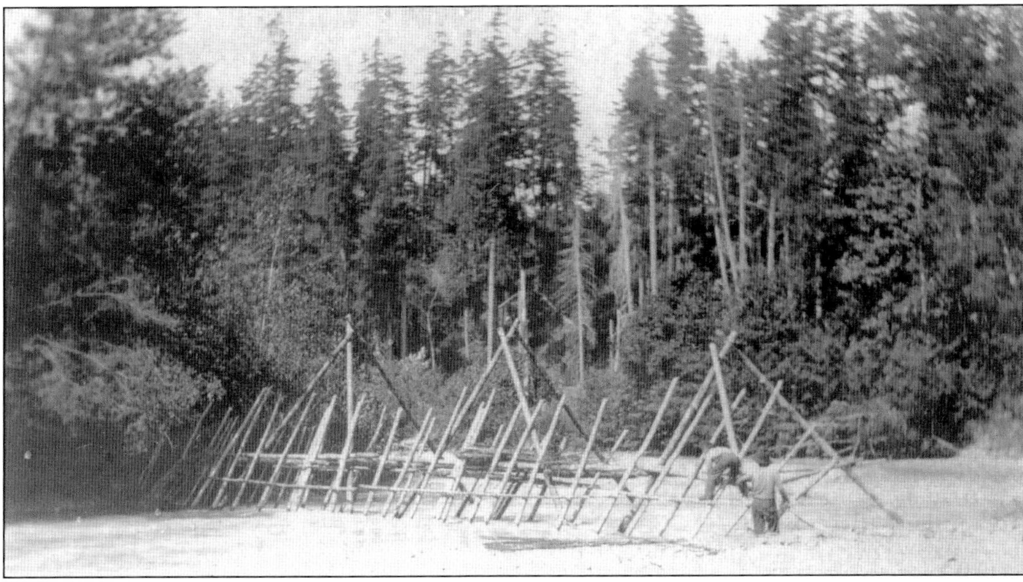

Salmon weirs, like the one being constructed here around 1903, were used to catch large numbers of salmon at once. Weirs acted as temporary "walls," trapping salmon in one section of the river. Fishers could then catch the gathered salmon using nets or spears. This weir was built on the White River, four miles south of what is now downtown Auburn.

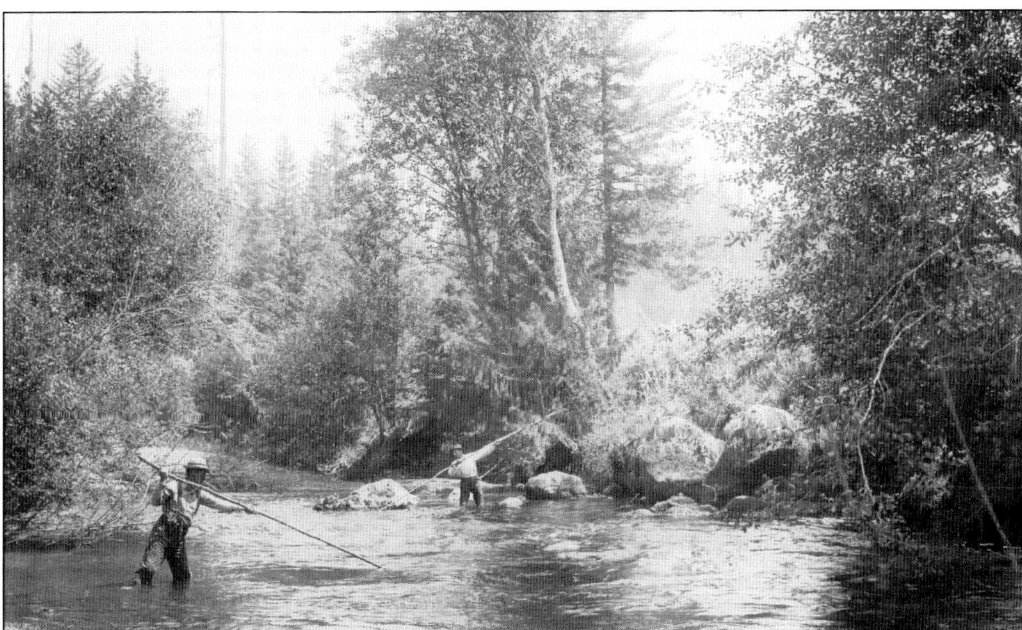

Fishing was vital to the survival of the Southern Coast Salish peoples. Here, Irving Alvord (left) and another nonnative settler demonstrate Native American spearfishing techniques on the Green River around 1900. Native fishers used spears from the shoreline or from canoes. Wood and bone hooks were also used.

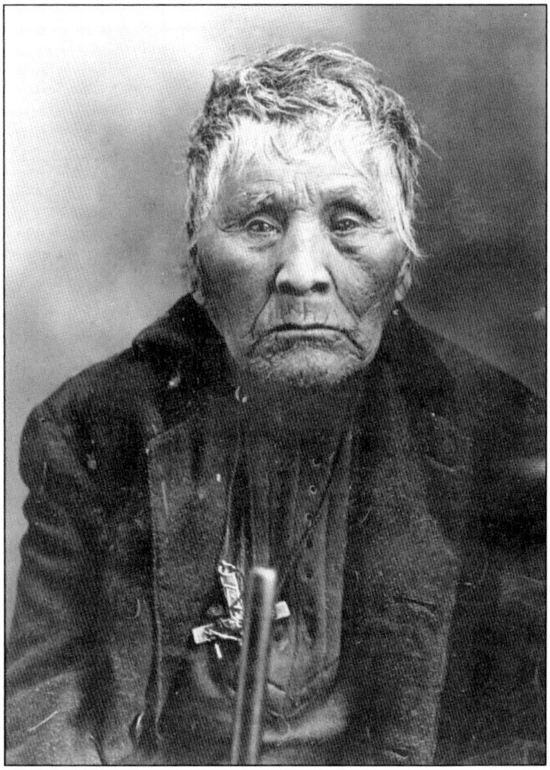

Wiletchtid, known to the early settlers as "Indian Tom," became famous throughout the region when he rescued three children after a violent encounter between Native Americans and a group of white settlers in 1855, now known as the White River Massacre. Wiletchtid took the children to Seattle by canoe under the cover of darkness to protect them.

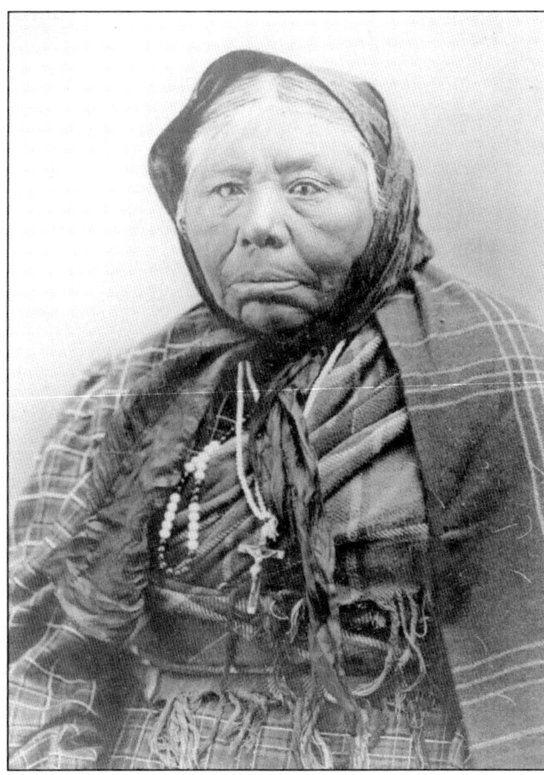

Elisa, the wife of Wiletchtid, was also something of a local celebrity due to her husband's popularity. In this 1914 portrait, she is wearing a crucifix on a beaded necklace, possibly indicating her participation with St. Claire's Mission, also known as the Muckleshoot Indian Church, the first Christian church built in the White River Valley.

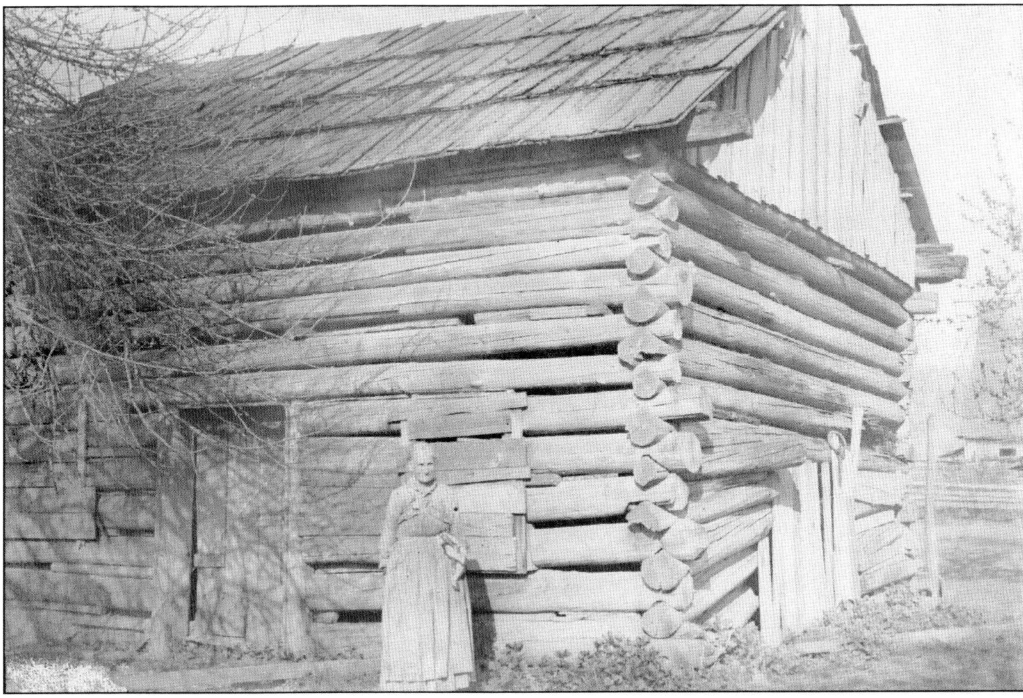

This log cabin was built by John and Rachel Faucett in 1864 on property near the current intersection of Seventh Avenue and Auburn Way in Auburn. Rachel is seen in front of the cabin. The Faucett family moved to the area in 1862 following the passage of the first Homestead Act, which encouraged settlers to claim land in the western territories.

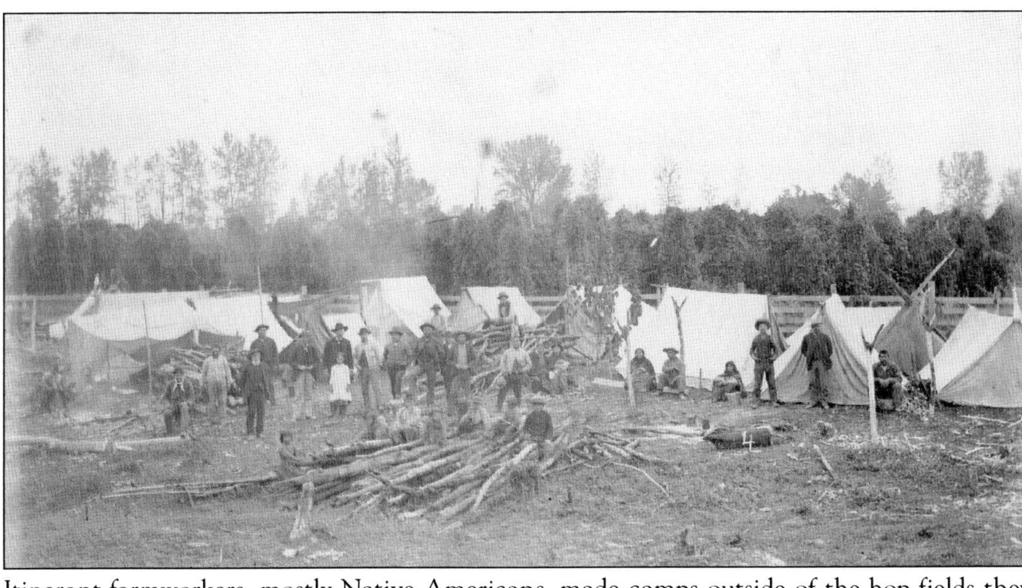

Itinerant farmworkers, mostly Native Americans, made camps outside of the hop fields they were hired to harvest. Without access to their traditional fishing and food-gathering sites, native peoples were forced to find other ways to make a living. This often took the form of farm labor, but also included selling pelts, baskets, and other trade goods.

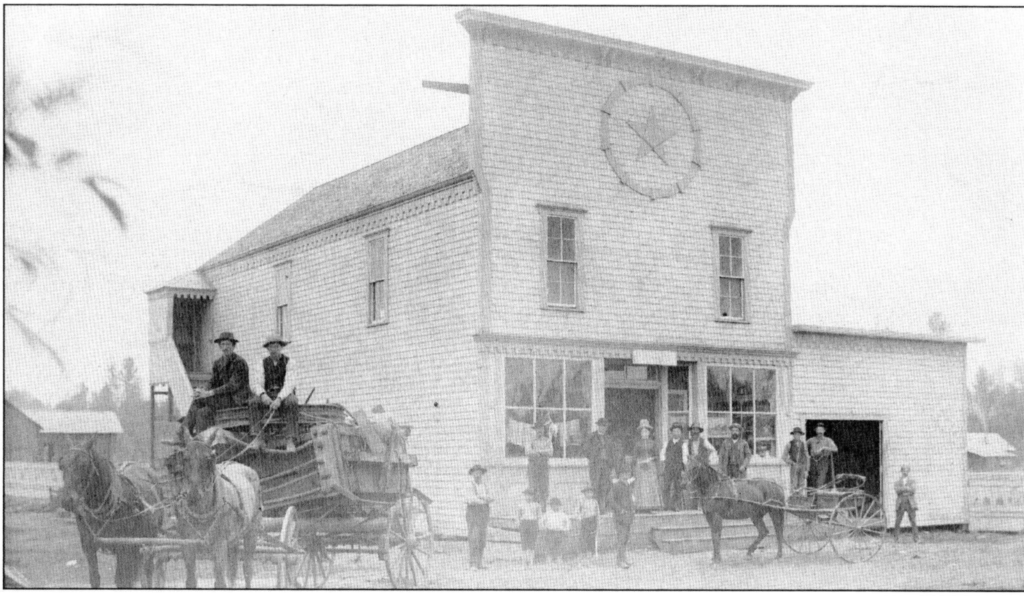

This general store, known as Portway's Store in 1885, was the first commercial building constructed on Main Street. Prior to being purchased by R.C. Portway, the store had been owned and run by Dr. Levi Ballard. The large decorative star on the front of the building was painted blue and was a local landmark.

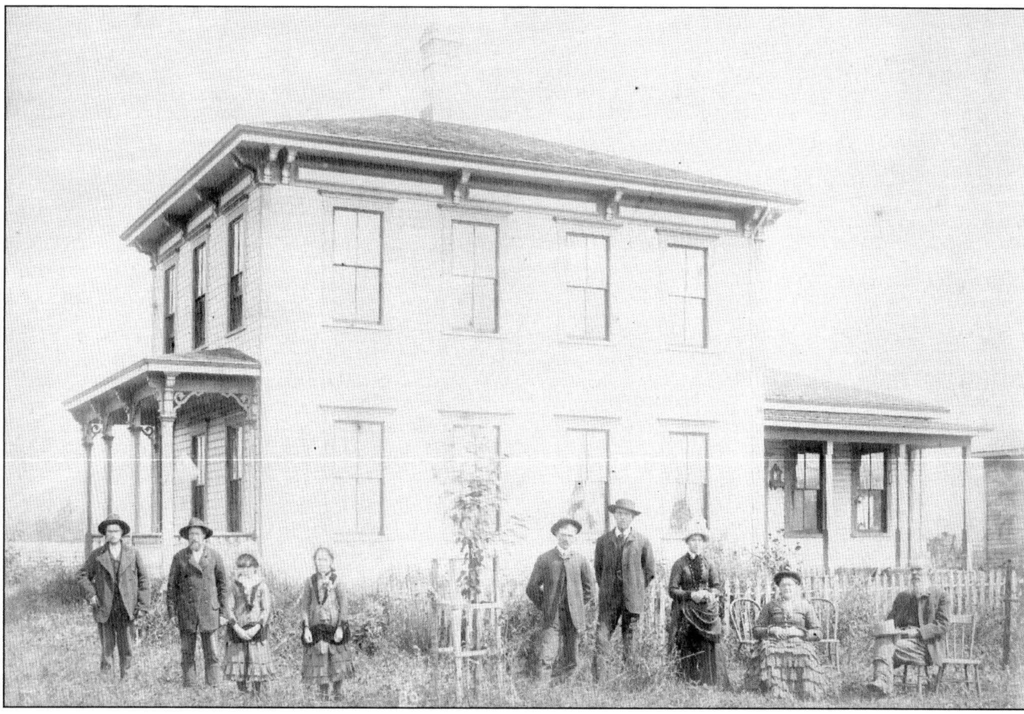

Several small communities besides White River existed in the area that would become Auburn. The village of Christopher, named for farmer Thomas Christopher, was located in what is today north Auburn. The Christopher house, seen here, was built in 1884 and stayed in the family until the 1960s.

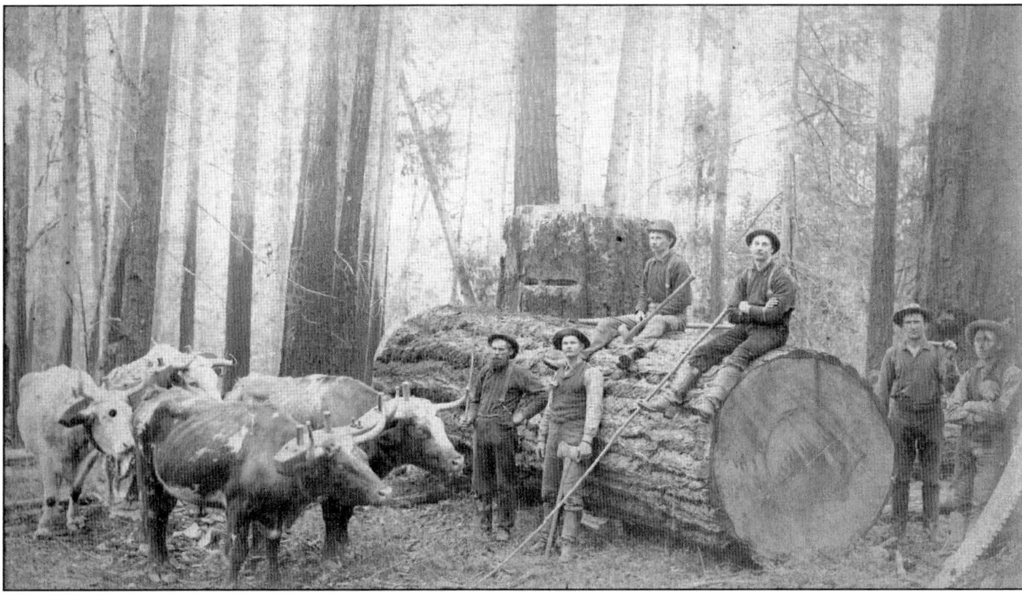

Timber was the first major industry of the new settlers of the White River Valley. Loggers like these men, seen outside Slaughter around 1890, felled huge trees using axes and handsaws. Logs were then pulled away by teams of oxen. Later, steam-powered engines and railroads made transporting the logs easier.

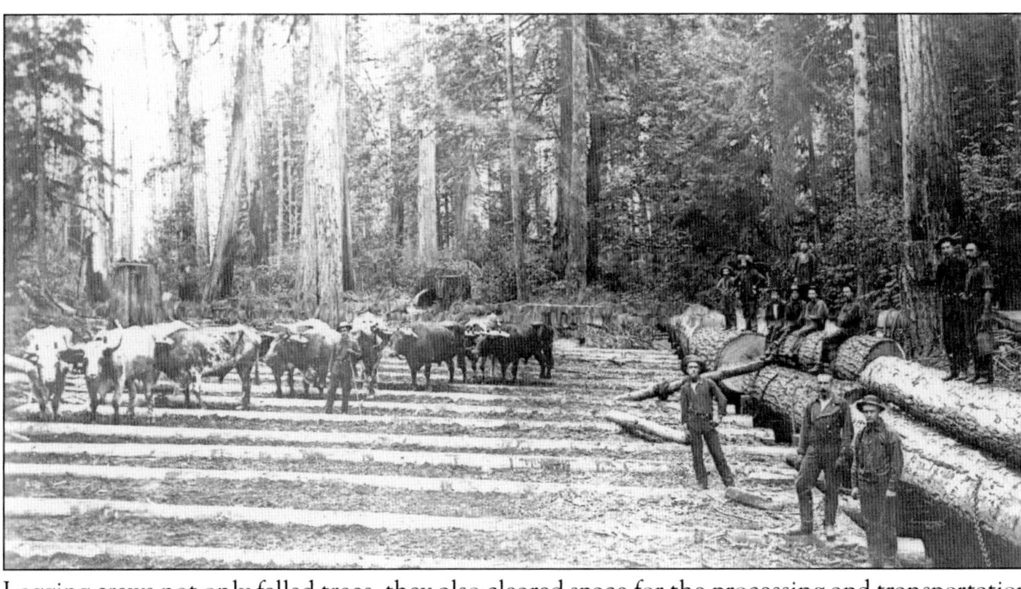

Logging crews not only felled trees, they also cleared space for the processing and transportation of the timber. The logs laid on the ground in this photograph acted as a sort of forest "pavement," keeping the ground from getting too muddy from the constant ox traffic and making it easier to slide logs.

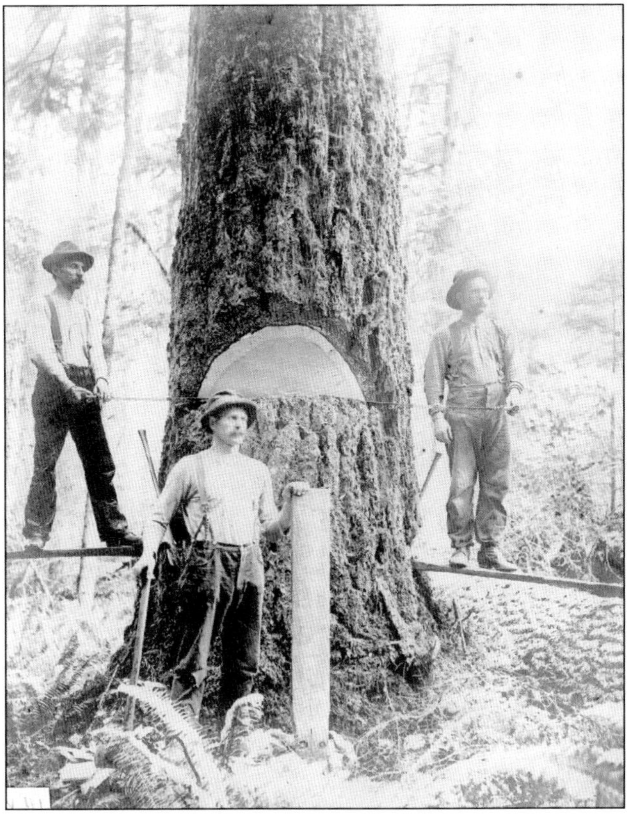

Logging operations were often conducted by large companies that bought the rights to cut large swathes of forest. Men were hired annually or seasonally to work on these areas, living in camps during most of their employment. Women were occasionally hired to act as camp cooks and launderers. It was difficult, backbreaking work, and unfortunately, injuries were common.

The timber supply in the valley allowed several other wood-product businesses to flourish as well. This 1891 shingle mill used wood from the ubiquitous red cedars to make shakes and shingles for building construction. Red cedar was best for this type of application because it was weather resistant and easy to split.

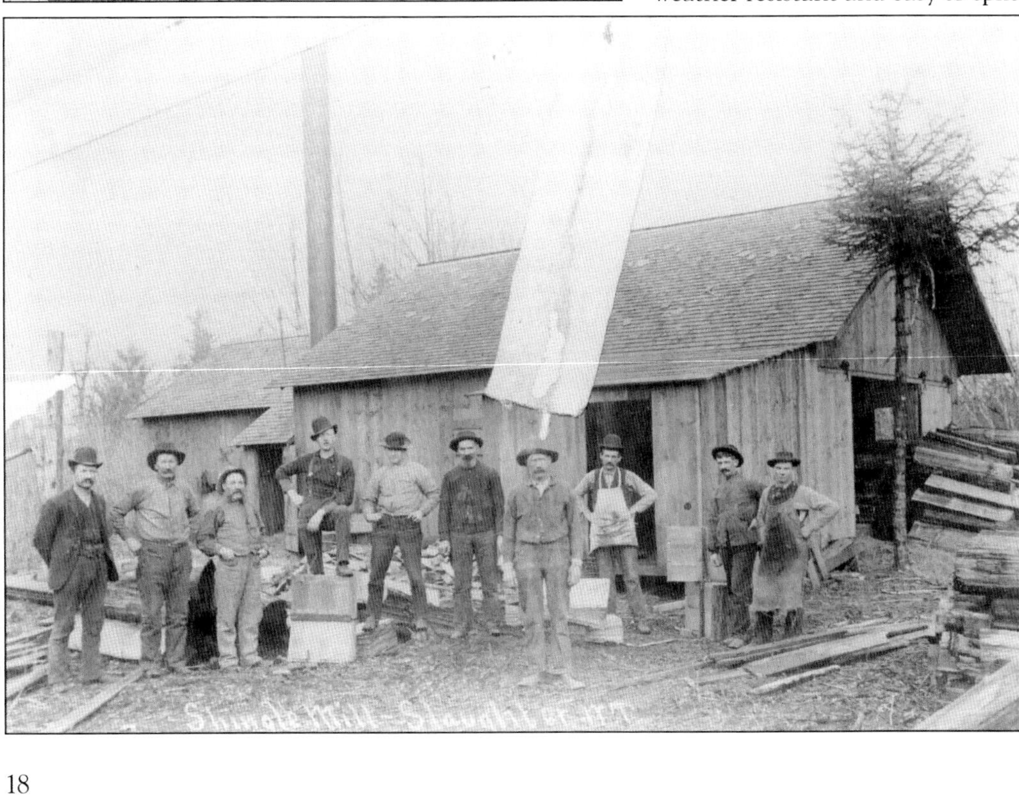

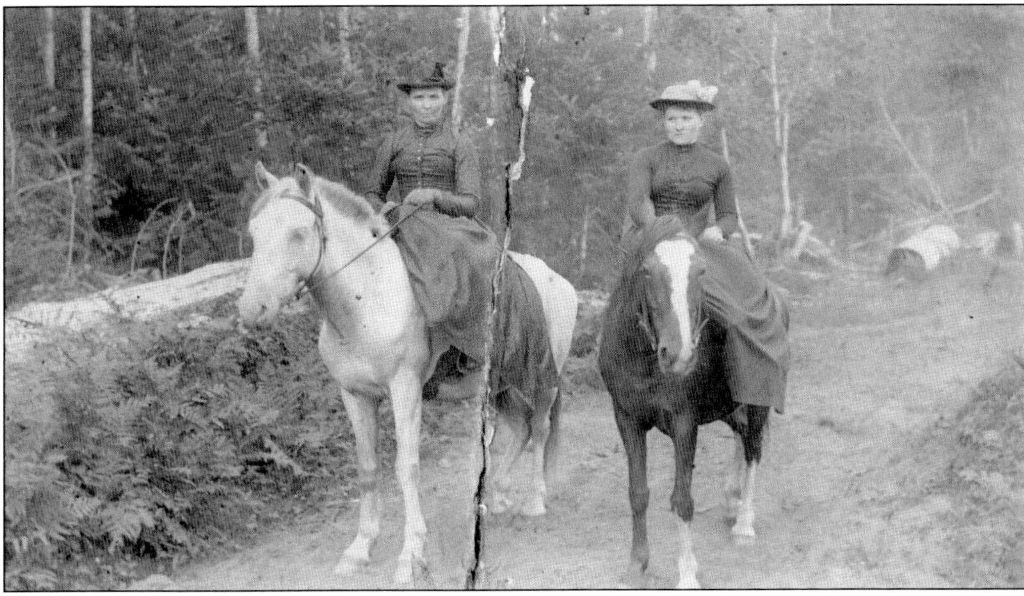

Logging operations provided more than just timber. Most of the first dirt roads in the White River region were made by timber companies, and felled logs were used to "pave" over low, muddy patches. Called corduroy roads, these roads were made of split cedar logs laid side by side. Here, around 1890, these two ladies enjoy a ride along a dirt logging road. Note the recently felled logs along the roadside behind them.

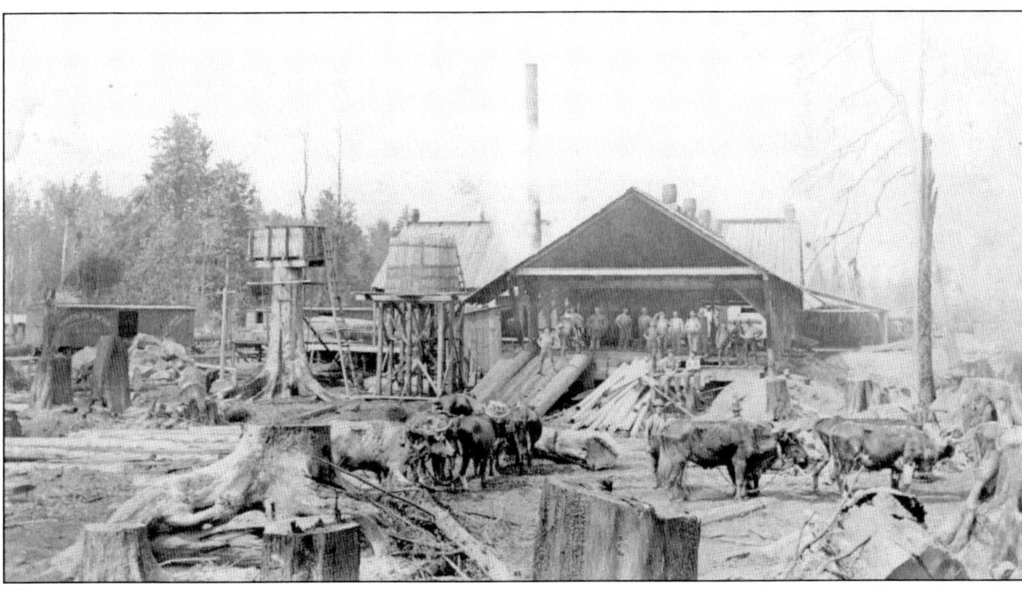

The Slaughter Lumber Mill was well positioned to take advantage of the new railroad line that ran through the valley beginning in 1885. Loggers could bring their raw timber to the mill, have it processed, and then load the new lumber directly onto railcars like the one seen here on the left, bound for Seattle or Tacoma.

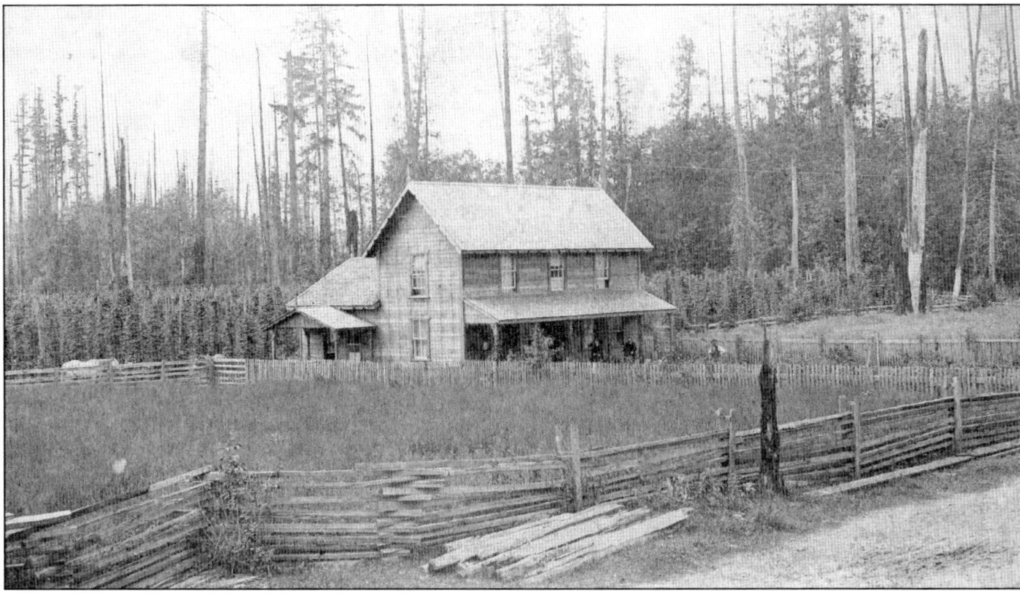

Early settlers had to diversify their crops to make ends meet on their new farms. Seen here around 1888, John Randall's farm on the south side of Slaughter has wheat growing in the foreground and hops growing up along hops poles behind the house. In the background, recently timbered trees show another potential source of income.

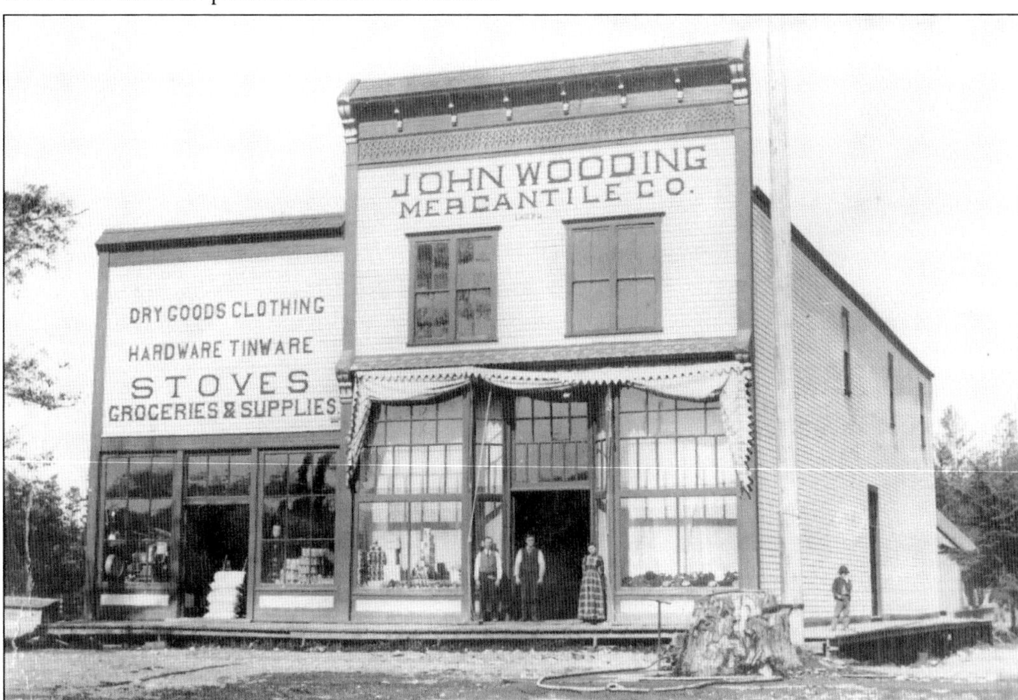

Valley settlers wanted to clear away the dense forest to make room for buildings and farms, like this general goods store seen around 1890. However, they often found themselves frustrated with the fast-growing native vegetation. Red cedar stumps like the one seen here were especially aggravating, as they were too strong to grub out and the wood was naturally resistant to weathering and rot.

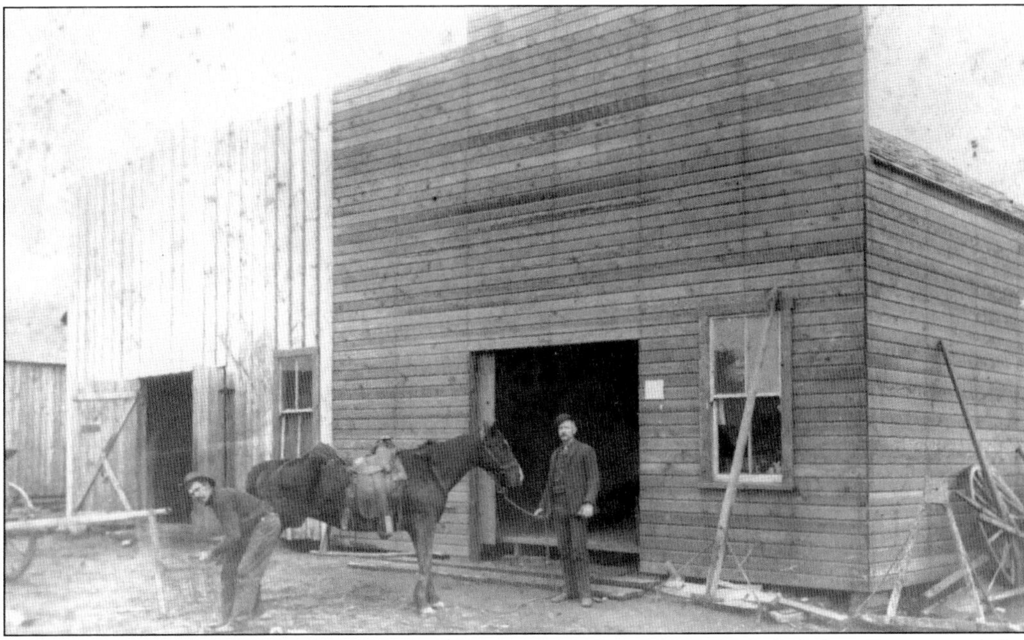

Blacksmiths were vital members of any frontier community. In 1890, C.P. Lacey operated this blacksmith shop in Slaughter, close to the intersection of present-day Main and South Division Streets. He is seen here shoeing a horse, but blacksmiths were also responsible for repairing wagons and ploughs and making metal architectural elements like doorknobs, hinges, and latches.

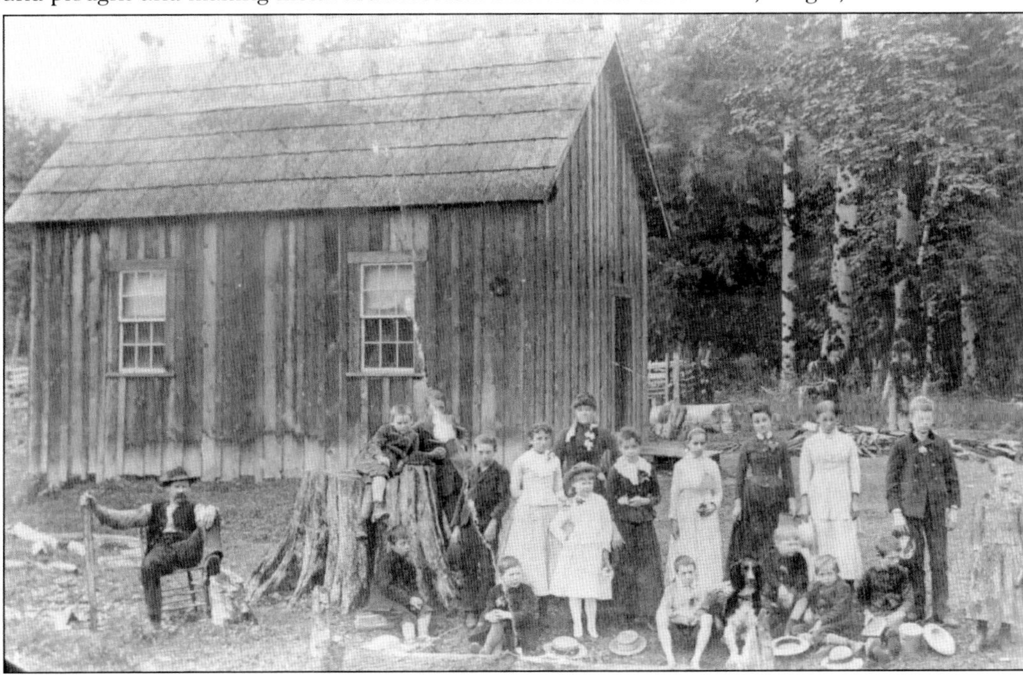

Schools in the White River Valley started as a mix between public and private education. Groups of parents joined together to provide a school building, hire a teacher, and pay for chalkboard slates and textbooks for their students. Teachers were "boarded round" by the students' families, meaning they spent a few weeks at each family's house during the school term.

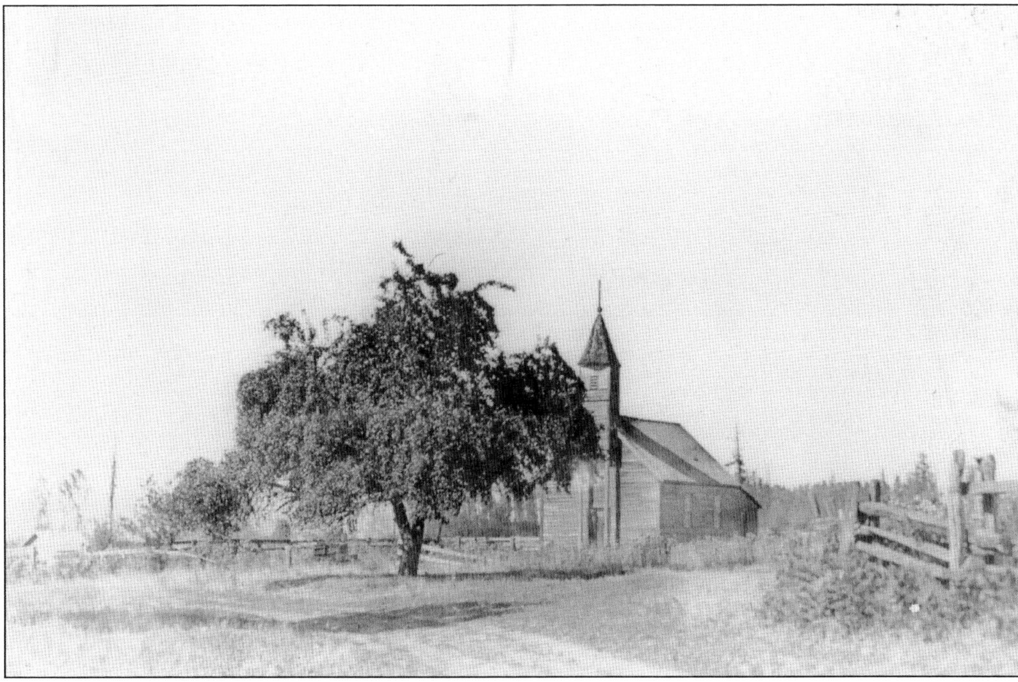

St. Claire Indian Mission, also called the Muckleshoot Indian Church, was built in 1874 by Catholic missionaries working to convert members of the Muckleshoot Tribe. Despite this early work, Catholicism was never the most dominant religious force in the White River area. That distinction was first held by Native American beliefs and then by the Methodist church.

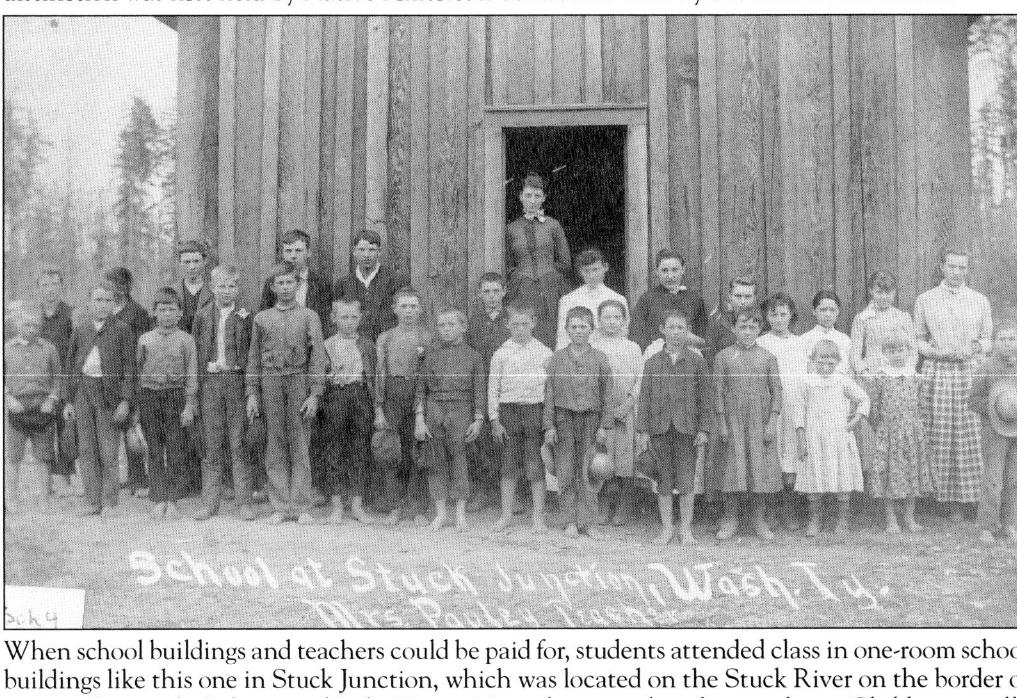

When school buildings and teachers could be paid for, students attended class in one-room school buildings like this one in Stuck Junction, which was located on the Stuck River on the border of present-day south Auburn and Lake Tapps. Note the many barefoot students. Children usually had to walk for many miles to get to their classroom, regardless of the weather.

Two

The Town of Slaughter 1886–1892

The town of Auburn was first platted under the name of Slaughter in 1886 by Levi and Mary Ballard. The Ballards were a prominent White River Valley family who made their fortune through agriculture and astute land deals. They chose the name Slaughter in honor of Lt. William A. Slaughter, an officer in the US military who was killed in the Puget Sound Treaty Wars in 1855. Though Lieutenant Slaughter was not a resident of the Washington Territory, the Ballards and many other White River families held him in very high regard.

Slaughter was formally incorporated as a town in 1891, two years after Washington became a state. Incorporation allowed the town to elect city officials, collect taxes, raise levies, and generally begin the work of independent governance, rather than having to rely on county government for their services. The first paid city positions included a town clerk, a treasurer, and a marshal, who was also the part-time poundmaster and superintendent of streets.

The 1880s and early 1890s were a relative boom time for Slaughter. Hops were in high demand, and the fertile river valley soil was found to be ideal for hops cultivation. While many other types of crops were grown in the area for subsistence purposes, hops were the first major cash crop to be successful in the valley. The money brought in from hops allowed Slaughter to grow, and dozens of new businesses opened their doors to take advantage of the growing population of residents with disposable income as well as the itinerant laborers who enabled the large hops harvests to get to market.

The Panic of 1893 and the introduction of the hops louse, a disastrous hops-destroying pest, in 1892 signaled the end of the hops bubble in the White River Valley. At the same time, Slaughter city officers were making big changes to the city itself. Slaughter was not a very inviting name for a new town hoping to attract new visitors and business, so, in 1893, the town's name was officially changed to Auburn.

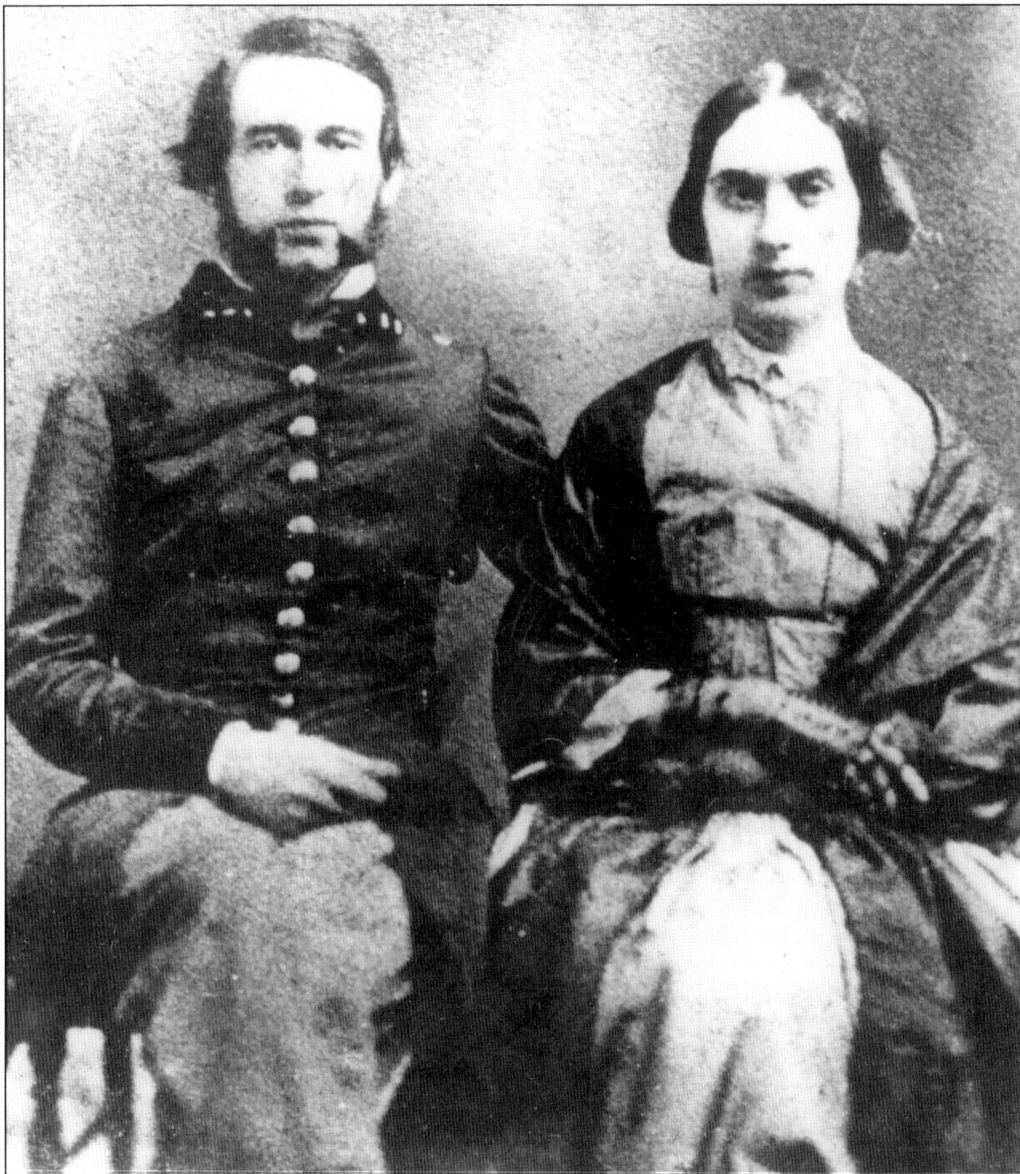

Lt. William Alloway Slaughter, seen here with his wife, Mary, was stationed at Fort Steilacoom in 1853. Slaughter made an impact on many early settlers in the southern Puget Sound, especially the new White River Valley settlers he was tasked with protecting during the Puget Sound Treaty Wars. Beginning in September 1855, Lieutenant Slaughter was sent out on patrol with 40 other soldiers to combat various opposing Native American groups, including the Yakima and members of the Duwamish tribe. He died in a 1855 ambush while camped on Brannan's Prairie, close to present-day Brannan Park along the Green River. Along with having the town that would become Auburn named for him, Slaughter was remembered fondly, with plaques and memorials throughout Auburn, into the 20th century. Kitsap County, situated to the east, was originally named Slaughter County after him. Within months, however, the name was changed to Kitsap, named for one of the opposing Native American leaders in the Treaty Wars. (Courtesy of the Washington State Historical Society.)

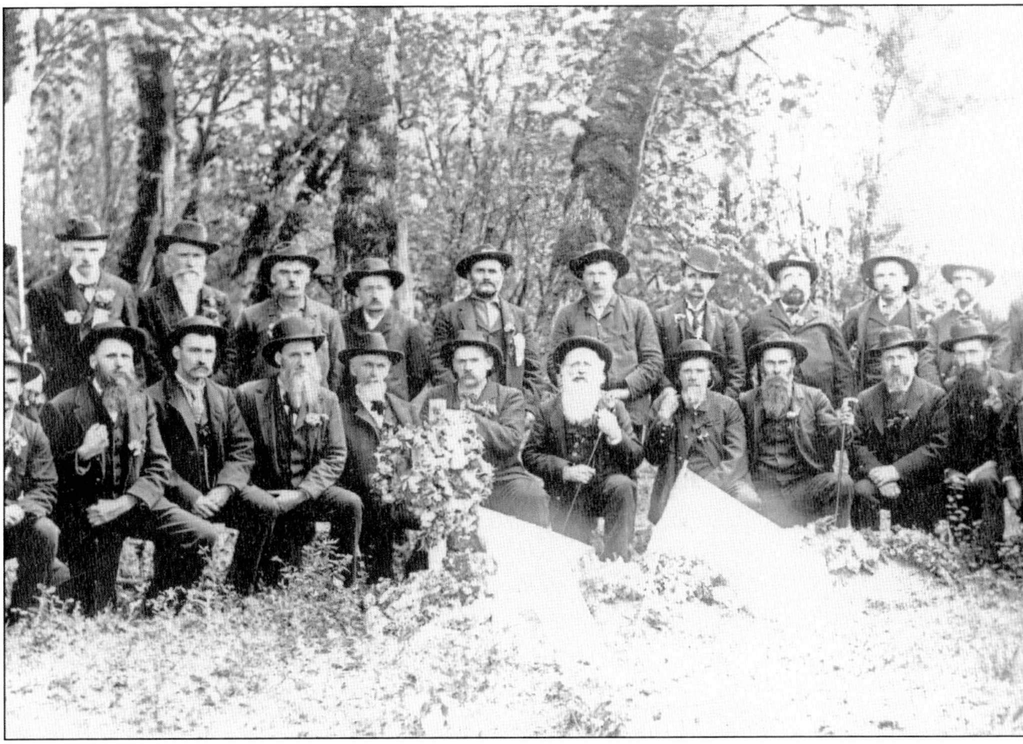

Slaughter was a soldier-friendly town from the very beginning. Many of the earliest settlers in the region had served in—or moved to Washington to avoid—the Civil War, and nearly every early resident was close to a veteran. These two photographs show gatherings on the first Memorial Day (then called Decoration Day) observances held in Slaughter in 1892. Decoration Day began being celebrated after the Civil War with the cleaning and decorating of veterans' graves. Above, a gathering of Slaughter men poses in front of flags and flowers prepared for the holiday. Below, the sons and daughters of veterans line up for a photograph.

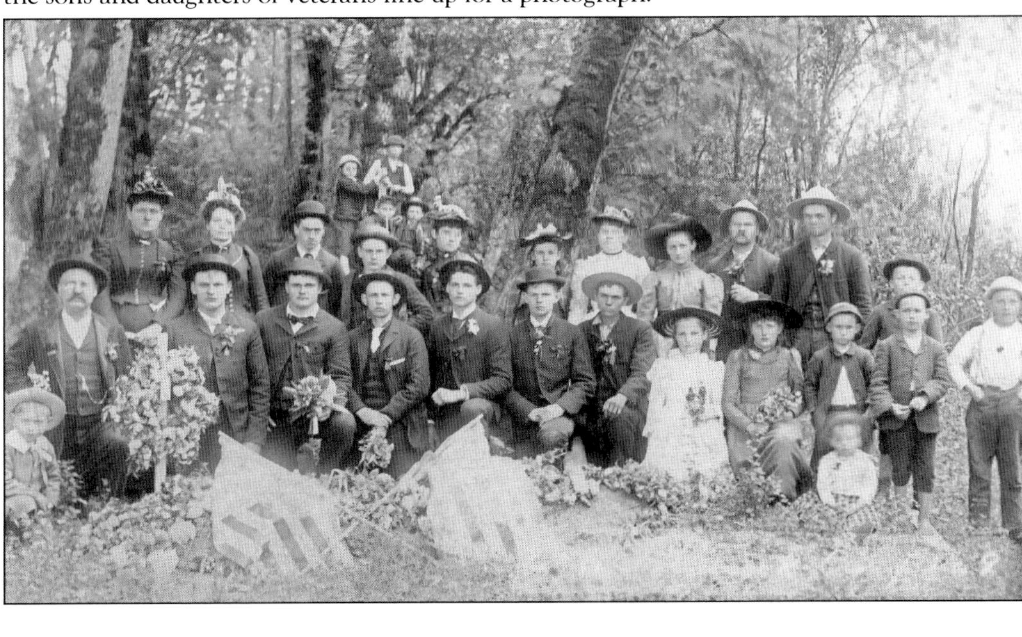

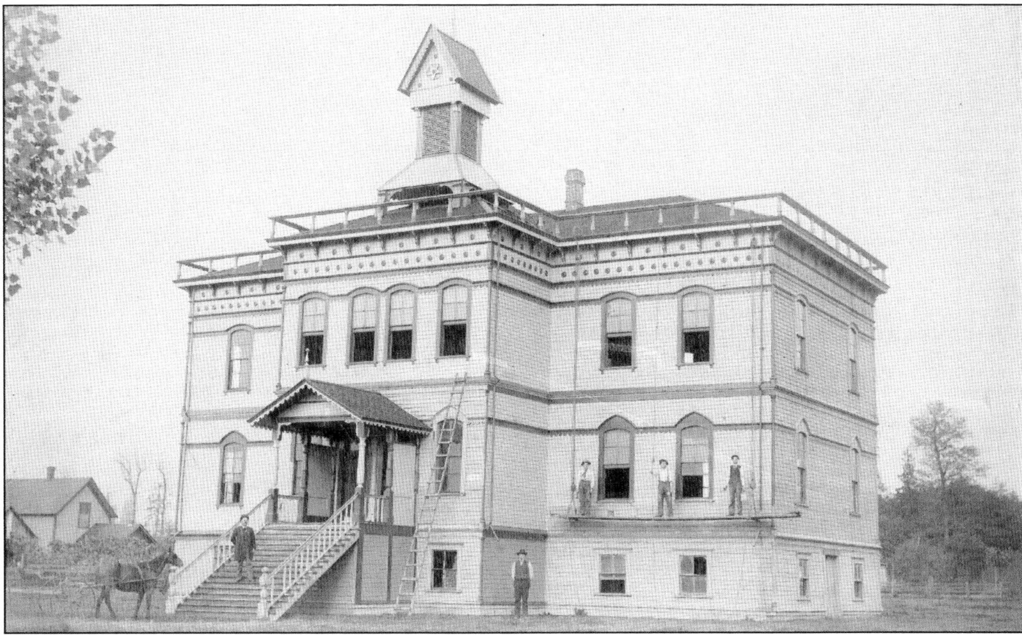

In 1889, Slaughter Central School was built to replace the patchwork of single-room schoolhouses dotted around the White River Valley. When it opened, this modern school offered lessons for 10 grade levels and held classes between six and nine months out of each year. Lessons focused on reading, diction, arithmetic, and penmanship.

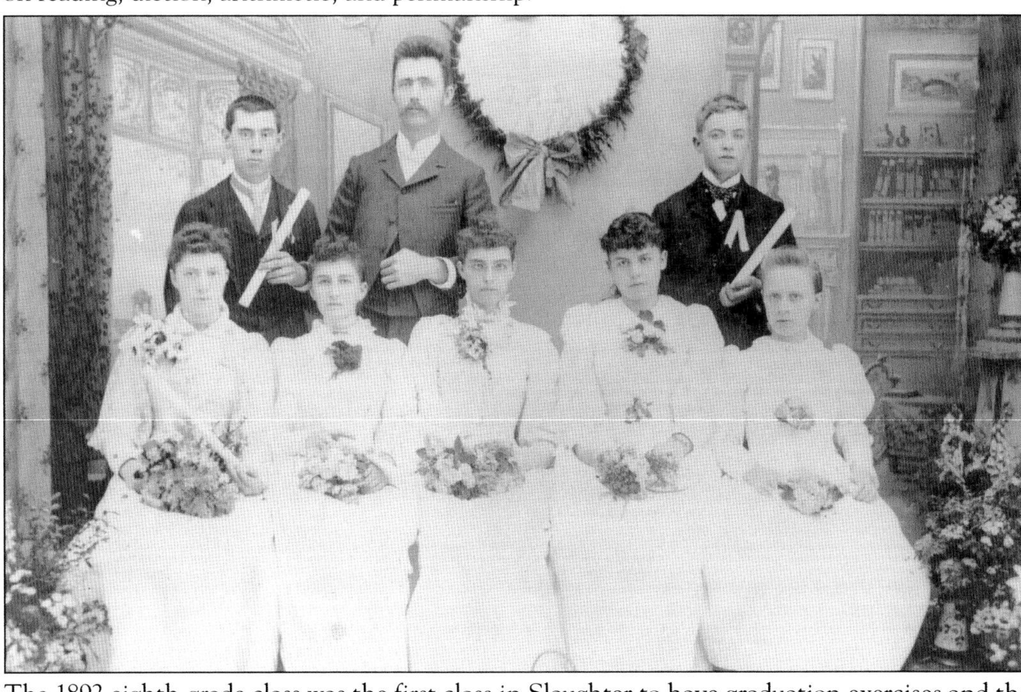

The 1892 eighth-grade class was the first class in Slaughter to have graduation exercises and the second class to formally graduate. Like most contemporary graduating classes, they chose their own motto ("Rest Not"), class colors (salmon and Nile green), and mascot (a salmon swimming upstream). They were also the last class to graduate while the town was still named Slaughter.

Virgil R. Bissell was the first mayor of Slaughter. He served from 1891 to 1892, during which time he oversaw many of the first improvements made to the town, such as the grading of streets, the building of sidewalks, and the management of the first town revenues, from street improvement taxes and license fees.

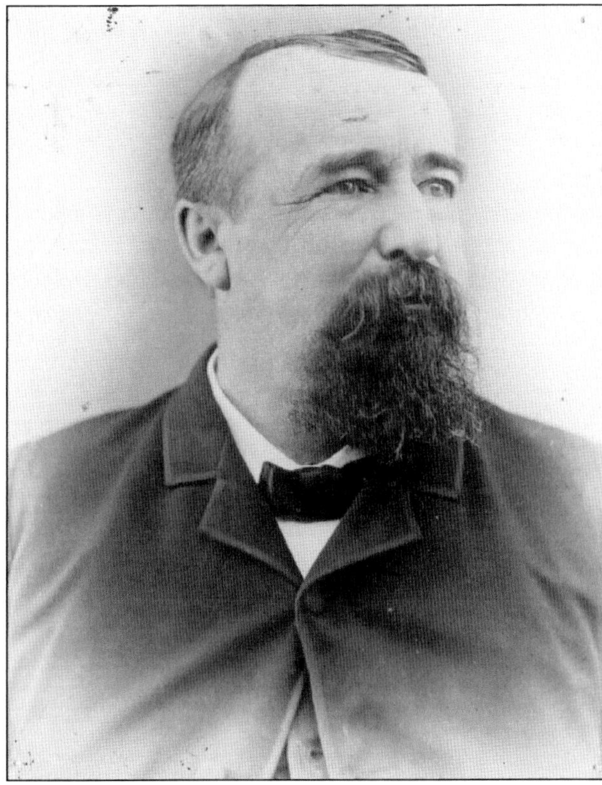

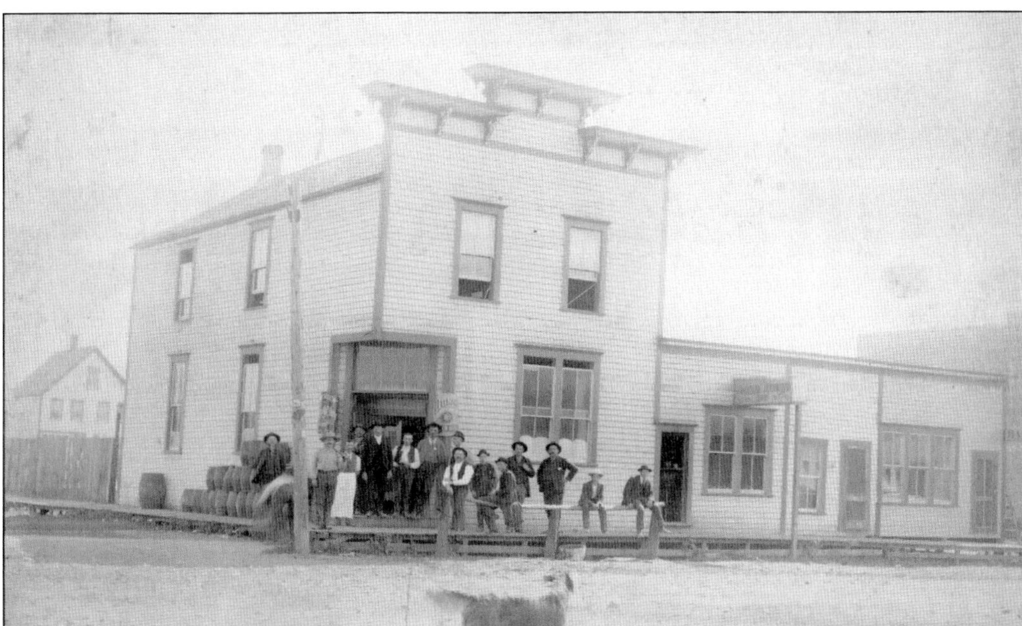

The first revenue-raising law passed in the incorporated town of Slaughter was a requirement to have all dogs licensed. Dog control was a serious problem in many frontier towns, and licensing allowed the city to fund a dogcatcher, officially called the poundmaster. In 1891, dog licenses cost $2 per dog, and unlicensed dogs could cost their owners up to $20 each in fines.

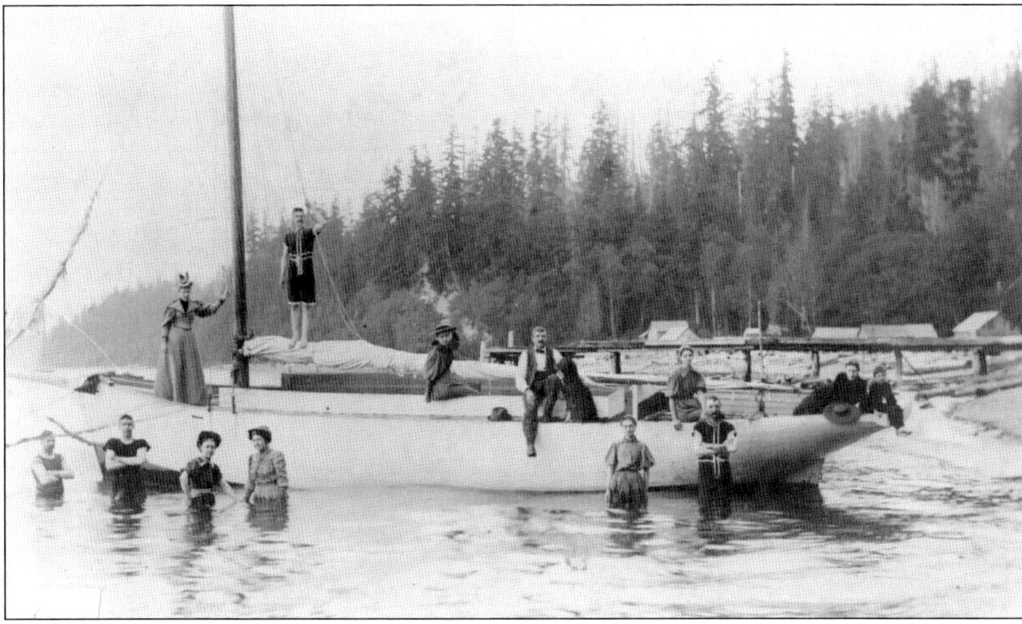

Even schoolteachers got to have fun on occasion. This photograph was taken during a 1890s picnic attended by the Slaughter schoolteachers and their principal, W.J. Meredith. The picnic was held at Redondo Beach, six miles northwest of Slaughter, a popular spot for ocean swimming, boating, and gathering shellfish.

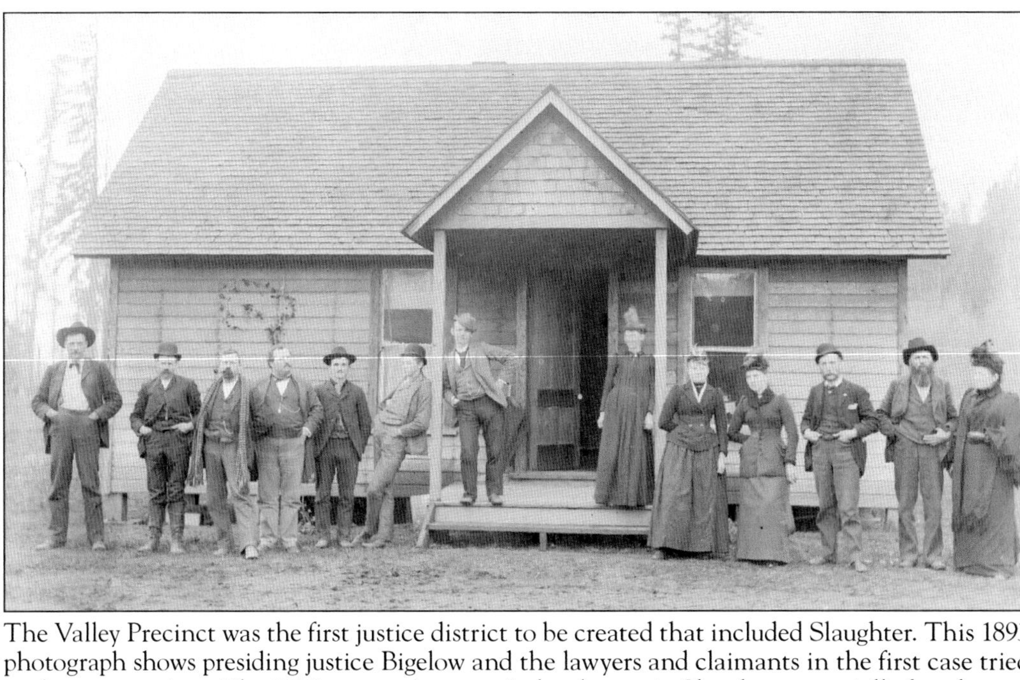

The Valley Precinct was the first justice district to be created that included Slaughter. This 1893 photograph shows presiding justice Bigelow and the lawyers and claimants in the first case tried in the new precinct. The 1890s saw an increase in legal cases in Slaughter, especially foreclosures and land disputes.

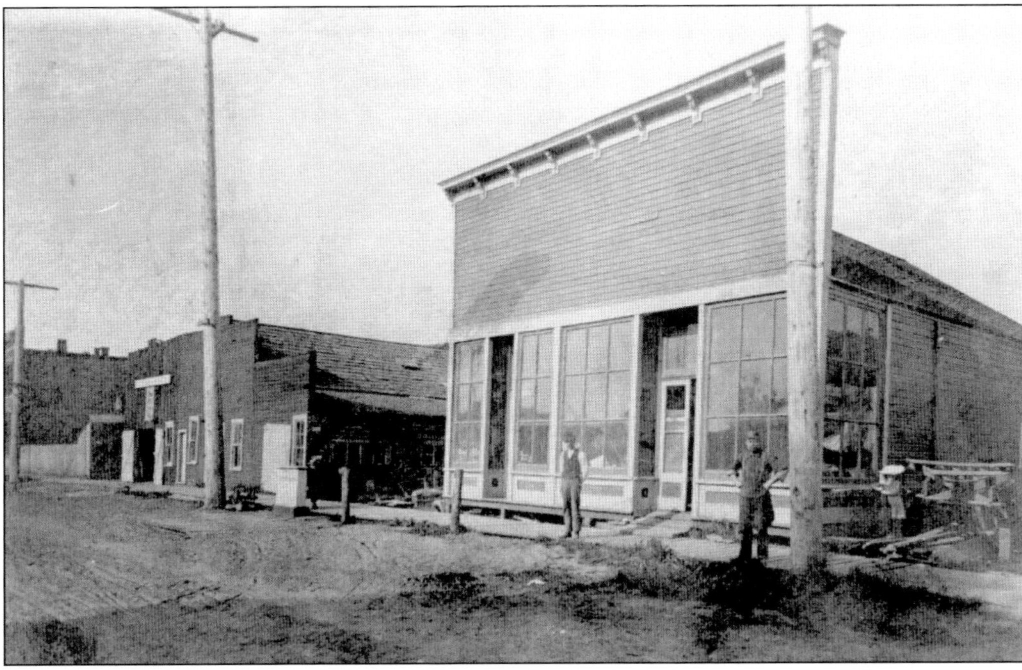

This 1889 photograph shows the first formal post office in Slaughter. The tall false front on the building was popular through the West at the time. Even the modest buildings next door have slight false fronts, though they lack the height and decorative trim of the post office's front.

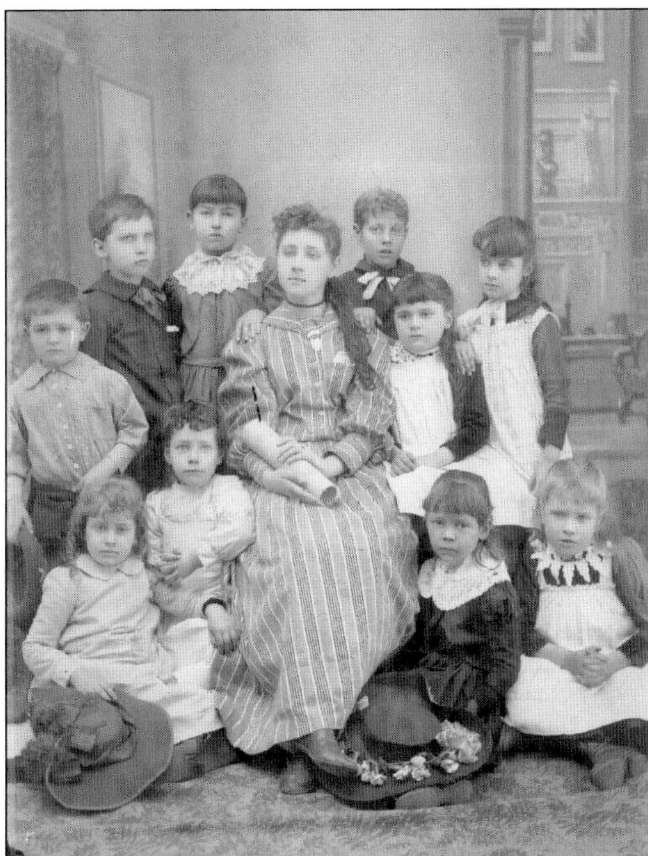

Most schoolteachers in Washington were young, unmarried women. School districts found they could pay female teachers less than male teachers. Teaching was one of the few nondomestic occupations available to girls who graduated from the eighth grade. This 1890 photograph shows teacher Rebbie Kerr Beach surrounded by her young students.

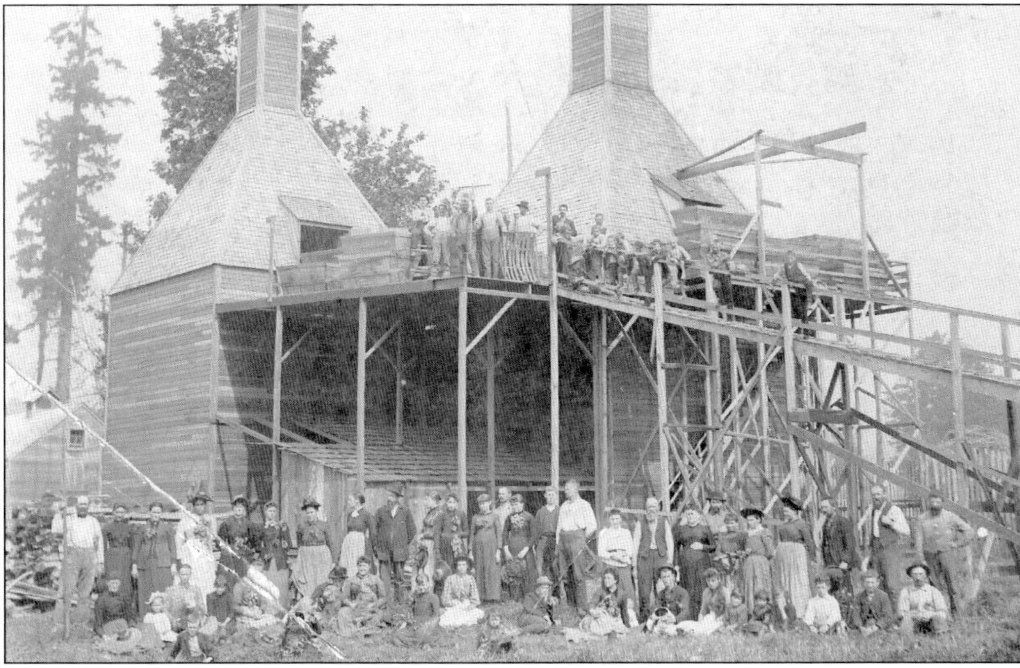

Any large hops-growing operation required this specialized building: a hops kiln. Freshly picked hops flowers, called cones, were put into this kiln, which was kept very warm by a fire on the ground level. Excess heat and moisture escaped from the tall chimneys. Once dry, the flowers could be bagged up, weighed, and sent to market.

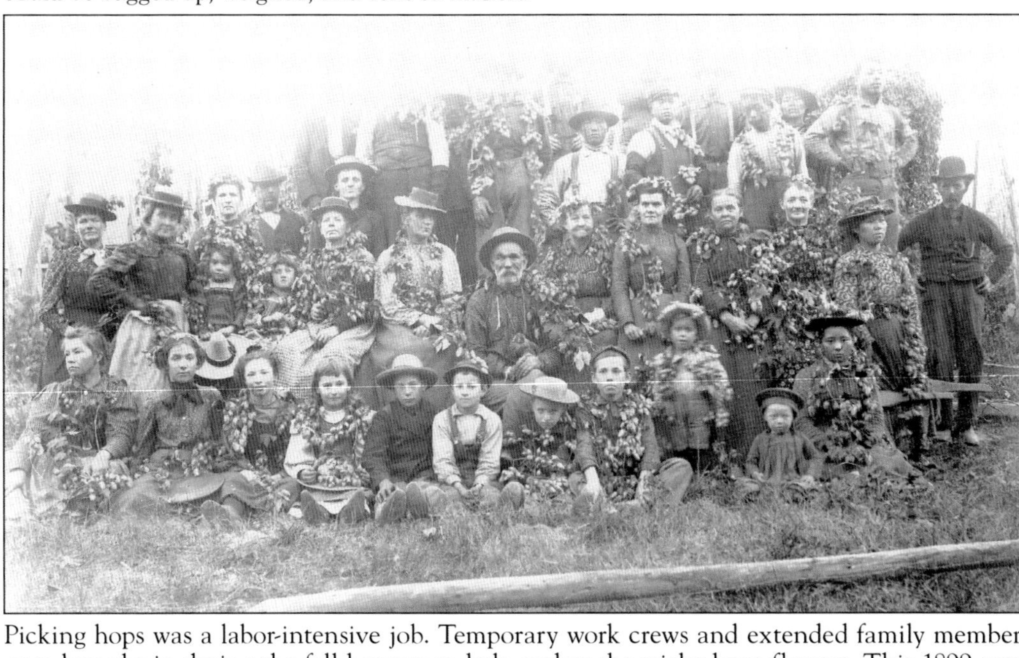

Picking hops was a labor-intensive job. Temporary work crews and extended family members were brought in during the fall harvest to help gather the sticky hops flowers. This 1899 crew was made up of hired local workers, migrant workers, and members of the Shuttleworth family. The Shuttleworths operated this hops farm for six years on land that later became the Auburn Golf Course.

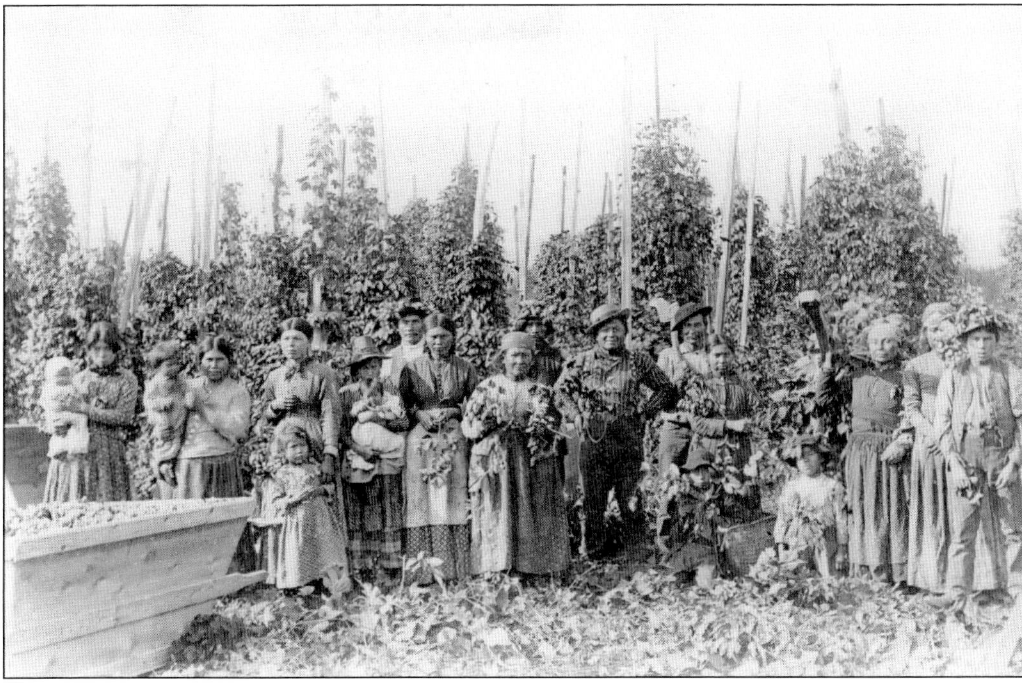

This group of Native Americans from the Muckleshoot Reservation poses around 1890 in front of mature hops vines they are about to harvest on a farm in Slaughter. Traditional berry-gathering baskets, like the one between the two kneeling children in this image, were easily converted into hops-gathering baskets. This kind of basket was worn on the back, hanging from the forehead with a tumpline.

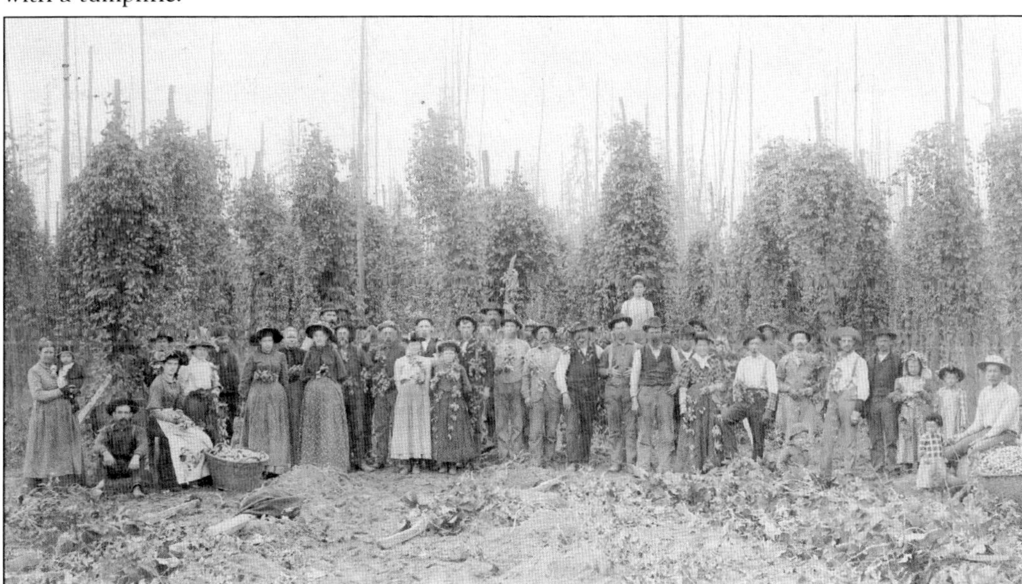

Hops were a huge commodity crop in the White River Valley in the 1880s and 1890s. An influx of German and other European immigrants to the United States fueled the national market for beer, and the mild climate and fertile soil of the valley were perfect for the fast-growing vine. This field belonged to the Traeger family of Slaughter in 1893.

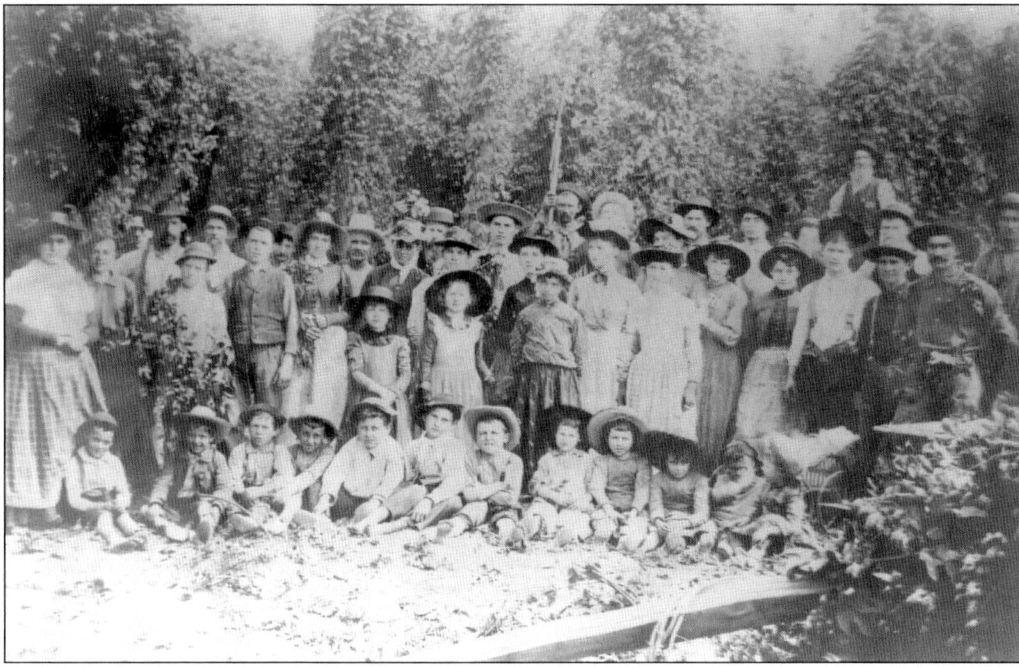

This 1892 hop field, owned by Pete Buckley, was located very close to town, on what is now the site of Washington Elementary School on East Main Street. Early school schedules often did not start until after the hops harvest was taken in to allow children to help without missing too many lessons.

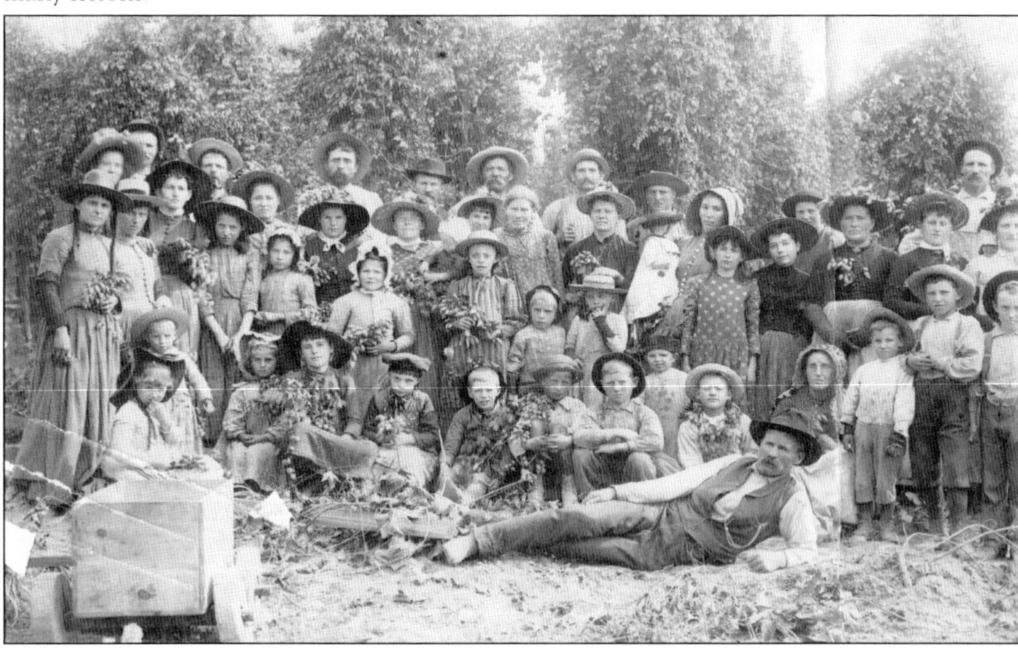

The yearly hops harvest was a busy time of year. Most hops growers recruited their entire families to assist in the harvest, an event worth commemorating with a photograph. In 1882, a pound of hops could be sold for 70¢—about $16.40 in today's money—and a single acre of hops vines could produce between 1,100 and 1,500 pounds of hops flowers.

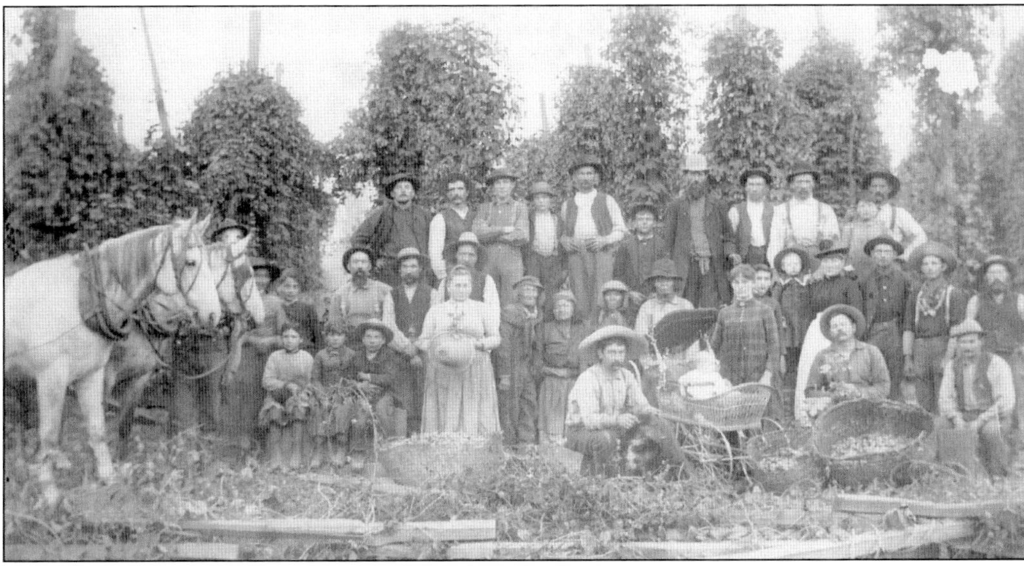

Hops were a relatively easy crop to grow in the wet Pacific Northwest. They grow very quickly after sprouting in the spring and only require a post or rope to climb up during the summer. The hops flower, called a cone, is the useful part of the plant. After harvesting, the vines are discarded, like the vines in the foreground of this 1889 photograph.

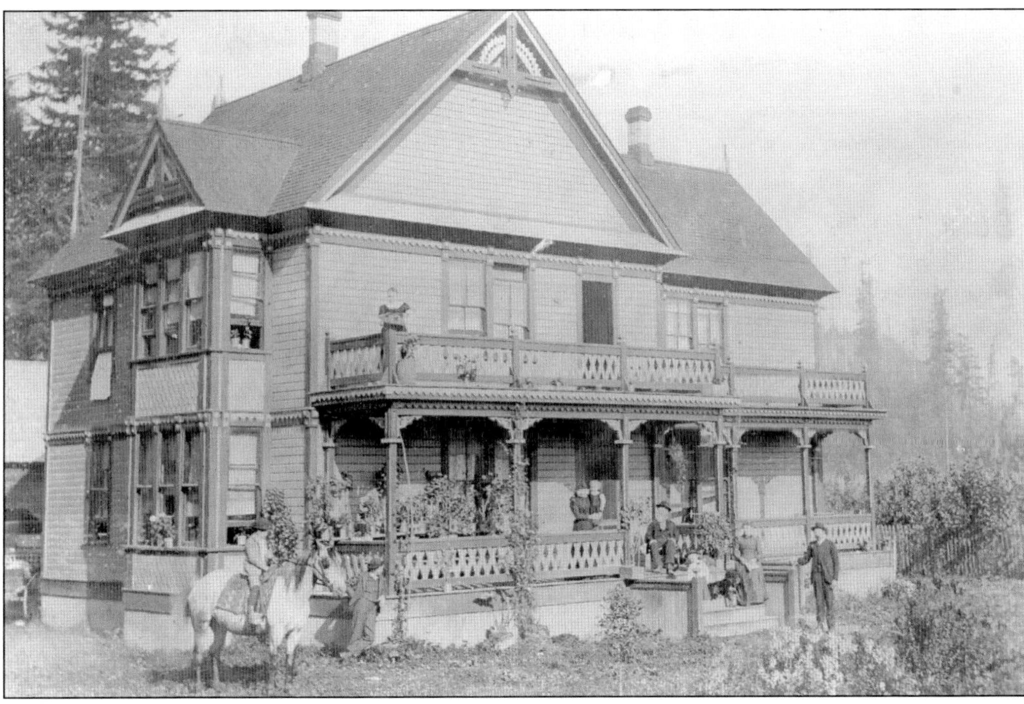

The influx of money from the hops trade allowed many families to expand their homes or build new ones. This home, belonging to the Crisp family of Slaughter in 1891, shows many of the signatures of Victorian houses in the area: all-wood construction with lots of decorative trims as well as decorative shingles in the gingerbread style below the bay windows.

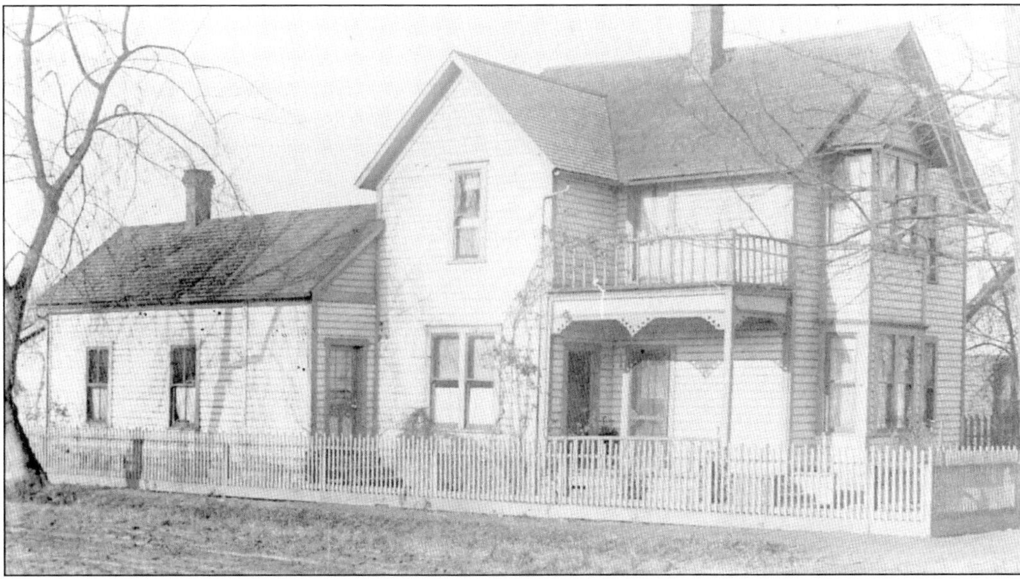

The Bronson-Smith home, seen here in 1890, features a less ornate exterior (above) than some of the other large houses from this era, but its interior (below) makes up for it. Wallpaper was a popular decorative choice because it allowed homeowners to cover up cheaper, less attractive wood on the inside of a building. The furniture in the house, like the small table in the center of the image below, was of the heavy, German-inspired style that was popular in the late Victorian period. This house was located at the present-day intersection of Third Avenue and C Street in Auburn.

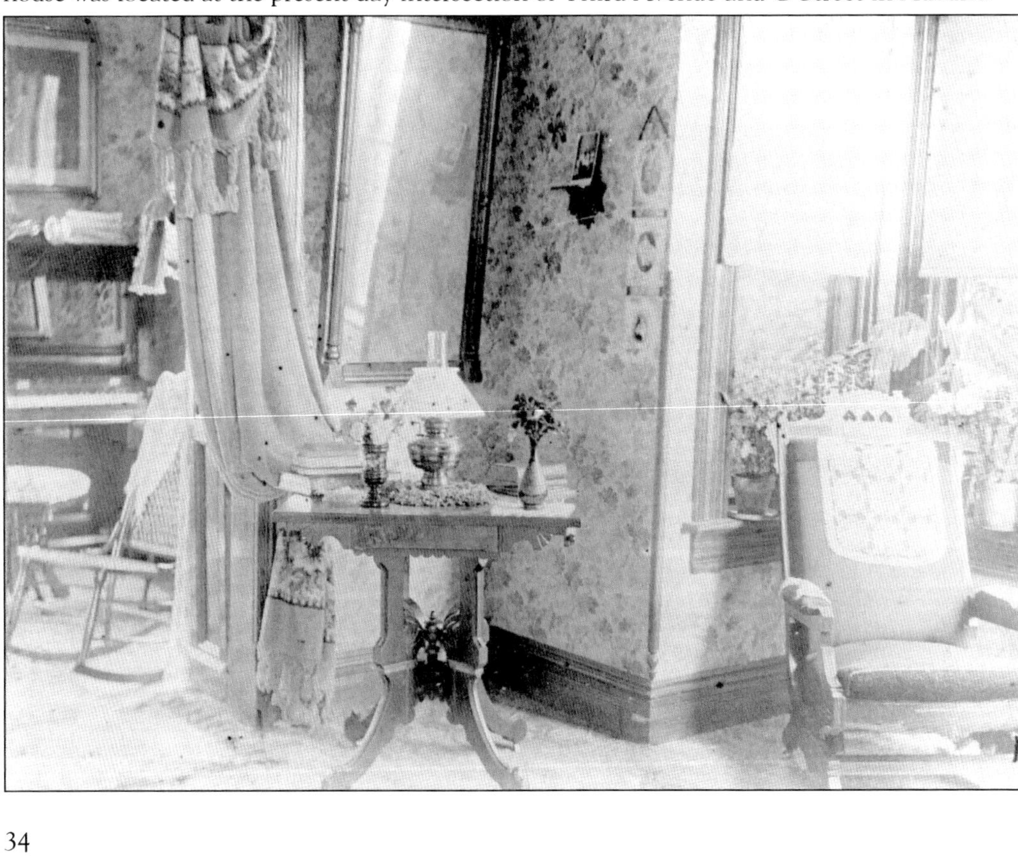

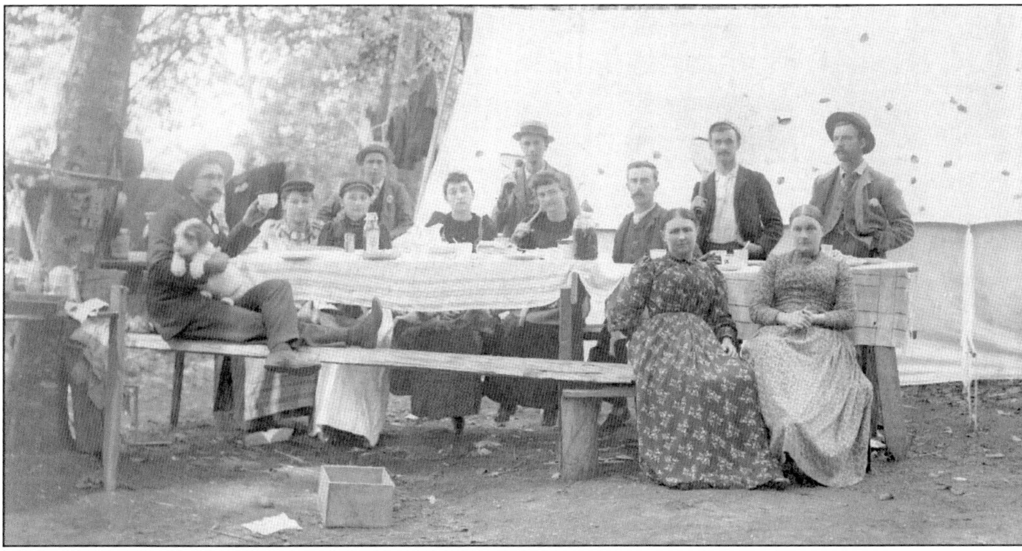

More money and more business allowed time for recreation and leisure for some families in Slaughter. This 1893 camping group from Slaughter seems to be in pretty good spirits, and the tennis racquets being held by three of the adults imply that at least one outdoor game was being played that day.

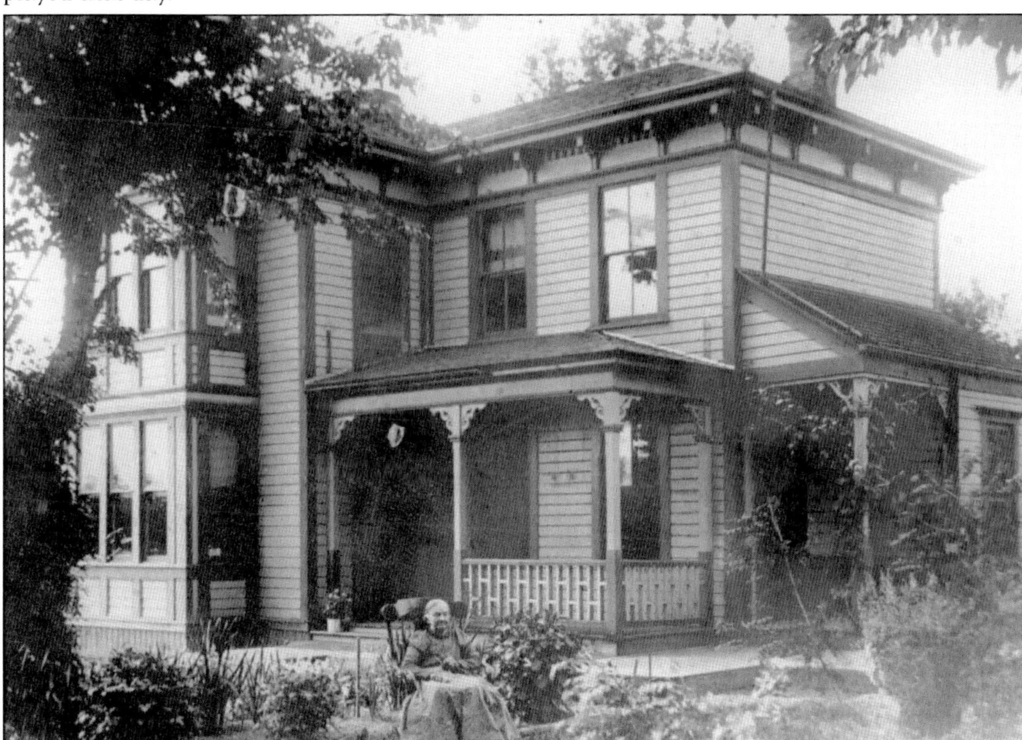

This house, built in about 1890, was the home of Dr. Alexander Hughes. His wife, Sarah, sits in the rocking chair in front of the porch. The house has the same decorative elements of other period homes, including the delicate scrollwork braces on the porch. This home was located across the street from the Auburn Pioneer Cemetery.

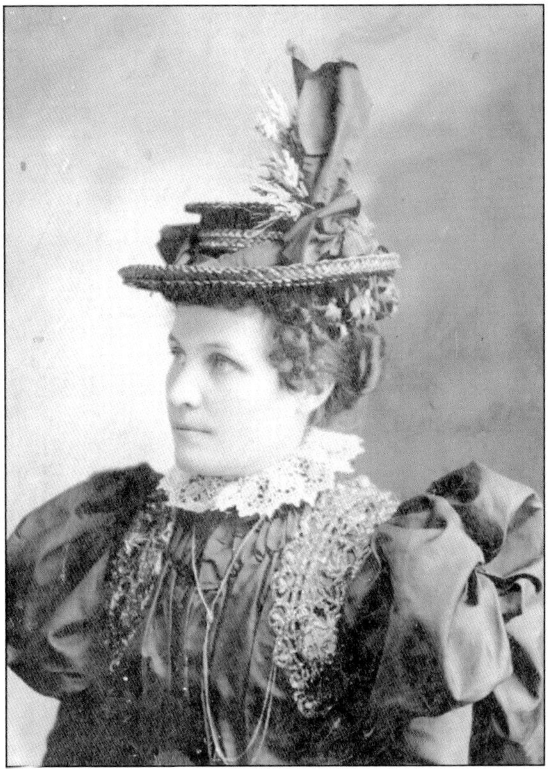

Despite living in rural Slaughter, women of means still found ways to acquire the latest fashions from Tacoma and Seattle. Mrs. Pillman, the wife of the town mortician, poses in this photograph from around 1890 in a silk dress and elaborate hat. Auburn would not have its own ladies' hat shop for another two decades.

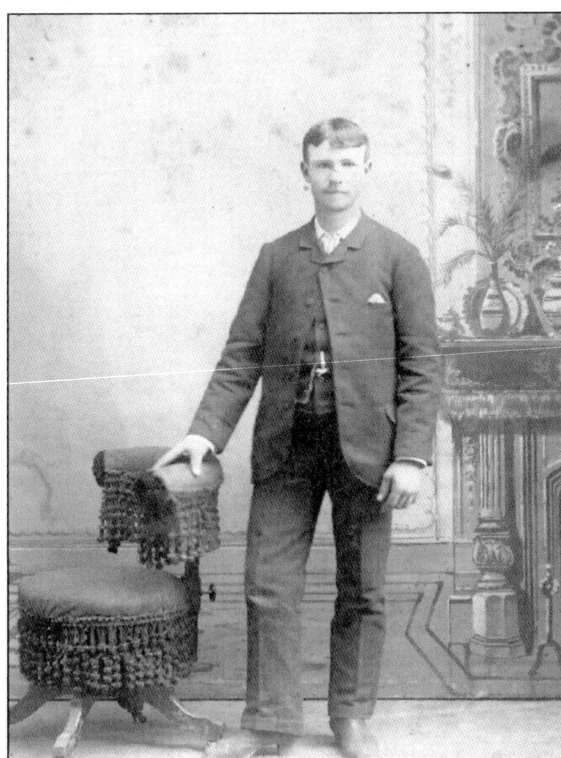

Charlie Pautzke was one of the first professional photographers to set up a studio in Slaughter in the 1890s. He and his son Clarence took portraits and scenic photographs throughout the White River Valley, including many of the early photographs featured in this book. Before the advent of personal cameras, professional photographers were the primary producers of all photographs in America.

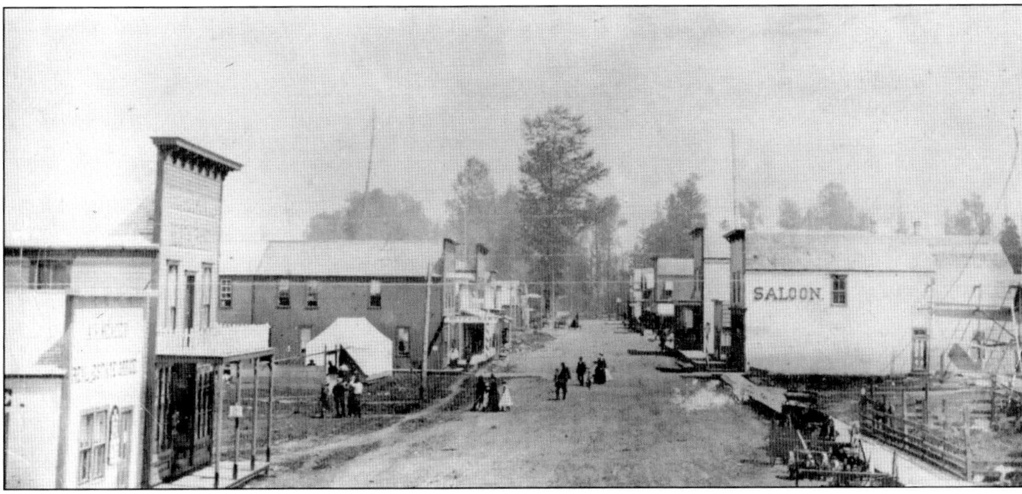

This is the earliest known image of Main Street in Slaughter, taken in 1891. This portion of the street is now called West Main Street. The trees in the background mark the banks of the White River before it was redirected; the dry riverbed later became a main thoroughfare. Despite its small population, Slaughter was still big enough in 1891 to support two restaurants and many other specialty businesses.

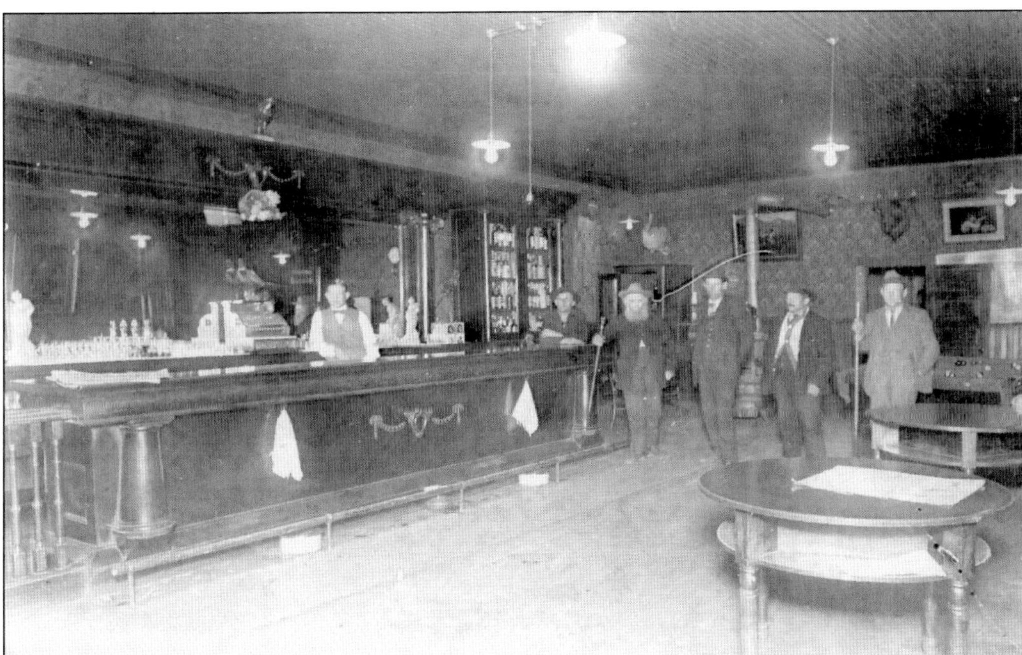

Saloons were more than just bars in the early days of Auburn; they were also cash cows for the town's tiny coffers. Dad Goodrich's Saloon, seen here around 1895, was one such establishment. Saloon owners were required to purchase a $500 saloon license from the city government—over $13,000 in today's money. Pool table licenses cost extra.

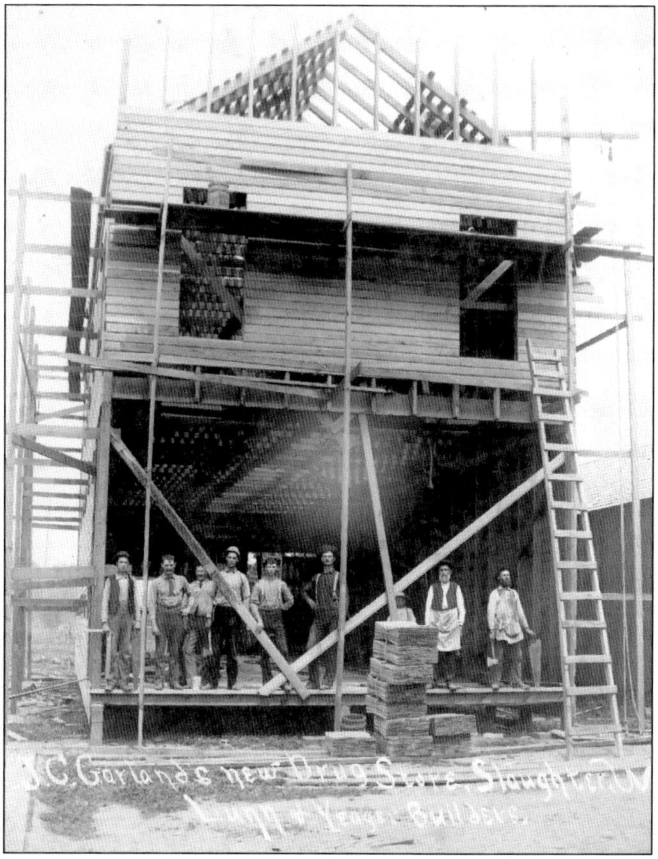

Lumber was the most widely available and affordable construction material in Slaughter. This drugstore, built around 1893, is made up entirely of wood, including its foundations. The clapboard siding, wooden shingles for the roof, wooden boardwalks, and even wooden scaffolding and ladders show how vital timber was for the early town.

The Bissell Drug Store, seen here around 1890, was one of the longest continually operating businesses in Auburn. Opened by Edwin Bissell, the store went through several name changes throughout the 1900s, including stints as the Peckenpaugh & Manson Drug Store and Manson's Rexall. The store was located at East Main and Division Streets.

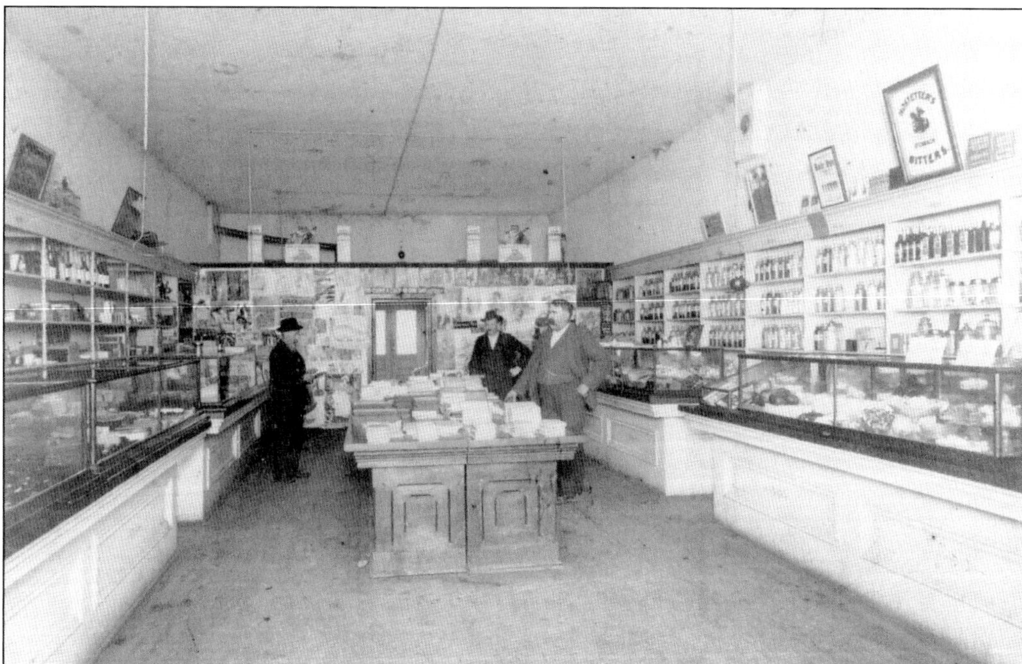

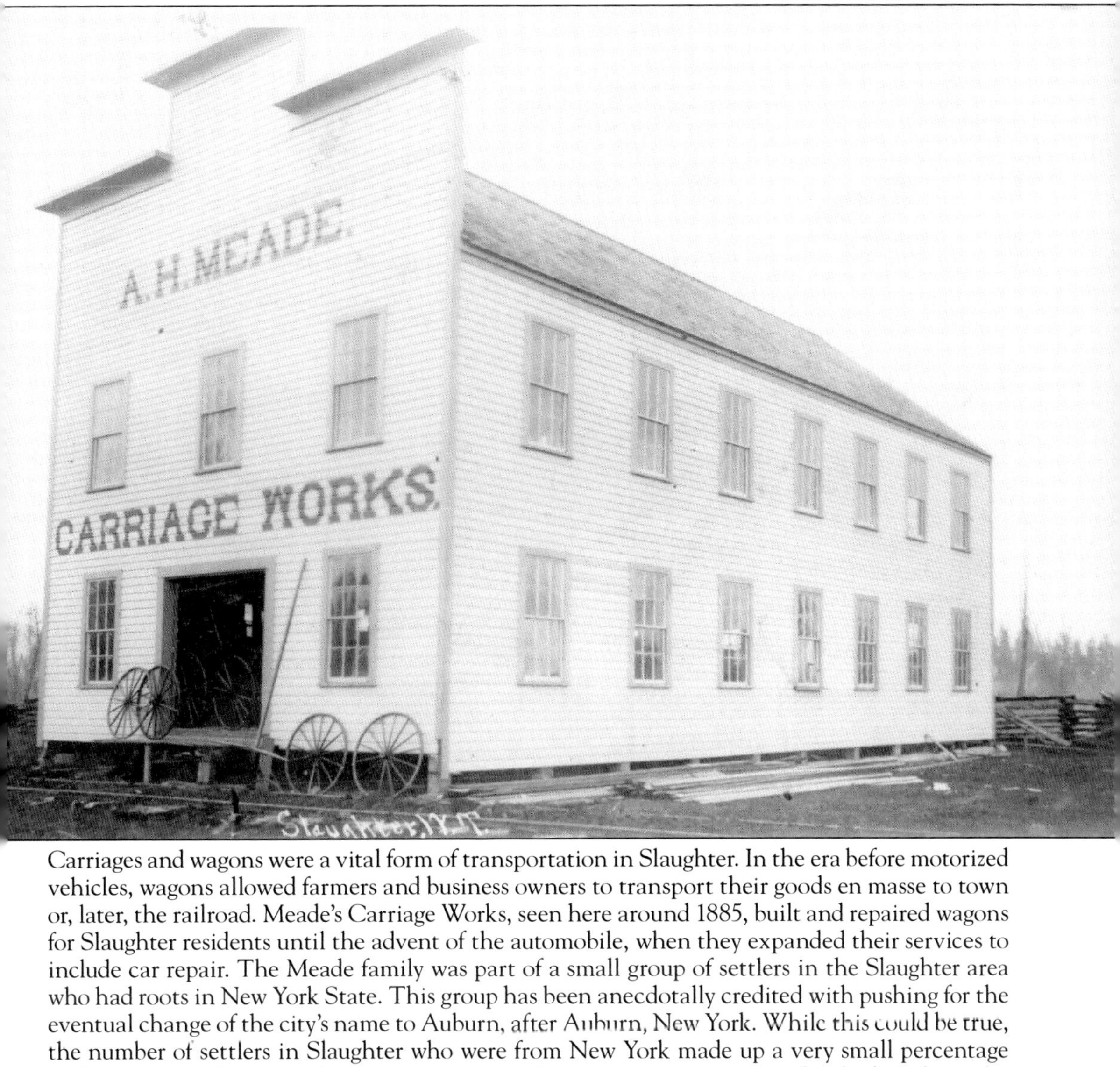

Carriages and wagons were a vital form of transportation in Slaughter. In the era before motorized vehicles, wagons allowed farmers and business owners to transport their goods en masse to town or, later, the railroad. Meade's Carriage Works, seen here around 1885, built and repaired wagons for Slaughter residents until the advent of the automobile, when they expanded their services to include car repair. The Meade family was part of a small group of settlers in the Slaughter area who had roots in New York State. This group has been anecdotally credited with pushing for the eventual change of the city's name to Auburn, after Auburn, New York. While this could be true, the number of settlers in Slaughter who were from New York made up a very small percentage of the total population, and no documentary evidence exists to prove exactly which Auburn the new city name was meant to emulate.

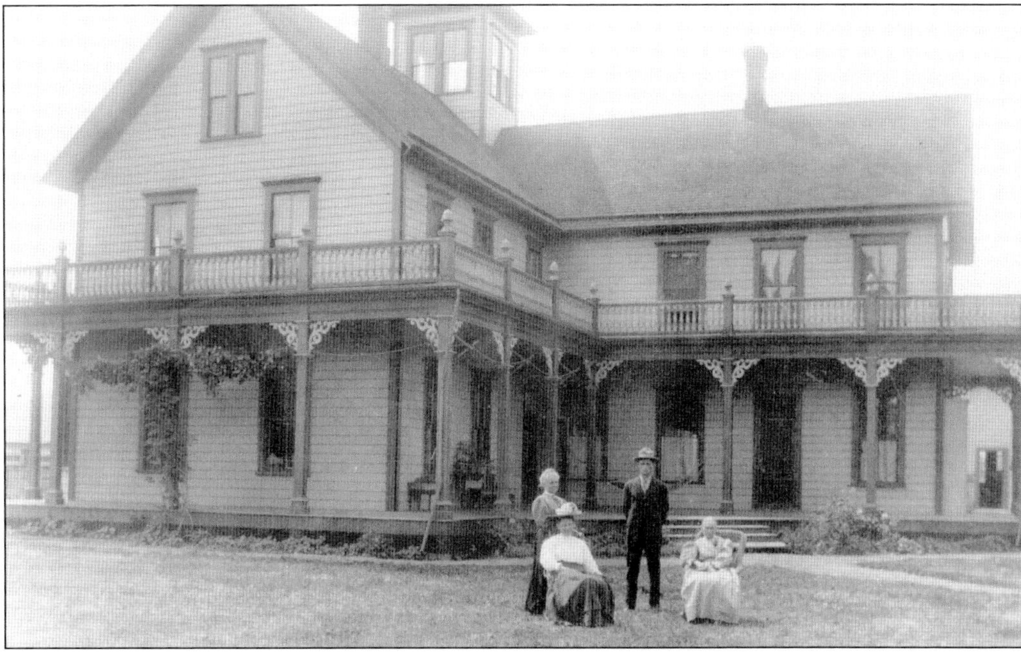

The Alvord home, seen here around 1885, was located in Thomas, a town that once existed exactly halfway between Slaughter and Kent. The area of the town has been split almost in half by modern borders, leaving the north part—including where the Alvord home stood—in the Kent city limits and the south part in the Auburn city limits.

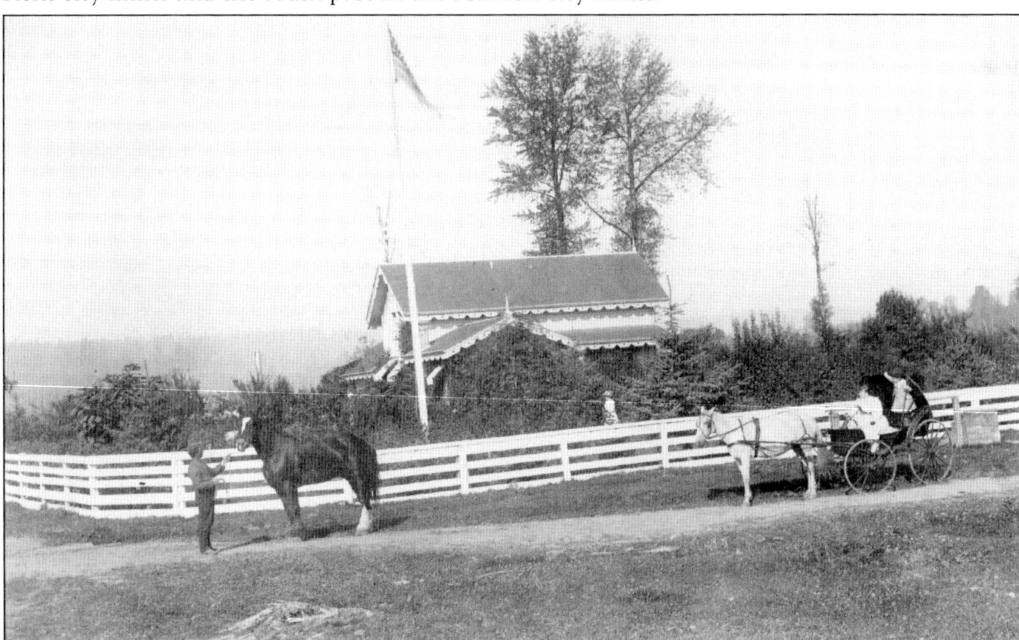

This 1891 photograph shows the Hart family home, located on the corner of what is now Auburn Way North and Thirtieth Street Southeast. It was one of the few homes located in the now extinct town of Christopher, which was between Kent and Auburn and was eventually absorbed into the north side of Auburn.

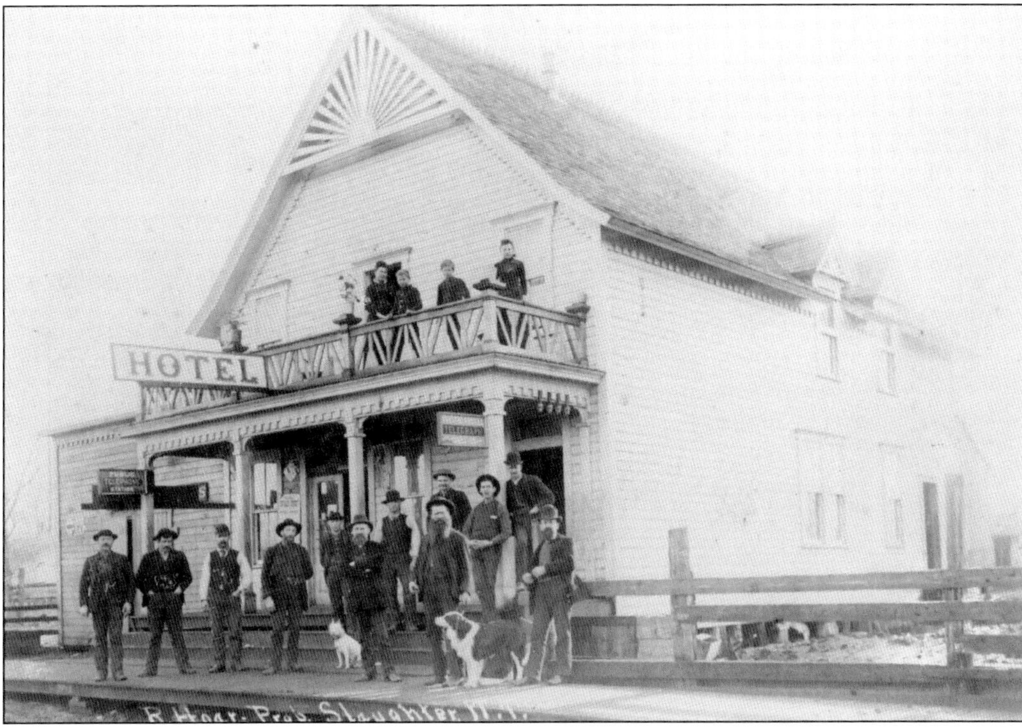

The Ohio House Hotel, run by William and Maggie Hoar, was the first hotel in Slaughter. Despite the large hotel sign in this 1887 photograph, local legend claims that the hotel was often referred to as the Slaughter House or the Hoar House, neither of which were very popular names with city leaders. Incidents like this encouraged the city's name change in 1893.

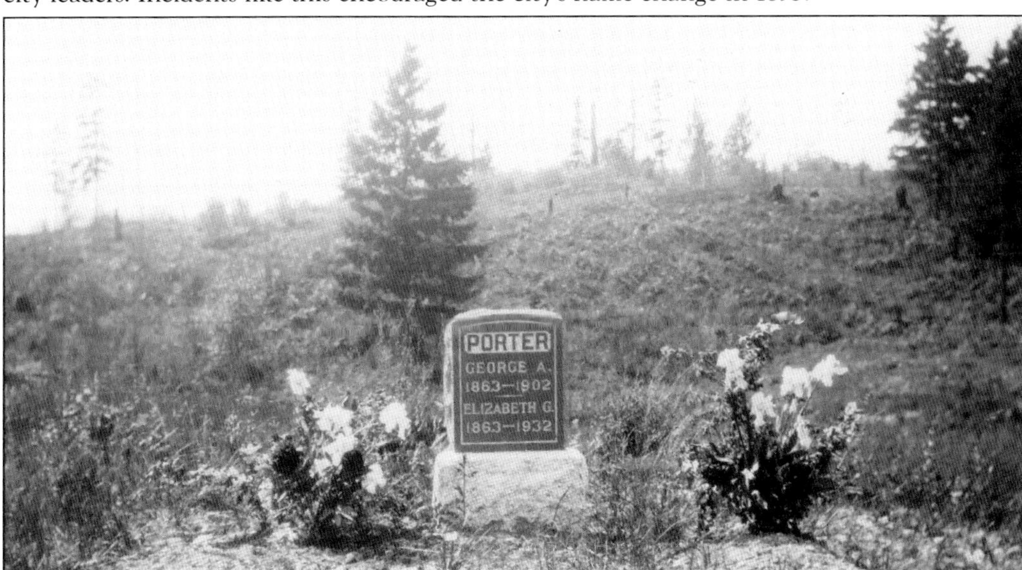

Mountain View Cemetery was established in 1890 on the west hill of Auburn. Constant flooding in the valley caused the older cemetery, now known as the Auburn Pioneer Cemetery, to become a less desirable final resting place for most of Auburn's Christian population. The oldest burials, along with Japanese Buddhist burials and unmarked burials, remained at the older cemetery.

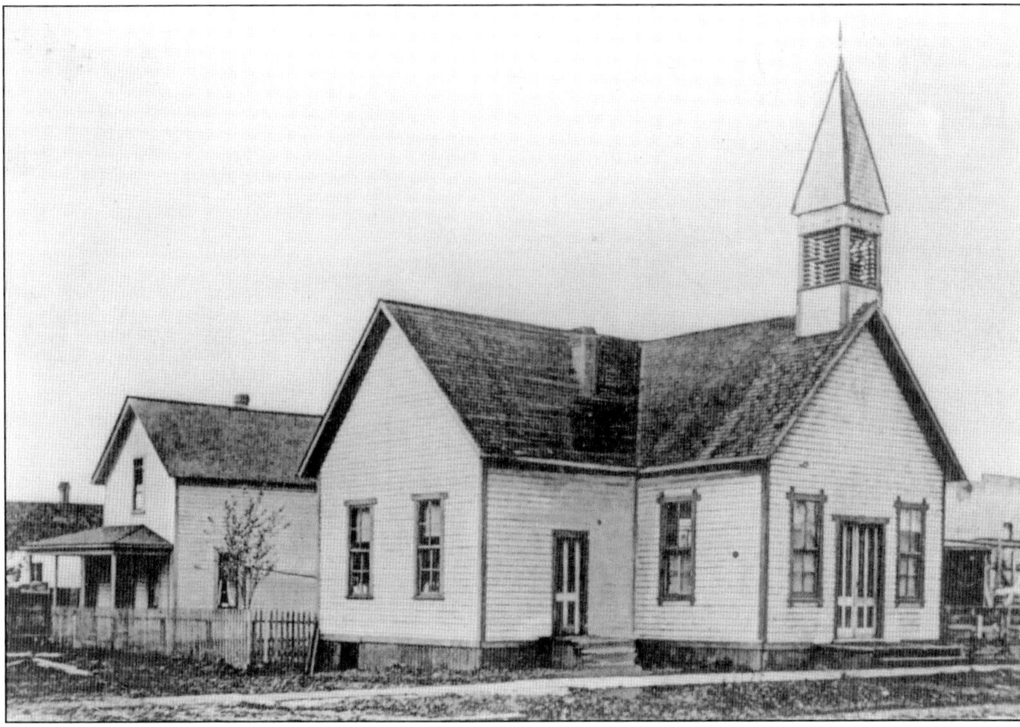

The Auburn Methodist Episcopal Church was built in 1886. The congregation was one of the first organized in the Auburn area. Before they had a formal church building, members met at private homes to worship, sometimes receiving sermons from itinerant preachers who traveled throughout the Puget Sound region.

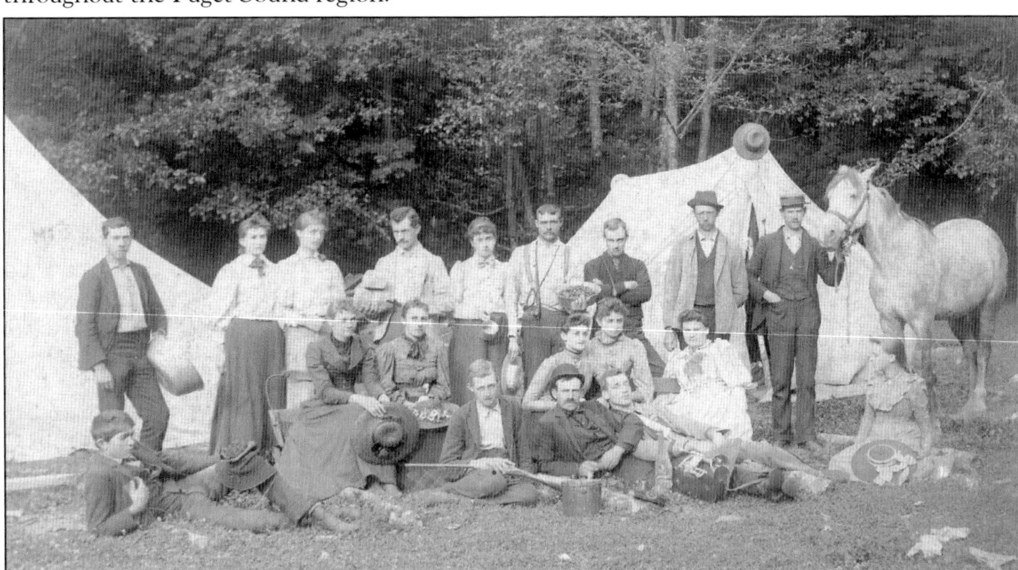

The White River Presbyterian Church in Slaughter was the first Presbyterian congregation in western Washington. This group of campers from the church is enjoying a camping trip to Redondo in 1893. Camping was a popular activity for church groups, which used them as an opportunity for a retreat and for religious instruction for young adults.

Three

The Town of Auburn 1893–1912

The switch from the name Slaughter to Auburn came at a time of significant change for the town. The Panic of 1893, a national financial crisis, hit Auburn very hard. Banks were run out of business, railroad companies went into bankruptcy, and financing for business development became almost impossible to obtain. The unemployment rate in King County shot up to 20 percent. At the same time, the hops industry in the Puget Sound region collapsed, forcing farmers to look for alternative sources of income. Without access to loans, many landowners, wealthy and poor alike, were forced to go into foreclosure or abandon their homes and land in the mid-1890s.

Luckily, it was not all doom and gloom. Enterprising farmers found that hops fields could be turned into pastures for dairy cows, and Auburn was able to establish itself as a center of dairying. New agricultural jobs brought in immigrants, especially from Japan, to work in the fields. In 1897, the Klondike Gold Rush brought a much-needed influx of money and commerce to every portion of the Puget Sound region, lowering the unemployment rate significantly. New leadership in the railroad industry led to an expansion of freight and passenger rail lines in and around Auburn, connecting Auburn to the rest of the region and encouraging new businesses and residents to put down roots.

City services in Auburn also expanded, along with the steadily growing population. Schools continued to be built, and school curriculums became more standardized. Telephone and telegraph services first reached Auburn in 1903, and streets and sidewalks began to be paved with concrete and gravel rather than mud and wood planks. Large civil engineering projects also began during this period, especially after a devastating flood in 1906 that put the Black, Green, White, and Puyallup River valleys underwater and caused the White River to completely redirect its flow after breaking through a barrier into the nearby Stuck River.

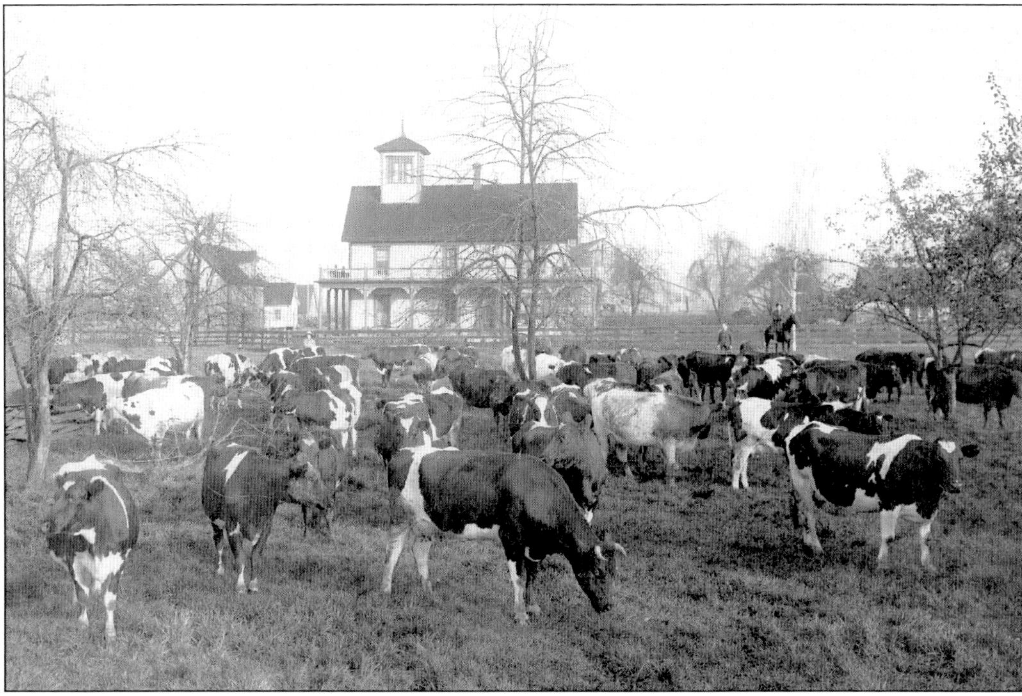

Dairy farming was one of the most popular forms of agriculture in the Auburn area in the early 1900s. Unlike grain crops like wheat and corn, cows did not stop producing during the long rainy season. The Alvord farm in Thomas, seen here around 1905, boasted a large herd made up of several varieties of dairy cows.

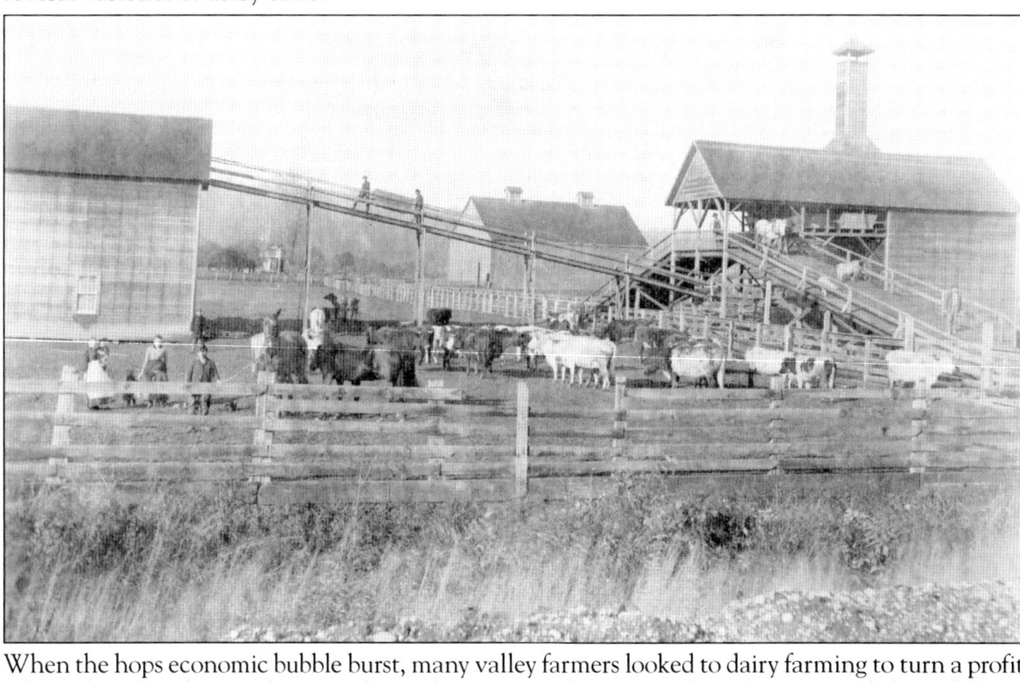

When the hops economic bubble burst, many valley farmers looked to dairy farming to turn a profit. The Nelson family, seen here on their Thomas-area farm around 1905, converted their old hops drying sheds (right) into multistory dairy cow barns with the addition of ramps on each side.

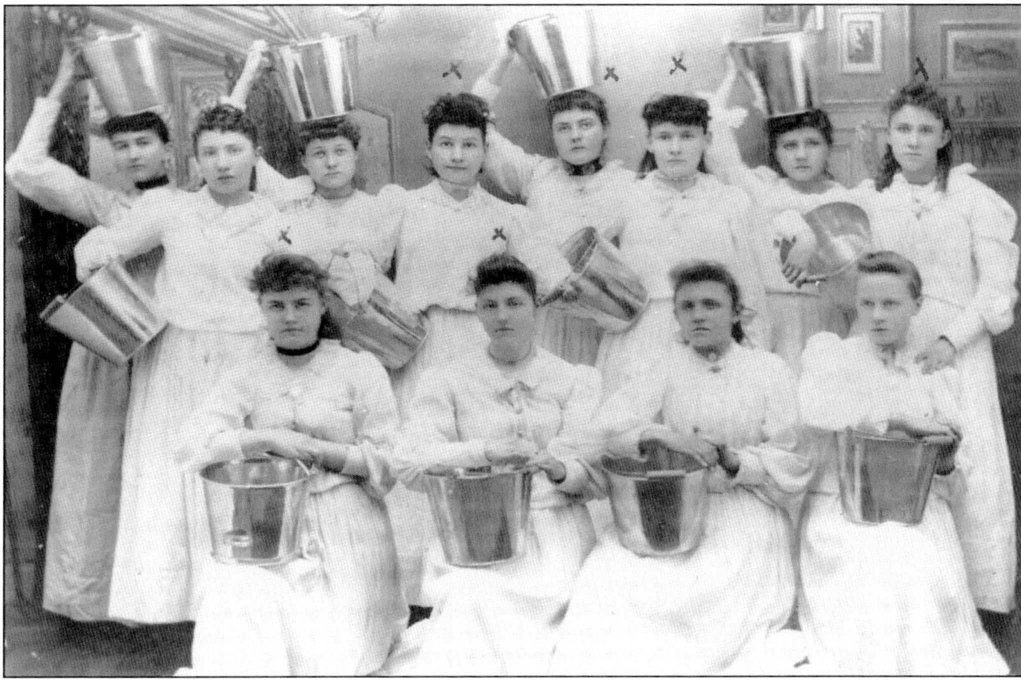

Dairying became such an important part of the economy in Auburn that the skills necessary to be a dairy farmer were publicly celebrated and formal education time was set aside for them. This group of young ladies, seen around 1893, was a milkmaid drill team made up of the daughters of several prominent farming families in the Auburn area.

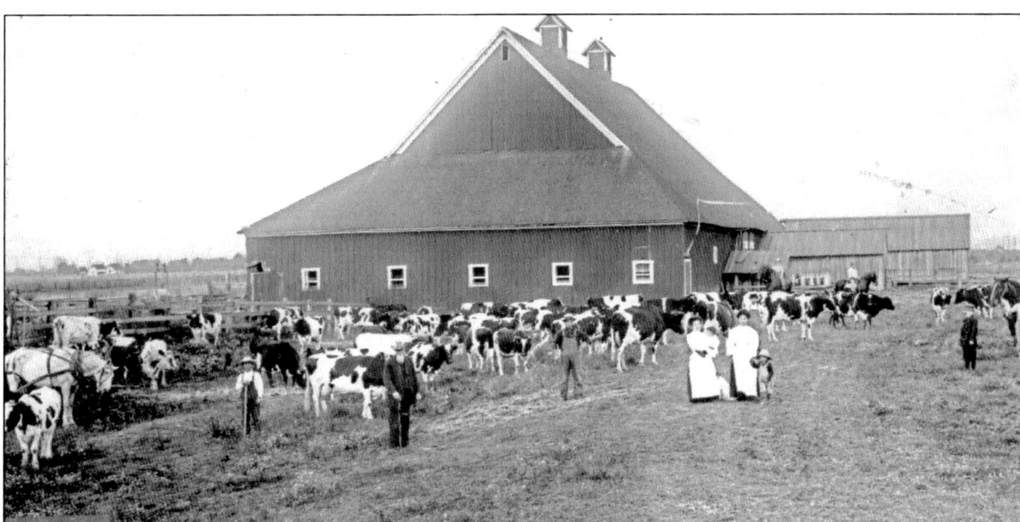

This large farm, owned by Thomas Christopher around 1907, was located in the town of Thomas. The large barn in the background was purpose-built for dairying, with a large lower story to allow for the maximum number of cows to be inside at once, as well as two cupolas and multiple windows to allow for ventilation.

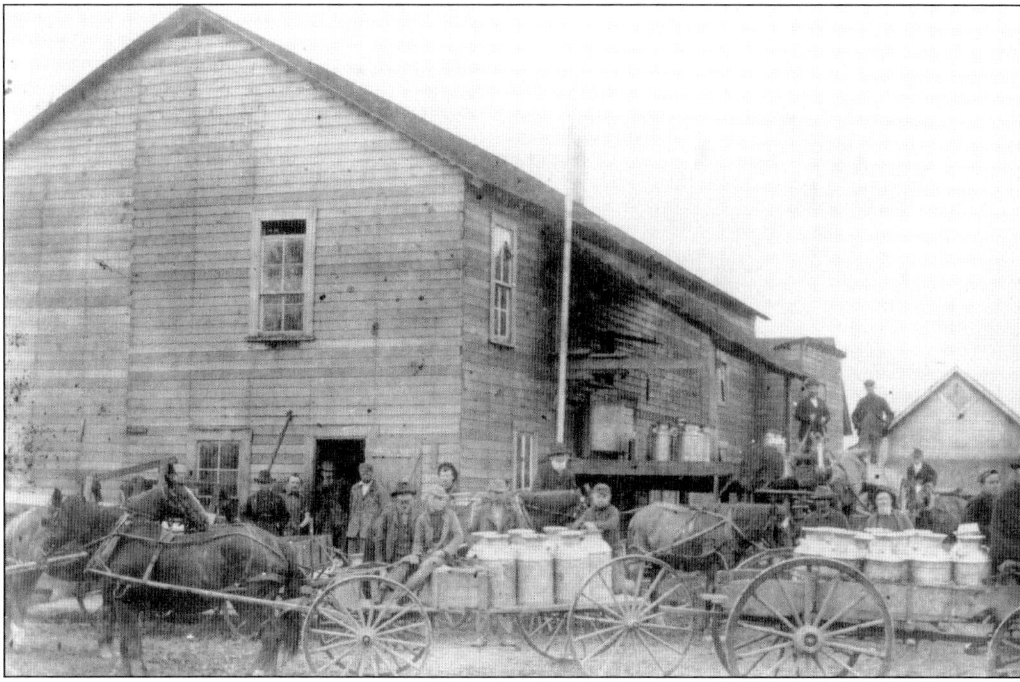

When the interurban railway began to travel through Auburn, products and people both began to move faster. Milk and cream from Auburn-area dairies could be loaded onto wagons and then directly onto trains. Within four hours, that milk could be sold to restaurants and residents in Seattle or Tacoma.

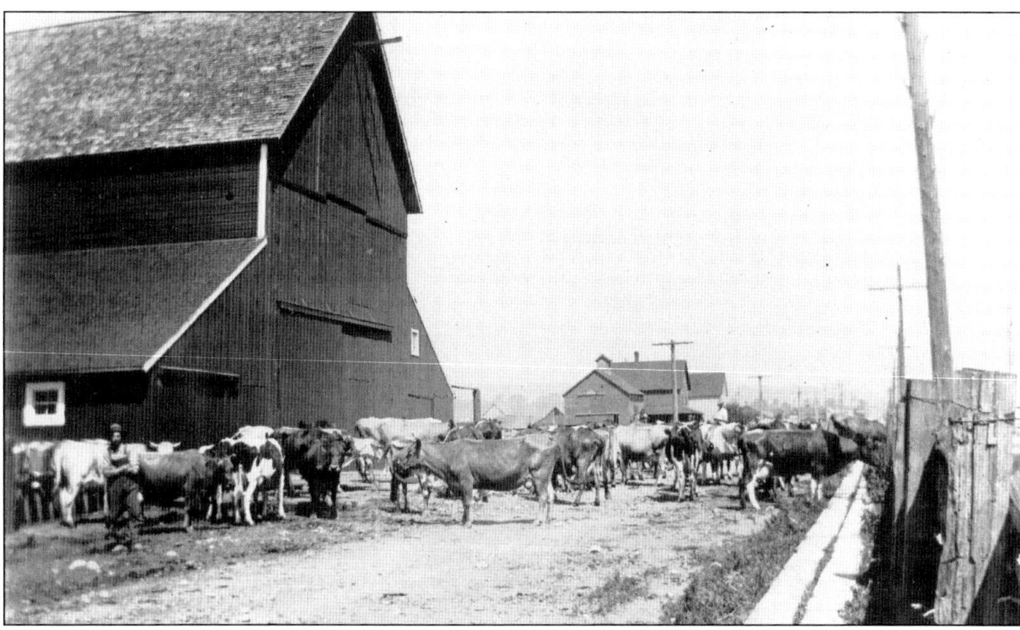

The Trott farm, seen here around 1906, was a diversified operation. Located directly on West Main Street, the Trotts raised chickens, potatoes, and corn along with their dairy cows. Cows and other crops could be transported directly up Main Street to be sold at auction or loaded onto train cars for delivery elsewhere.

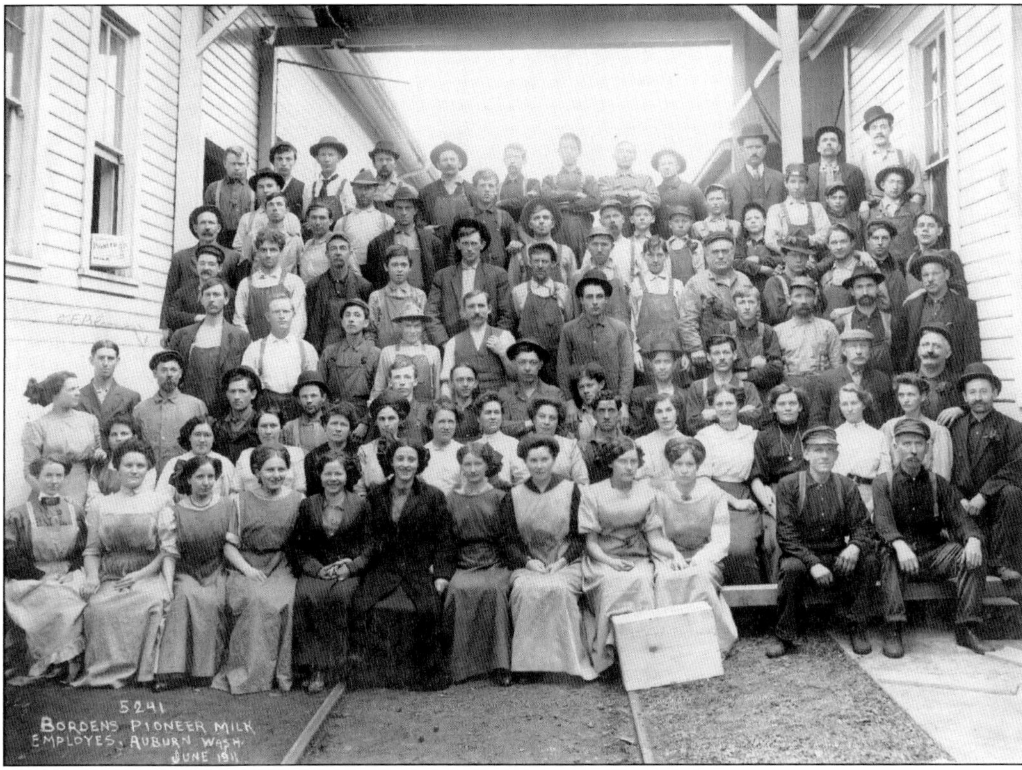

The Borden Condensed Milk Company opened a large factory in Auburn in 1903 under the name Borden's Pioneer Milk Company. At the time, it was one of the largest employers in town, second only to the railroads. In this 1911 photograph, every employee in the plant was gathered together.

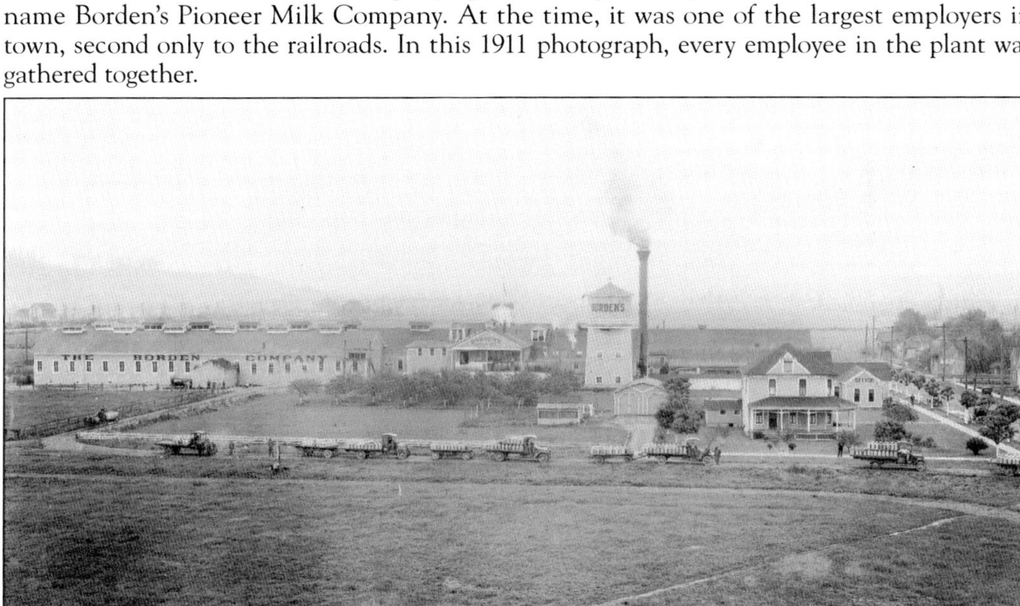

The Borden condensery complex was one of the largest factories in Auburn. It also bordered a large grass field, seen here in the foreground, next to the first Auburn High School. Many photographs of school athletic events from the 1900s and 1910s show the condensery's buildings in the background.

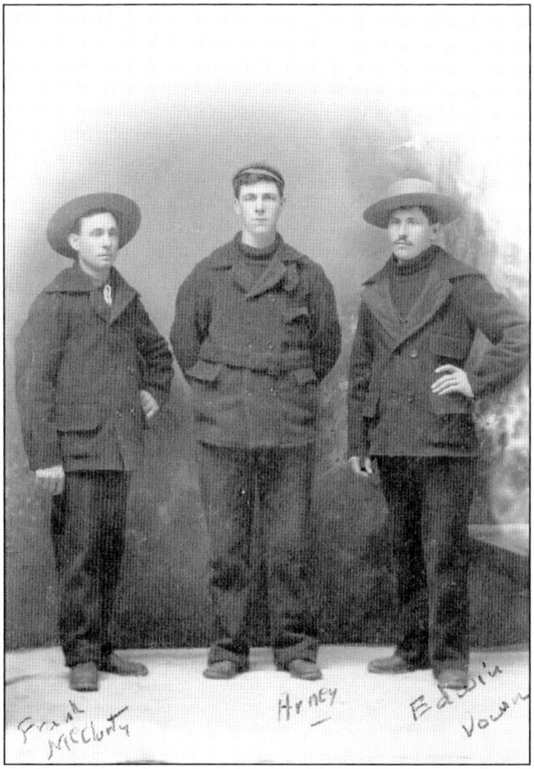

The Klondike Gold Rush brought many new residents and travelers through the Puget Sound region, but it also tempted many existing residents to try their luck at gold prospecting in Alaska. These three men were Auburn residents who had their photograph taken in Seattle before boarding a ship north to the Klondike around 1897.

Trains stopped in Auburn for a variety of reasons, including refueling and picking up new freight. This train, seen around 1908, is waiting in front of the coal dock, where coal mined in the nearby communities of Franklin and Black Diamond was stored until it could be loaded into railcars to be used to power locomotive engines or sold in other markets.

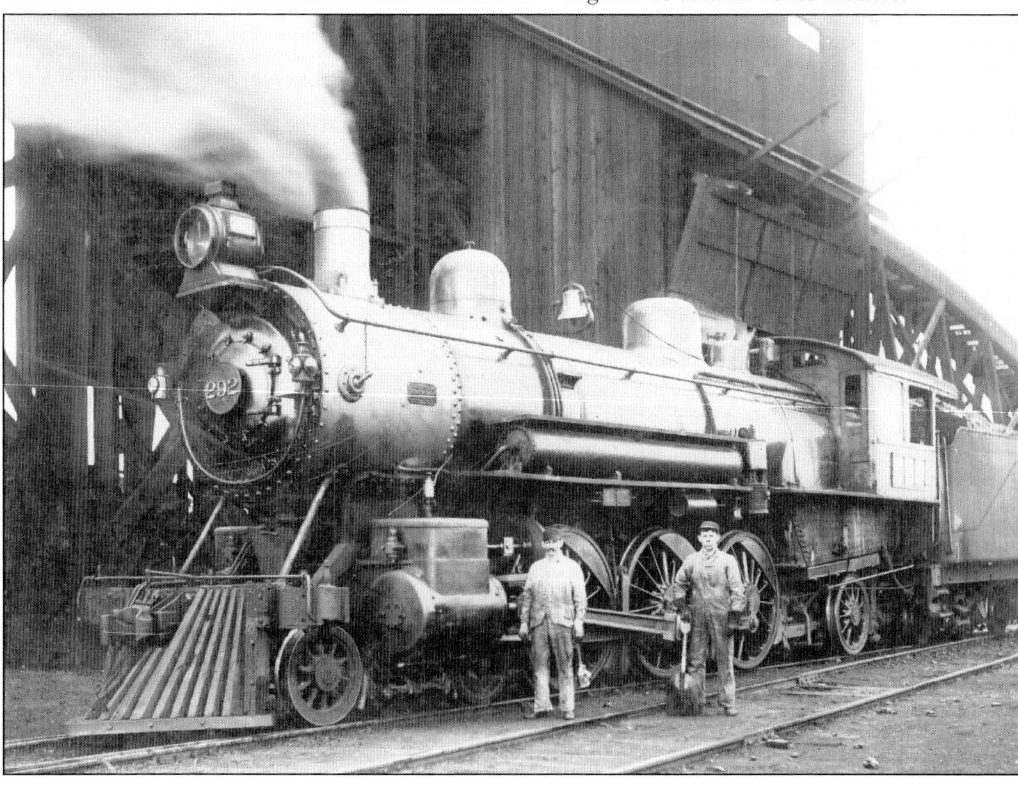

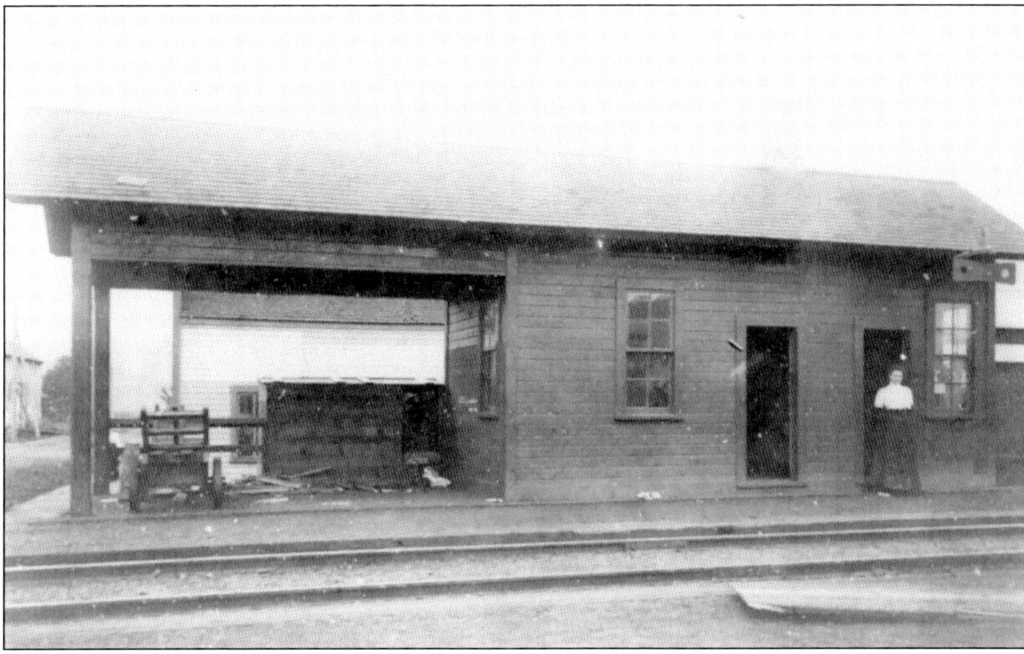

Auburn had several different railroad stations, each serving a different railroad line. This Northern Pacific Railroad station, seen here around 1908, was located on what was then the eastern edge of town, at the intersection of the Northern Pacific line and K Street. It was referred to as the East Auburn station to differentiate it from the downtown Auburn station.

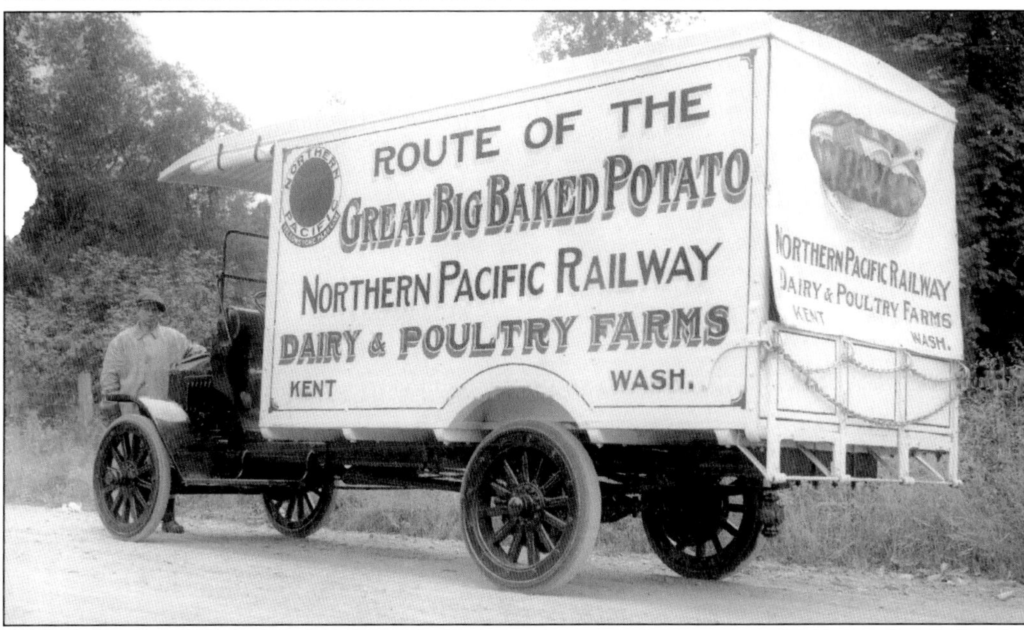

The Northern Pacific Railroad was largely responsible for popularizing baked potatoes in American cuisine. Farmers in potato-producing regions served by Northern Pacific had been throwing out the large, thick-skinned potatoes they harvested. Northern Pacific passenger services began cheaply purchasing them and made the baked potato a staple of their dining cars. This delivery truck from Kent is advertising this specialty meal.

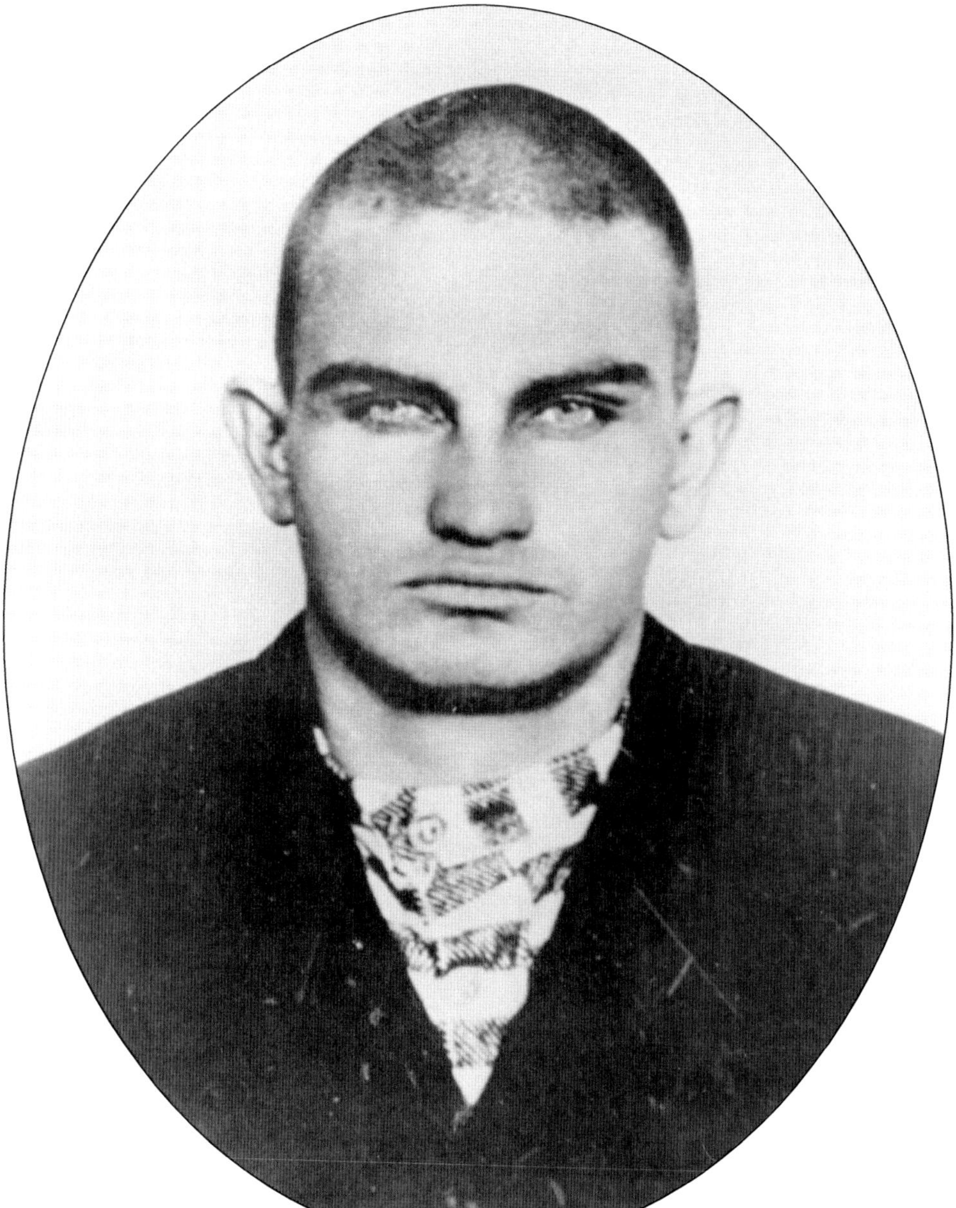

In 1902, Auburn was host to one of the most notorious outlaws of the era, Harry Tracy. After escaping from an Oregon prison and murdering three prison officers, Tracy and another convict traveled throughout the Puget Sound region. Tracy's visit to Auburn took place in July 1902 when the Johnson and Olson families, who lived on a remote farm along the Green River, were held hostage by Tracy. Tracy sent Eric Magnus Johnson into town to purchase a new revolver, threatening to harm his family if he contacted the police or failed to return. After resting and resupplying, Tracy left the farm to continue his cat-and-mouse chase with the local sheriff and federal agents. Tracy died while being apprehended a few weeks later in eastern Washington State. The farm these events took place on is now called the Mary Olson Farm and is listed in the National Register of Historic Places.

The Puget Sound Electric Railway, also known simply as the interurban, began operating the interurban line through Auburn in 1902. The line traveled between Seattle and Tacoma via Auburn, Kent, and Renton, transporting both passengers and freight. The interurban was a much more direct route to Seattle, shaving nearly 30 miles off the more circuitous Northern Pacific route.

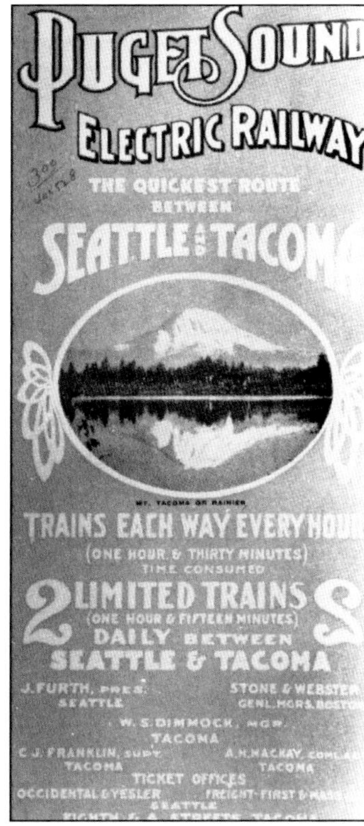

The speed of the interurban railway allowed people to both travel and communicate faster. This mail car, passing through the interurban's headquarters in Kent, was full of letters and packages bound for post offices through the White and Green River Valleys. Fast, reliable mail service encouraged more businesses and residents to settle in the White River region.

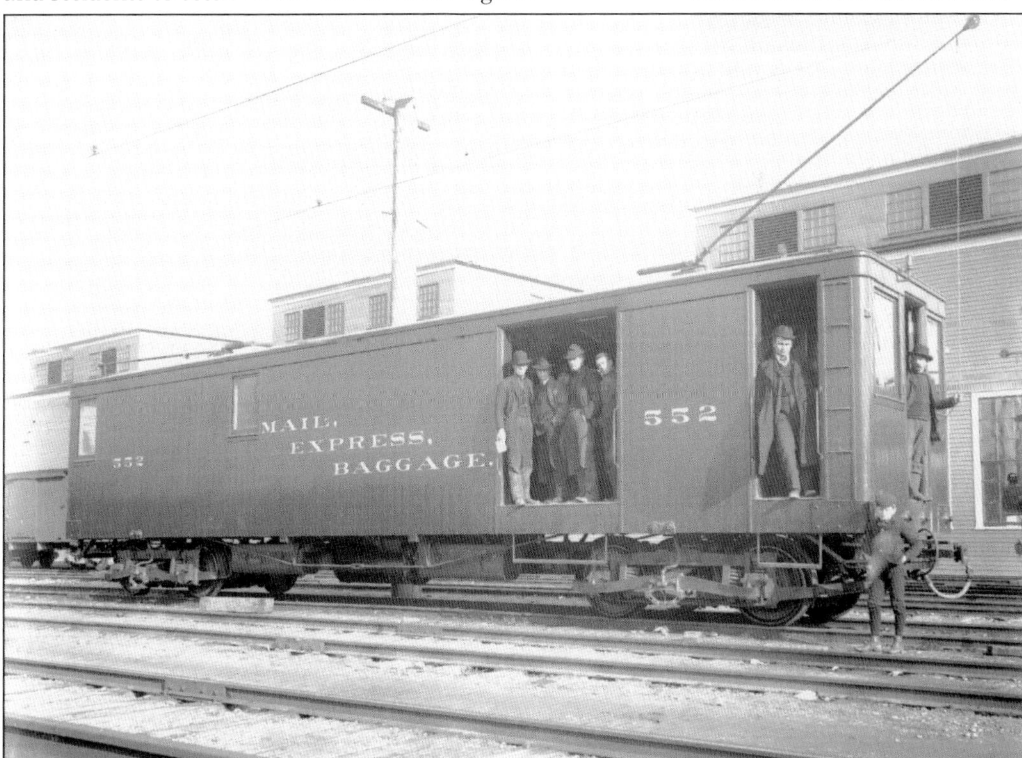

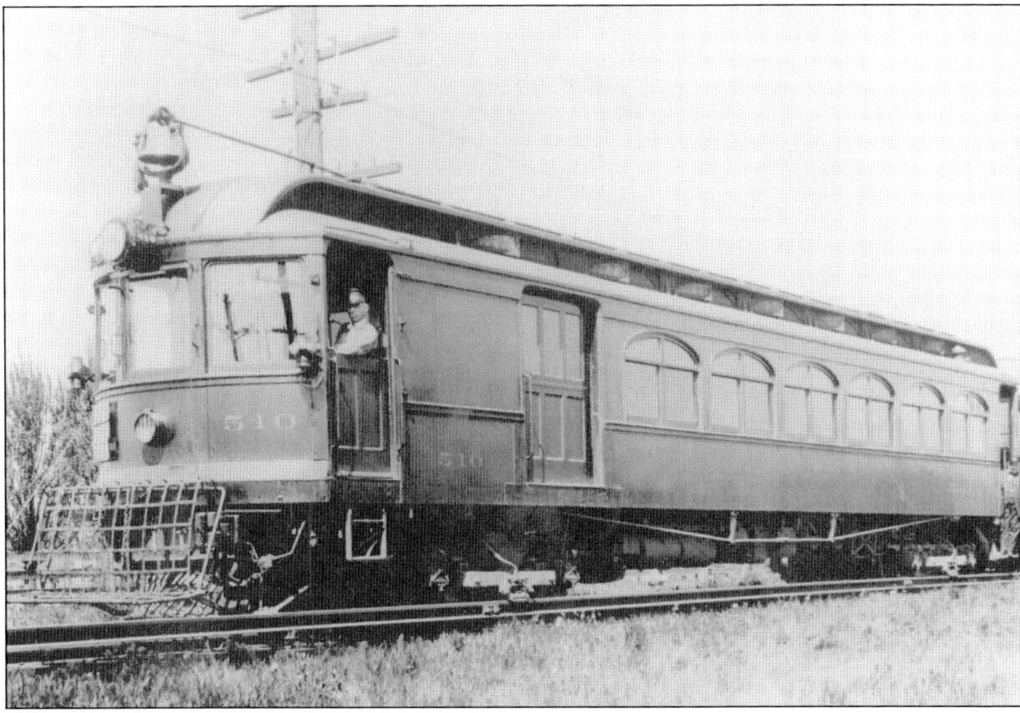

The interurban operated on electricity rather than the steam power that operated locomotives throughout the 1800s. Power was supplied to the train by a third rail, an electrified metal railing running parallel to the tracks. Conductors, called "shoes," extended from the bottom of the train to the third rail to supply power to the engine, as seen in this photograph from around 1920.

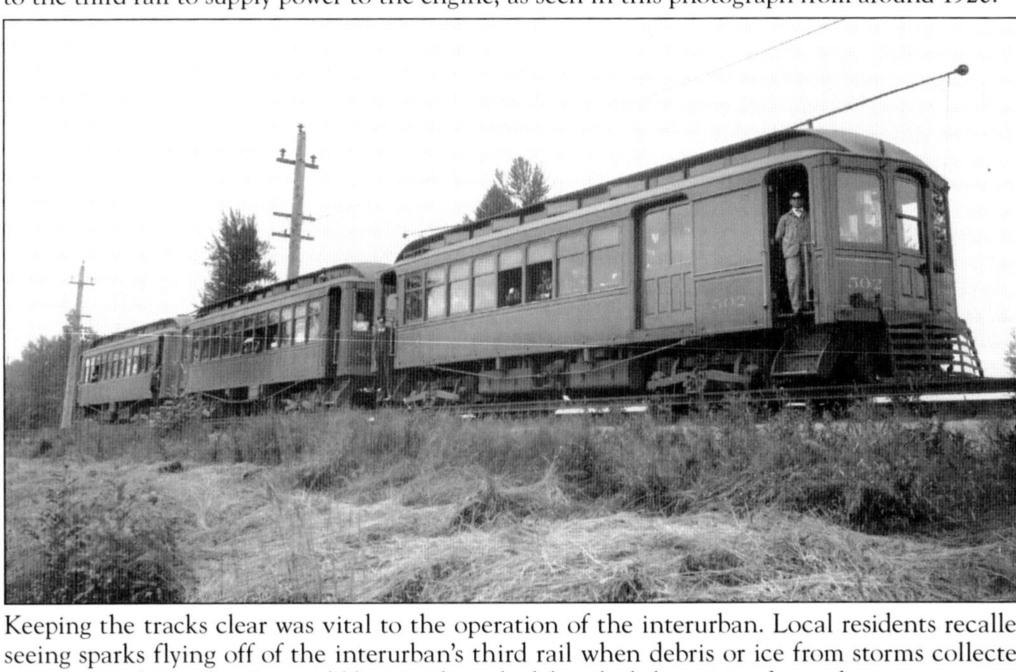

Keeping the tracks clear was vital to the operation of the interurban. Local residents recalled seeing sparks flying off of the interurban's third rail when debris or ice from storms collected over the tracks, and trains could be significantly delayed while waiting for work crews to remove hazards on the railroad line.

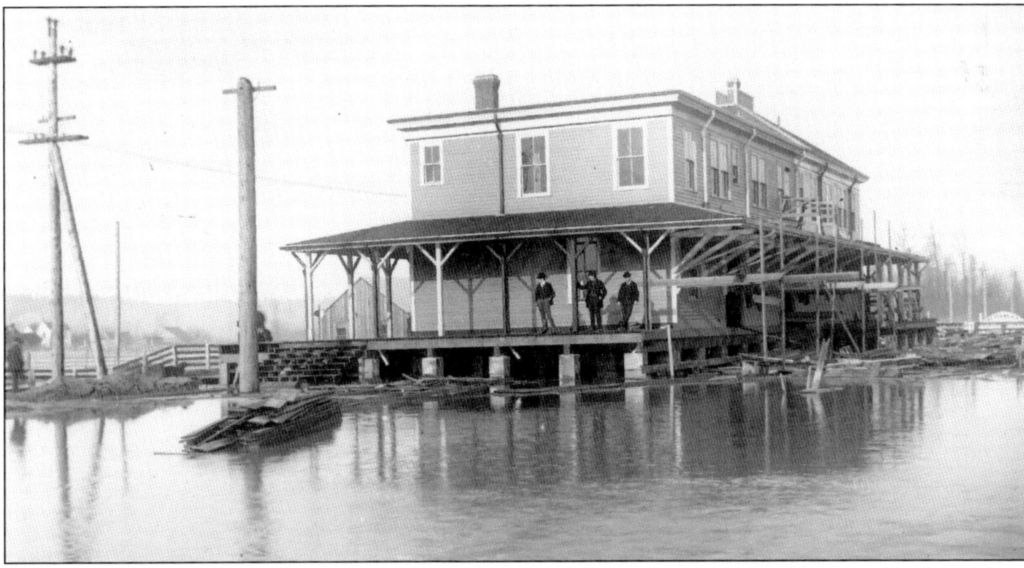

Flooding was a perennial problem for residents of Auburn and other valley cities. The White, Green, Puyallup, and Stuck Rivers flooded their banks on a nearly annual basis, often in the spring or fall, when snow began to melt and heavy rainstorms were common. Here, the interurban office is partially underwater during a flood around 1910.

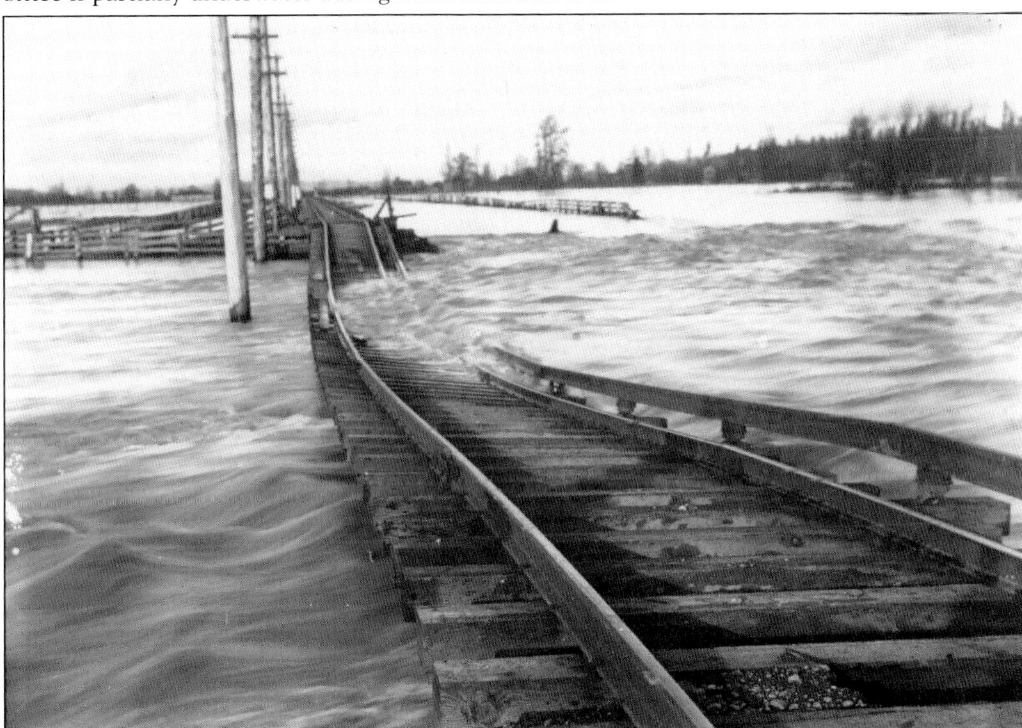

Flooding not only destroyed crops and buildings, but it also threatened the new infrastructure beginning to stretch toward Auburn. This section of the newly laid interurban track had its footing completely destroyed by floodwaters. The cleanup from floods like this one, around 1904, could take months or even years—just long enough to wait for the next major flood to strike.

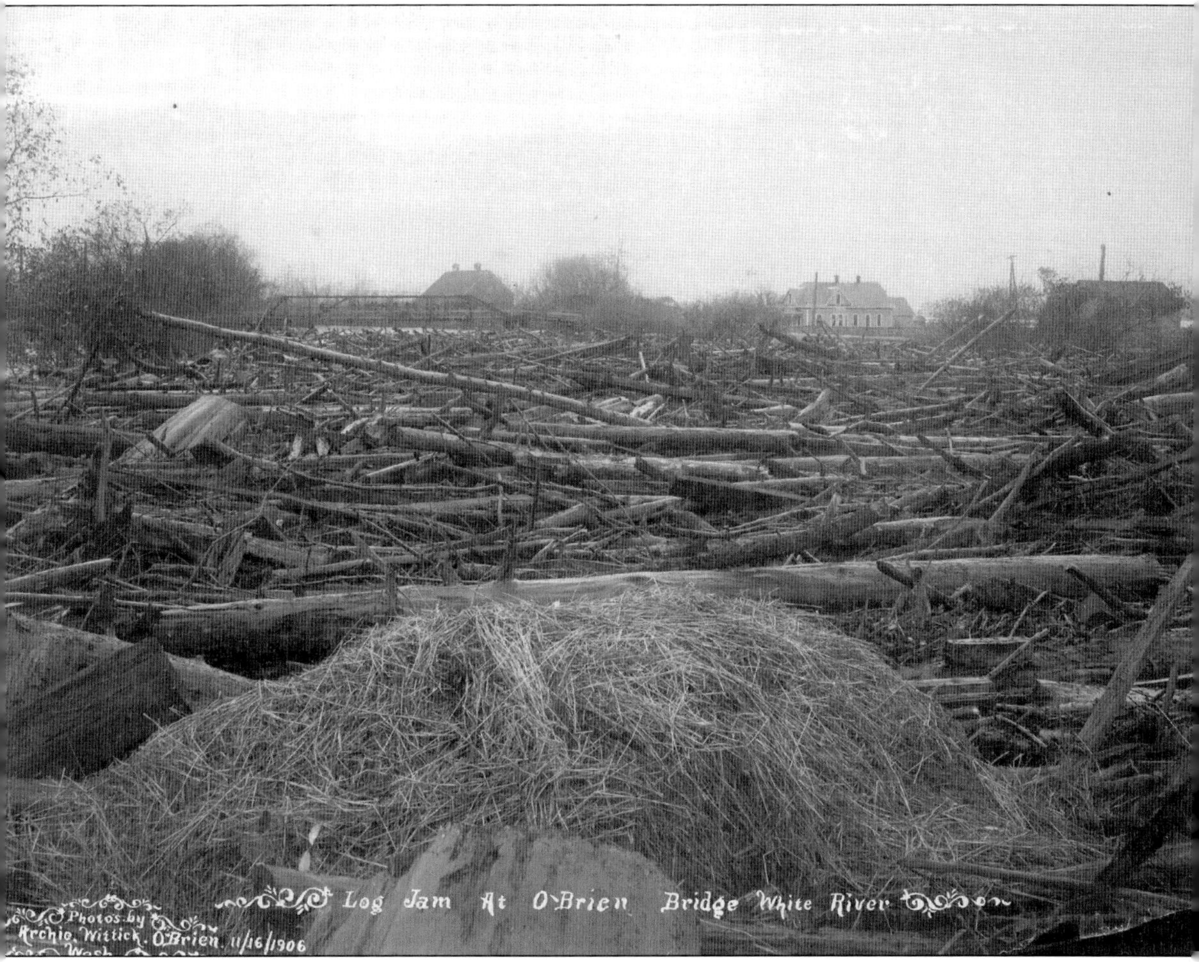

The most significant flood in Auburn's history took place in November 1906. After days of very heavy rain and storms, the White River flooded the entire valley, eventually crashing through the barrier between it and the Stuck River. This forced all of the water that had been flowing into the Green River to be redirected to the Puyallup, permanently changing the course of the White River. This cut the White and Green Rivers off from each other and forced most of the floodwaters south into the Puyallup River Valley. The receding floodwaters left massive logjams and piles of debris throughout the region, like this logjam left by the flood in the small valley town of O'Brien. This flood prompted efforts by city, county, and state governments to construct dams to better control the rivers surrounding Auburn, efforts which continue to this day.

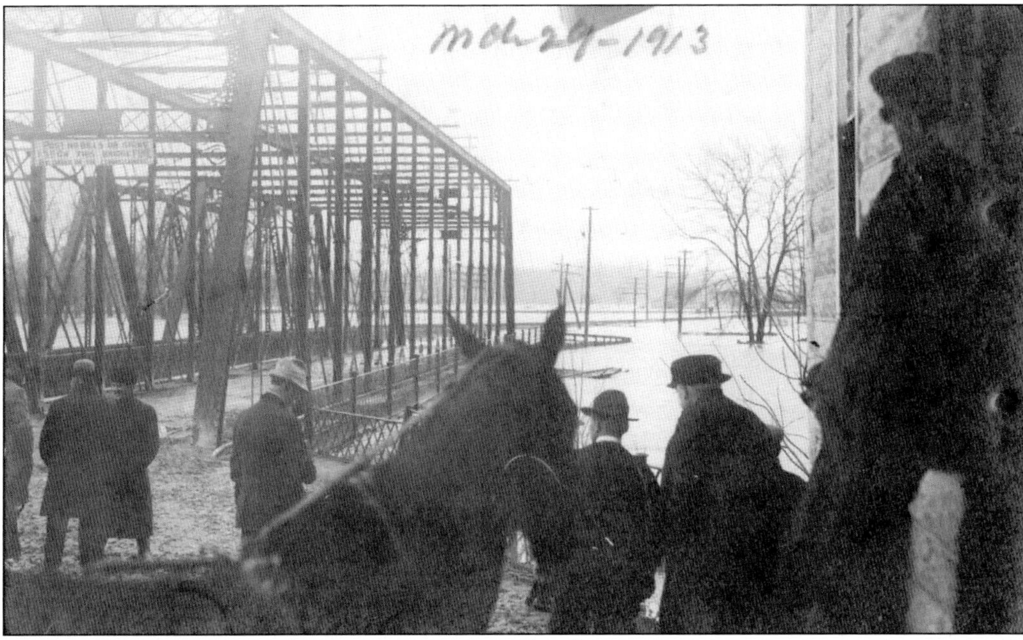

Despite the threat of flooding, people continued to live and settle in Auburn. This footbridge over the White River was well used, usually allowing foot and horse traffic to pass a dozen feet or more over the surface of the river. During this 1913 flood, the waters rose high enough to cover the deck of the bridge.

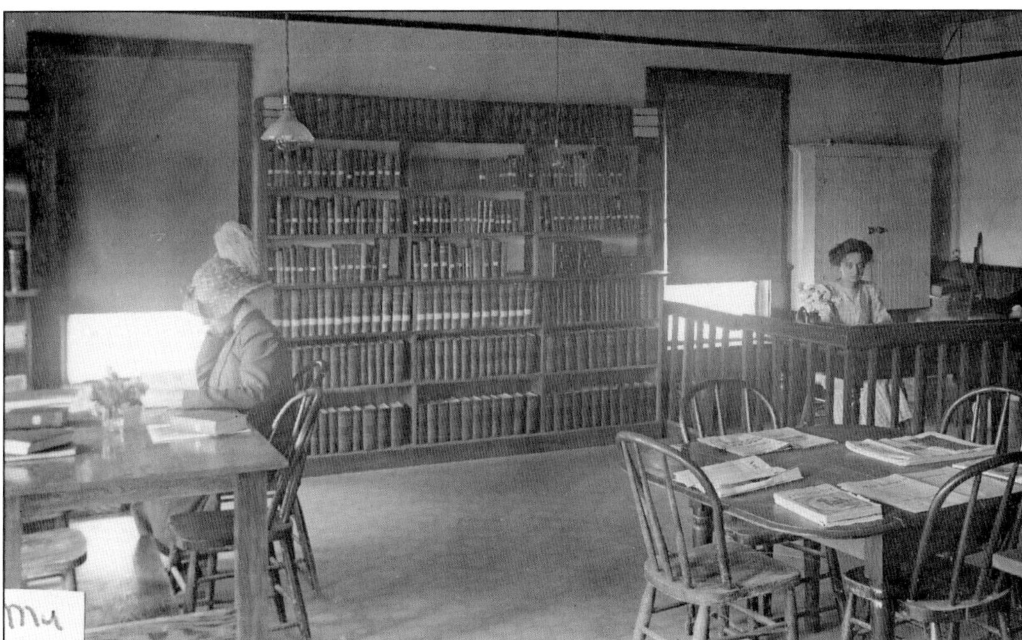

Auburn's first library operated out of a single room on the second floor of city hall. Librarian Mary Fife Smith is seated at the desk in this 1910 photograph. Most libraries in this era were not self-service operations; patrons would instead request a volume from the librarian, who would retrieve and shelve all books.

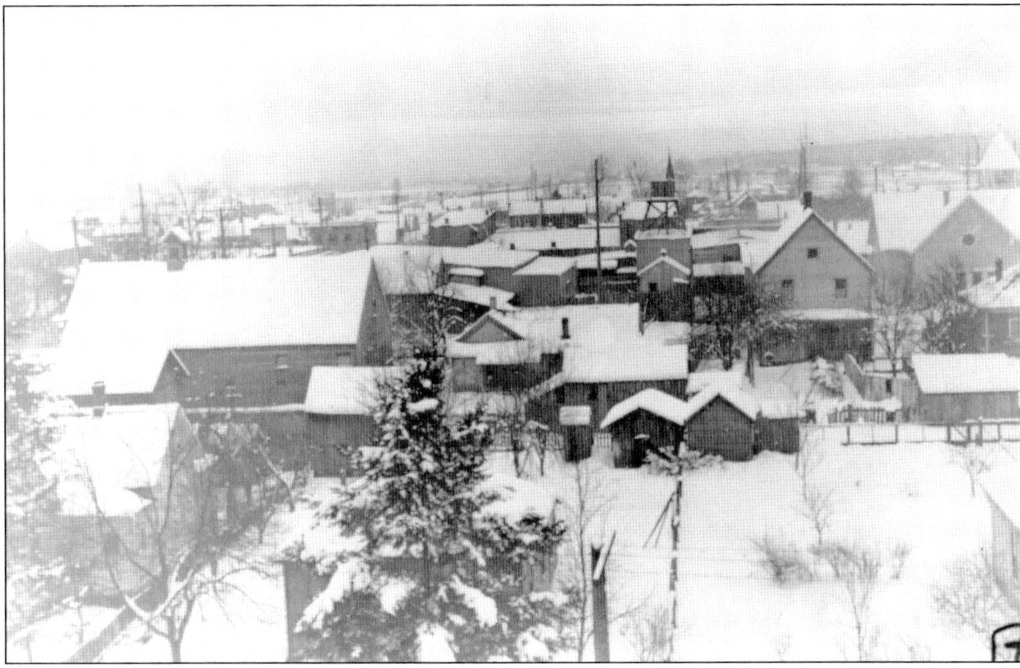

By 1911, telegraph lines carrying information and electricity could be seen throughout Auburn. Most new buildings in the center of town, as well as some old ones, had begun to make the switch to electric lighting. Most of the outlying houses and farms continued using kerosene lamps or carbide gas systems for lighting.

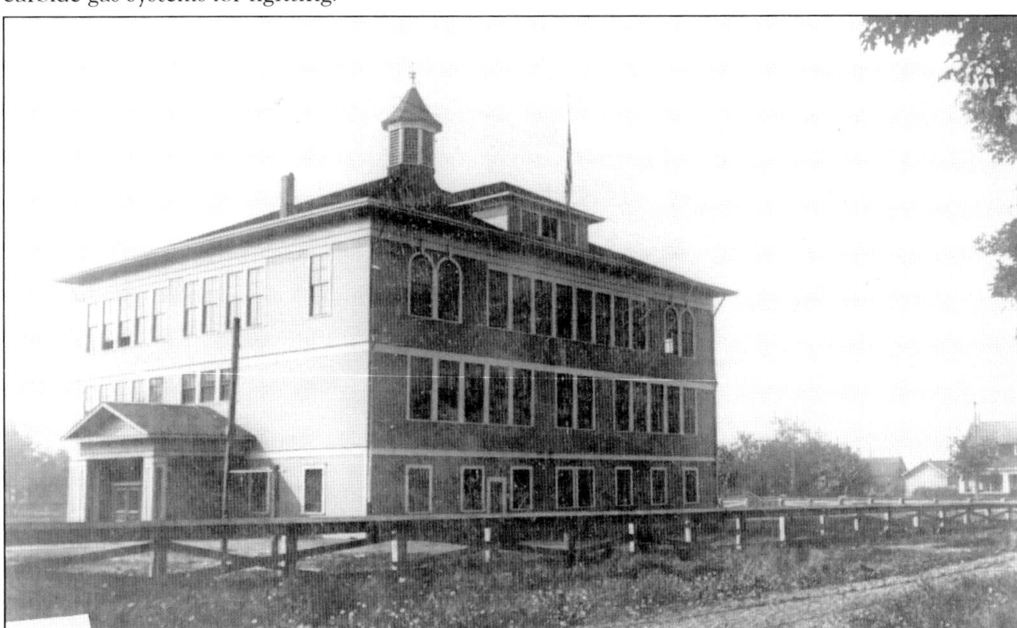

The Central School, built in 1889, burned down in 1903, and this similar, though not identical, building was raised in its place. The school served all grade levels until 1910, when the first Auburn High School was built and the older students moved from the upper floor of the Central School to their new facility.

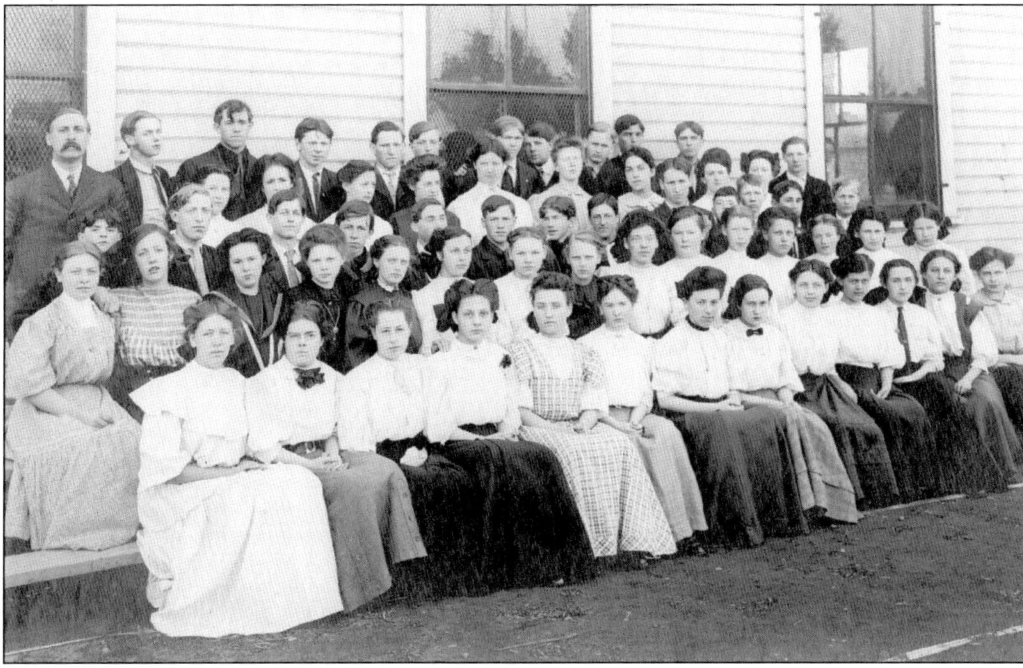

In this 1908 photograph, the assembled members of the Central School sophomore, junior, and senior classes pose in front of their school building. High school graduation was an uncommon achievement at this time due to a lack of demand for college education in the workforce, and many of these students would not go on to receive their 12th-grade diplomas.

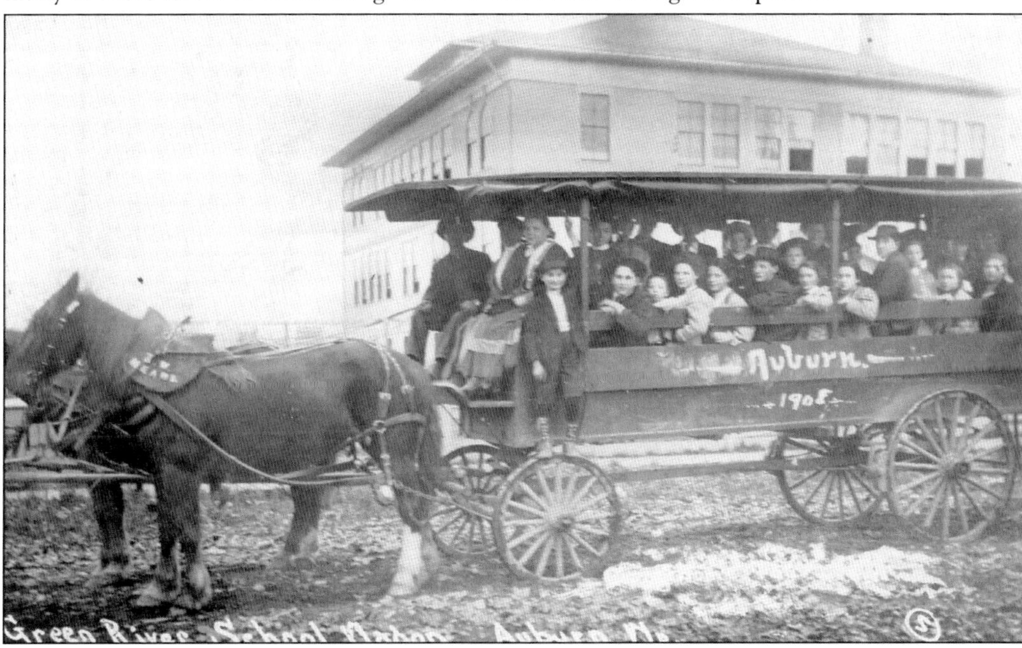

As the Auburn school district grew and consolidated one-room schools into the Central School, students from outlying farms and settlements had to travel farther to get to school than ever before. Meade's Carriage Works provided a horse-drawn wagon to bus children into town for their lessons, as seen in this 1908 image.

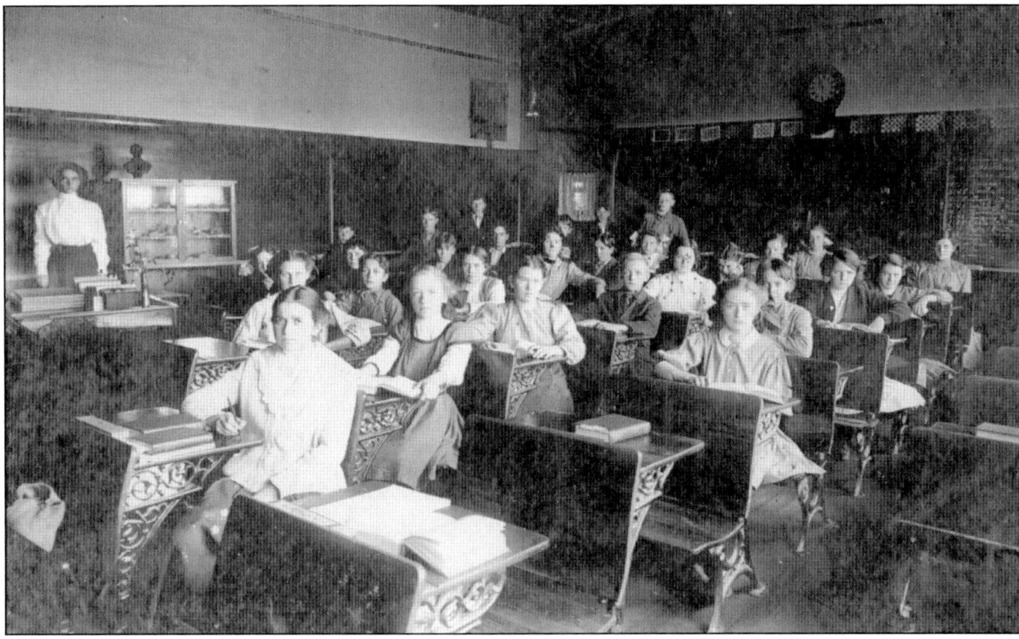

Students at the Central School were separated into classes of between five and thirty students, depending on grade level and age. These middle-school-aged students in 1909 studied arithmetic, grammar, literature, and recitation under the careful eye of their teacher, Miss Wiley, standing behind her desk on the far left.

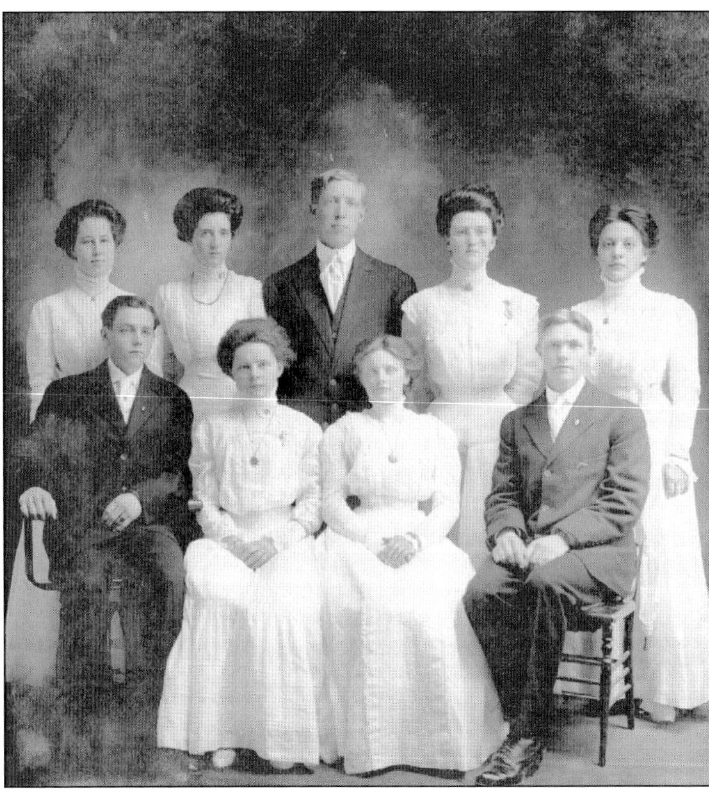

Reaching high school graduation was a cause for celebration in 1909, and these Auburn graduates dressed for the occasion. Elaborate white dresses were traditional graduation garb for young women. Graduation dresses eventually became so expensive as to be prohibitive, and many high schools adopted graduation gowns or other uniforms to ameliorate the issue.

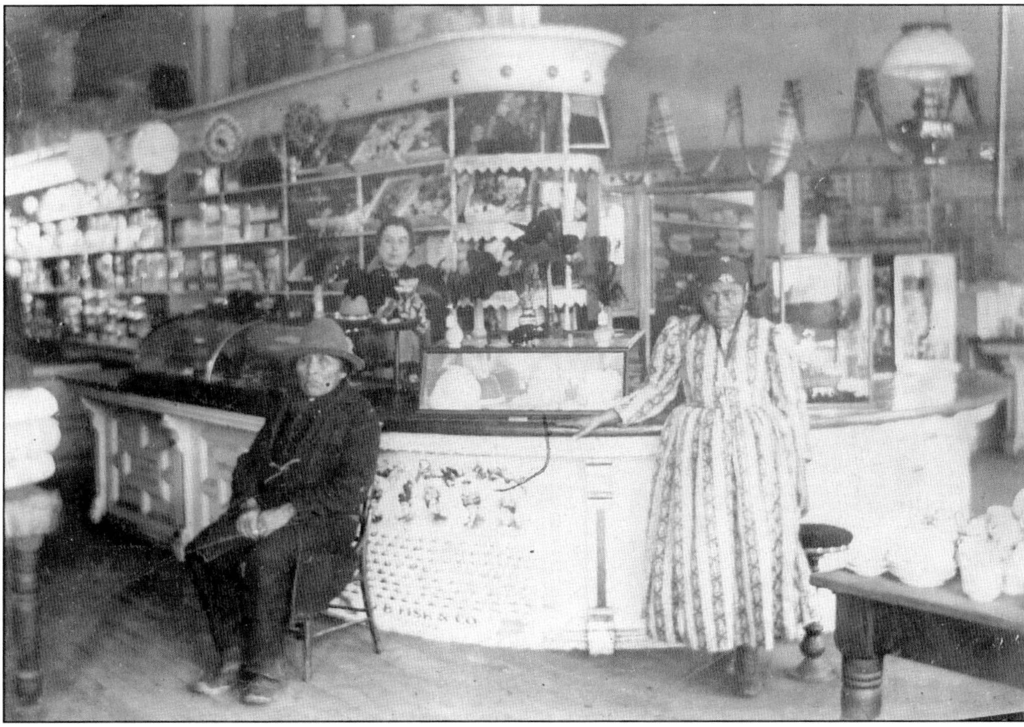

The growth of the economy after the gold rush allowed businesses such as Porter's General Goods, seen here in 1898, to expand their inventories to include decorative and luxury items such as china dishes and fine hats. Wiletchtid and his wife, Elisa, pose for this photograph next to a selection of feathers for decorating the hats in the glass case between them.

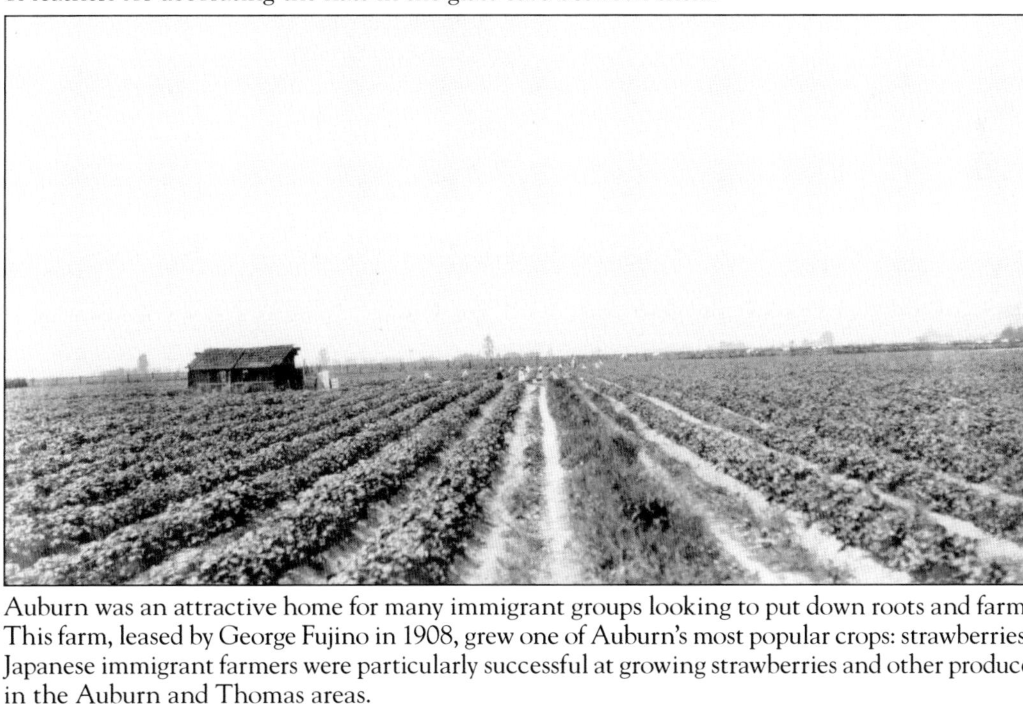

Auburn was an attractive home for many immigrant groups looking to put down roots and farm. This farm, leased by George Fujino in 1908, grew one of Auburn's most popular crops: strawberries. Japanese immigrant farmers were particularly successful at growing strawberries and other produce in the Auburn and Thomas areas.

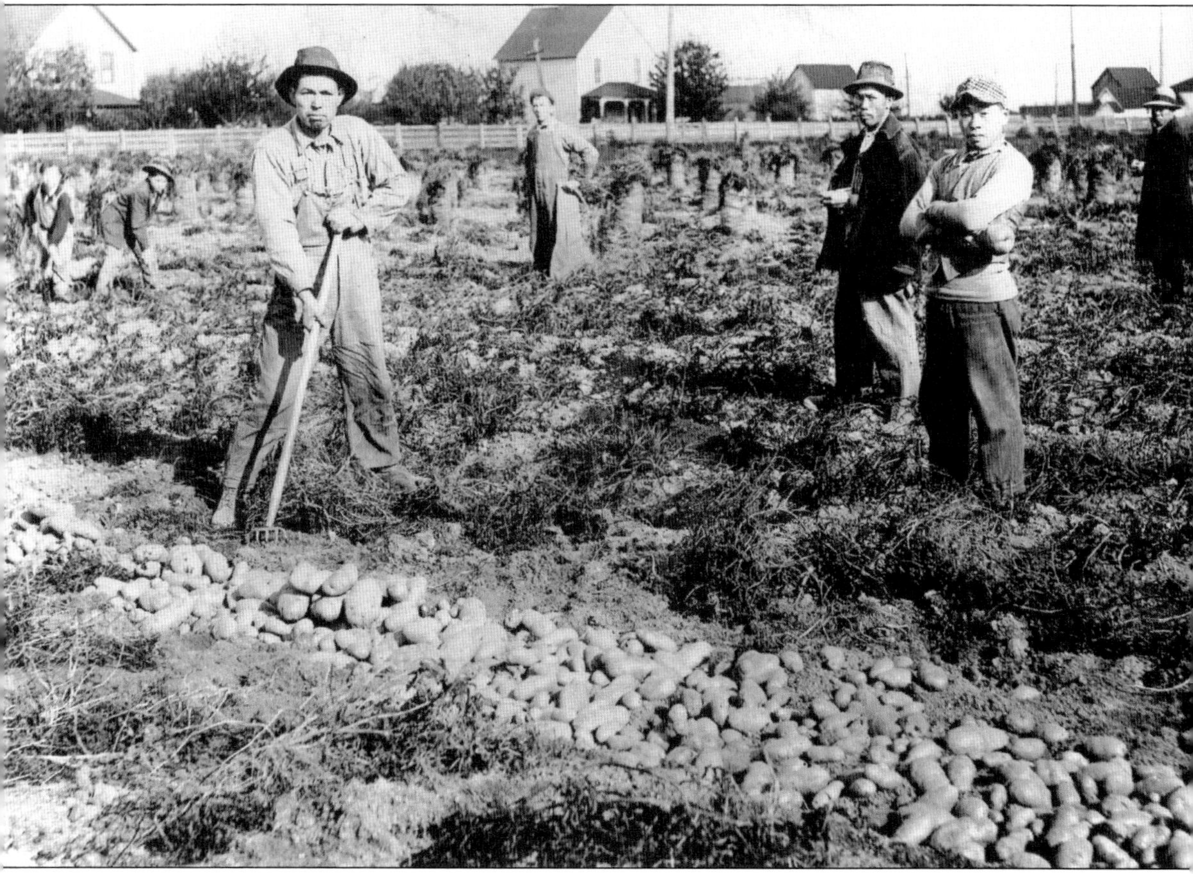

In the early 1900s, immigrants from Asian nations, most notably Japan and China, were not allowed to own land under Washington State law. These laws, collectively called Alien Land Laws, stemmed from racial prejudices against immigrant workers, who were incorrectly perceived to be "stealing jobs" from white laborers. Efforts to stop immigration were often spearheaded by labor groups. Additional prejudice was directed toward Japanese immigrants due to the care many families took to teach their children Japanese and instruct them in Japanese cultural traditions, leading to accusations that Japanese immigrants were refusing to assimilate into American culture. Despite this hostility from other workers and from the law, most Japanese immigrants in Auburn worked as farm laborers or leased land from white farmers. Here, unnamed Japanese laborers work with white farmer George Trott (left) on his potato farm around 1915.

Four

Auburn, Railroad Powerhouse 1913–1940

The period between World War I and World War II saw Auburn shift from an agriculture-based backwater into a fully industrialized city.

In 1913, the Northern Pacific Railroad opened the Auburn Yard, a massive complex of facilities built to repair and maintain Northern Pacific engines and railcars. The advent of World War I caused an economic boom in Auburn, as resources like timber, coal, and agricultural products grew in demand. When the United States entered the war in 1917, the railroads were nationalized, leading to more efficiency in the railway system and better wages for railroad workers. Farmers and local business owners benefited from all of these changes, as money continued to be made and spent by Auburn residents.

Railroad strikes in the 1920s spearheaded the labor movement in Auburn, which became known as a prosperous city where workers could earn fair wages and live comfortably and safely. Many new industries were established or expanded in the 1920s, especially the terra-cotta industry. Easy railroad access made transporting goods to larger cities or ports simple and cost effective.

Not every citizen of Auburn benefited from this prosperity equally. Amendments to Washington's Alien Land Laws unfairly discriminated against immigrant workers, especially those of Japanese descent. Racism was rampant in the region, and some organizations actively lobbied against the growing Japanese American population by attempting to deny them business or access to services—sometimes even with outright assault.

Much of the economic value gained in the 1920s was lost during the Great Depression. Businesses laid off workers, new jobs were scarce, and construction work of any kind ground to a complete halt. Luckily for Auburn, agricultural products like milk, lettuce, and berries were still needed, so farming continued. Workers looking for jobs could usually find seasonal work helping to bring in the harvest, even if no other job opportunities were available.

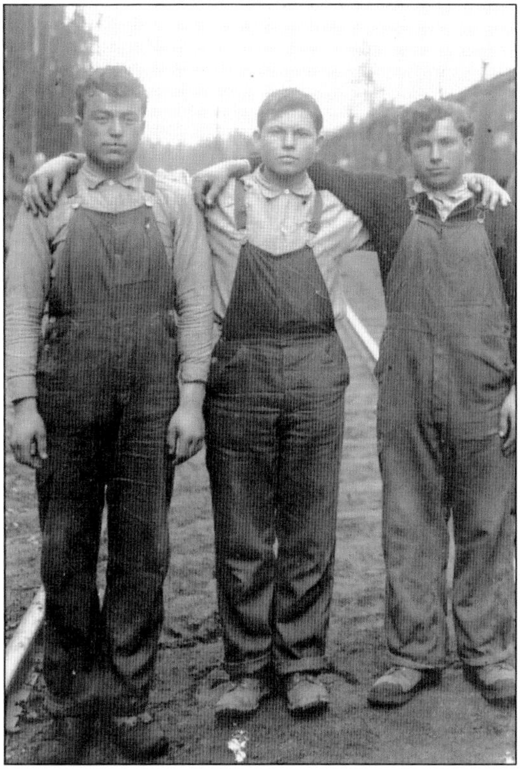

The construction and operation of the Auburn Yard brought approximately 600 new residents to Auburn, including Greek and Bulgarian laborers who were brought in by Northern Pacific to work as cheap labor. While many of these workers moved on to new job sites after the yard was completed, some stayed on in Auburn, adding to the rich mix of immigrant groups calling the town home.

These Auburn Yard workers take a break to pose for a photograph around 1921. Most workers at the Auburn Yard were engaged in repair work on the dozens of locomotive engines that came through the Auburn depot every day. Though these workers are all men, young women were also occasionally hired to assist with locomotive cleaning and maintenance.

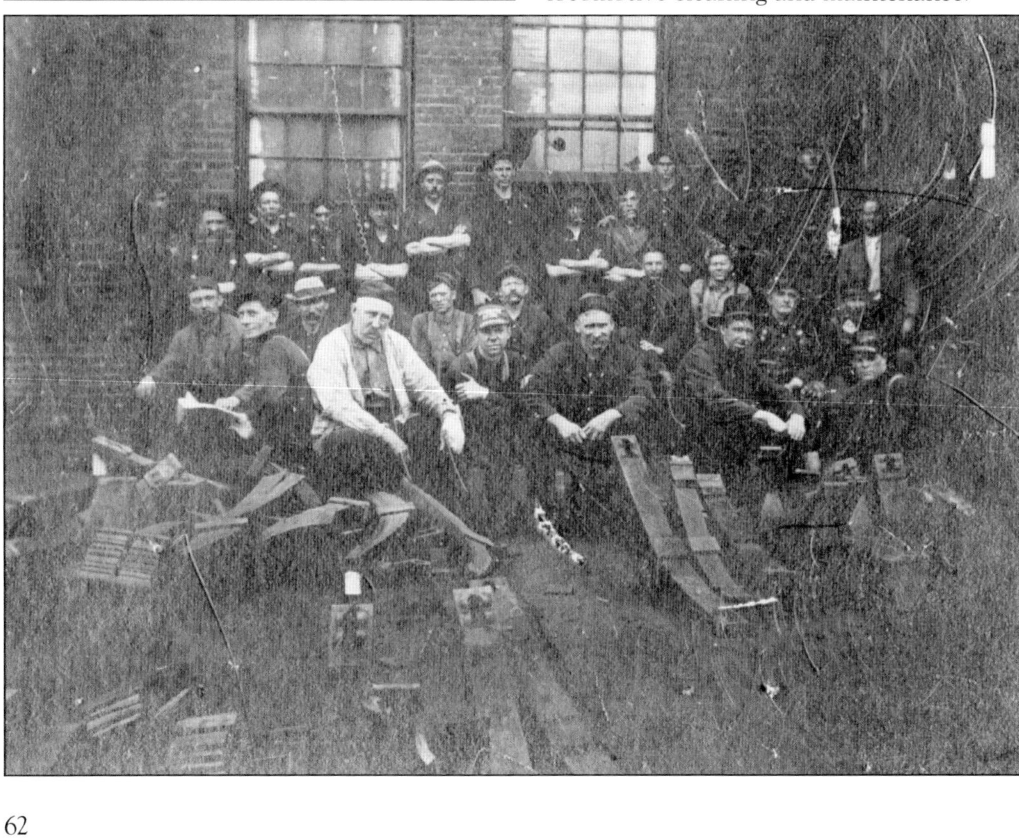

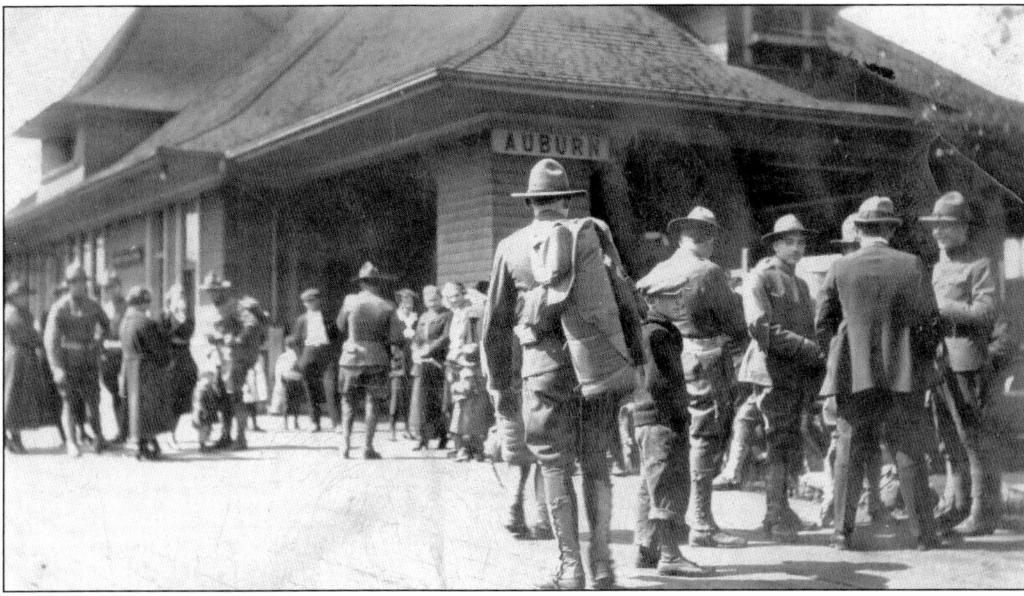

The Northern Pacific Railroad was the major line in Auburn for long journeys. In this photograph from around 1923, local members of the 41st Division of the National Guard prepare to leave on a training exercise. The US National Guard was founded in 1903, and members were mobilized for combat in World War I.

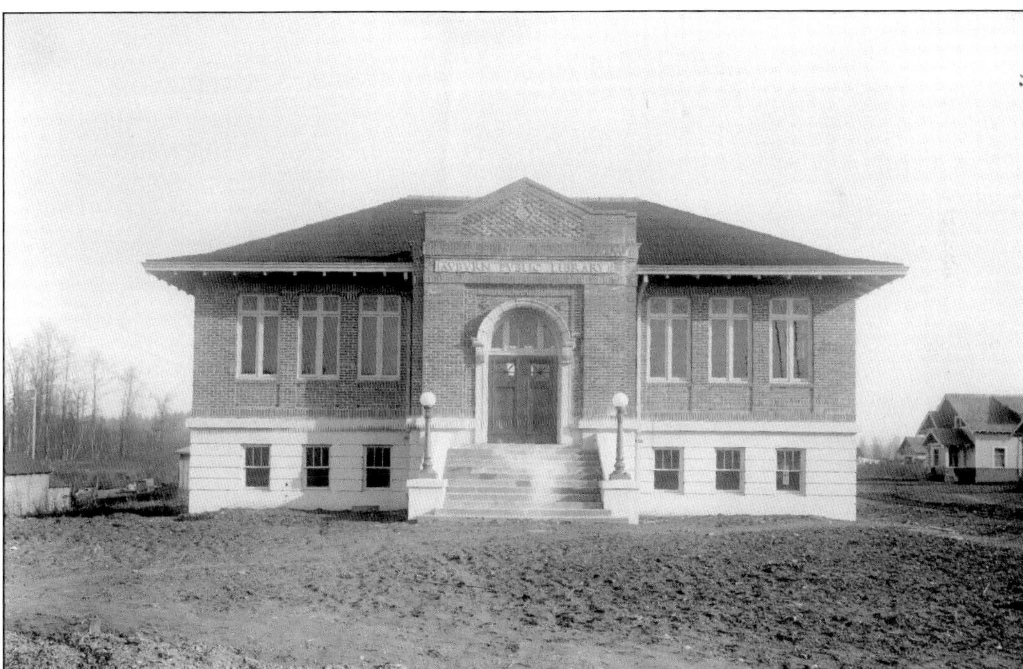

The first library in Auburn was a Carnegie library, built in 1914 on land donated by the Ballard family. The library cost $9,000 to construct and was funded by a grant from the Carnegie Foundation, like many other small libraries throughout the country. Though no longer used as a library, this building still stands at the corner of Auburn Avenue and Third Street Northeast.

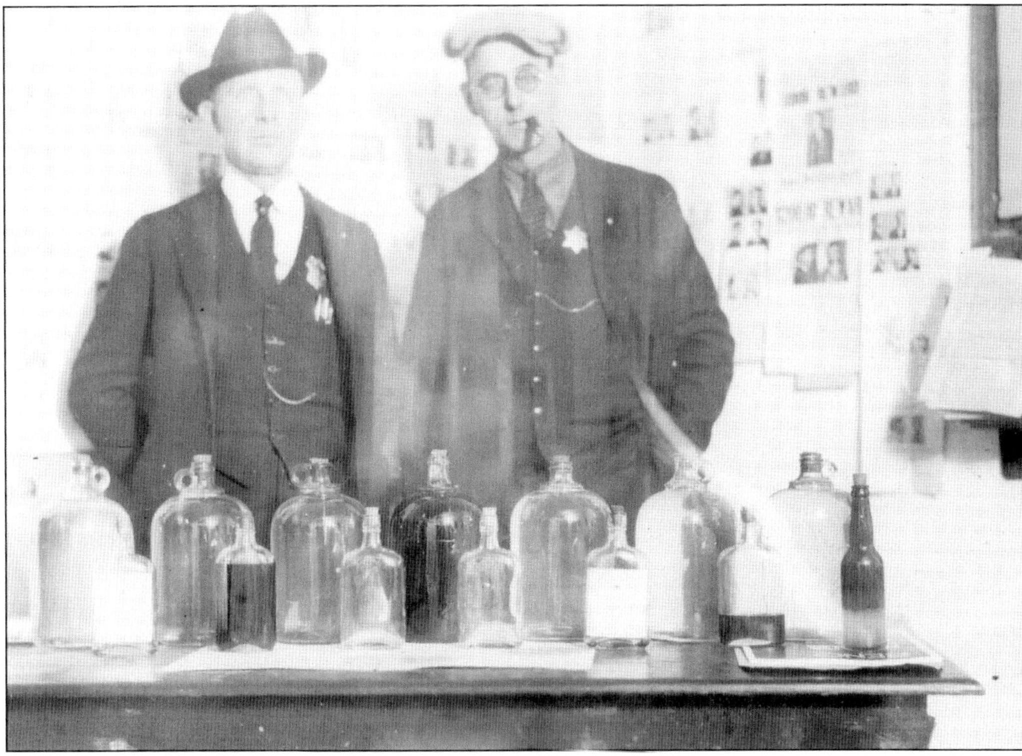

Prohibition took effect in Washington State in 1916, three years before the 18th Amendment made the production and sale of alcohol illegal nationwide. Auburn police had their hands full responding to reports of illegal still operations. Here, around 1924, two members of the Auburn police force pose with jugs of confiscated alcohol.

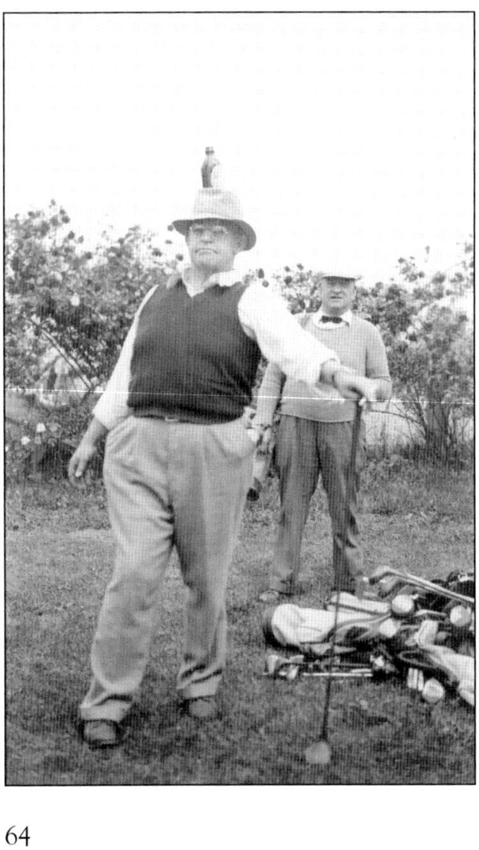

Prohibition was notoriously difficult to enforce. Even upstanding Auburn citizens like Dr. Robert Palmer (left) and Dr. George Scott enjoyed the occasional drink in private. Citizens were allowed to drink alcohol that had been purchased prior to 1916 or small quantities of self-produced wine and beer. Many more opted to purchase illegally produced gin or moonshine.

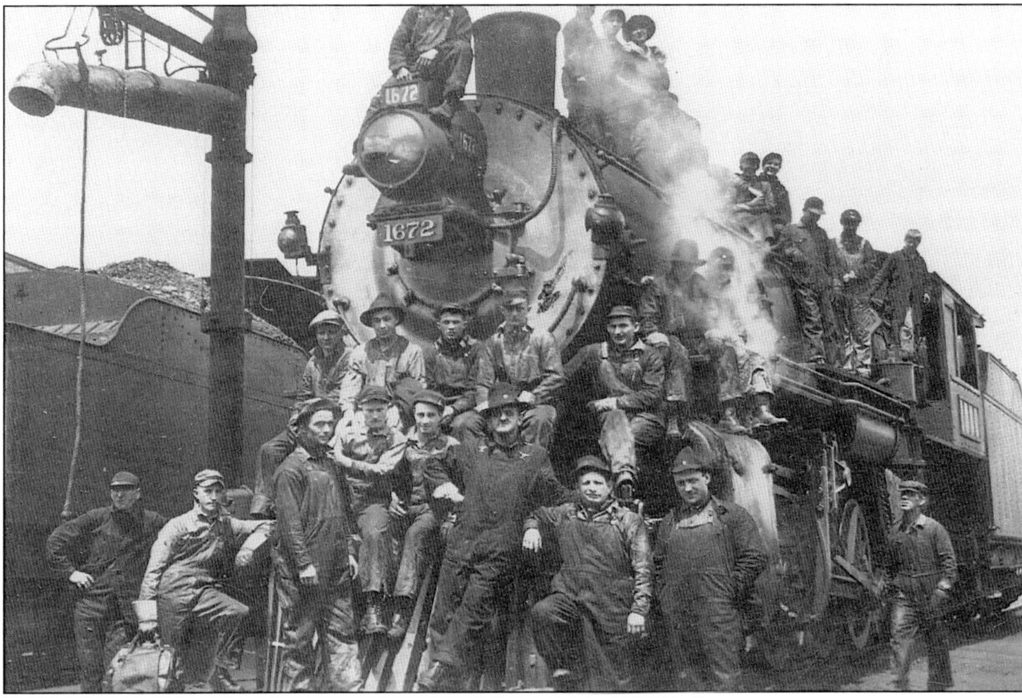

The nationalization of railroads during World War I led to greater efficiencies and better wages for railroad workers, like this group posing at the Auburn roundhouse in 1918. When private ownership resumed, company leaders tried to reduce wages to prewar levels, which led to massive labor strikes. The unions were victorious, and wages stayed high throughout the 1920s.

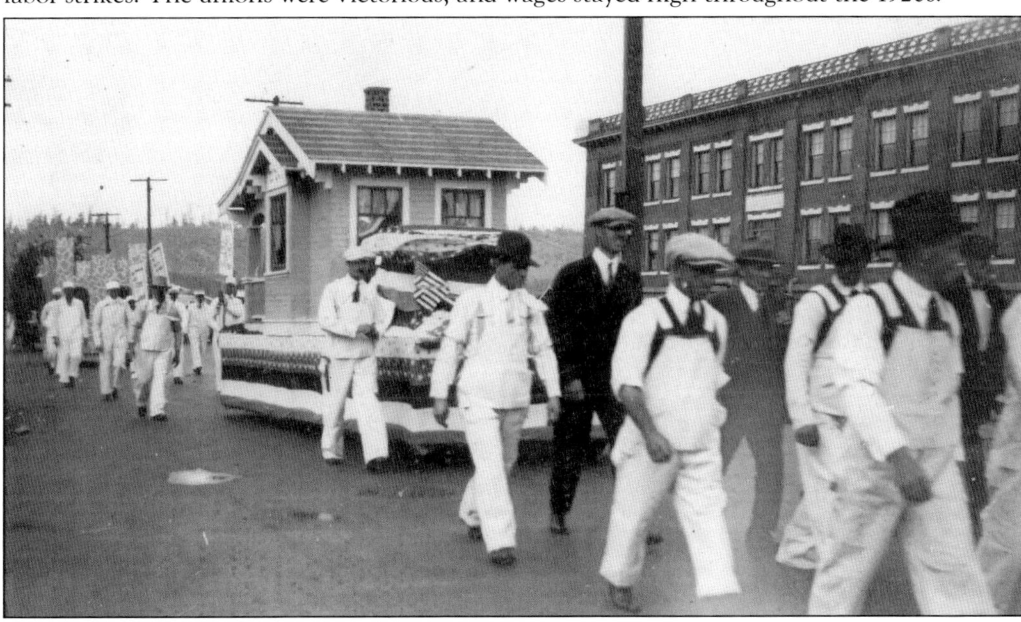

Many labor unions found Auburn to be a great place to live and work in the years following World War I, and the community and social activities they provided were a part of the fabric of the city. The United Brotherhood of Carpenters and Joiners Local 1708 produced this elaborate float for an Auburn Day parade around 1925.

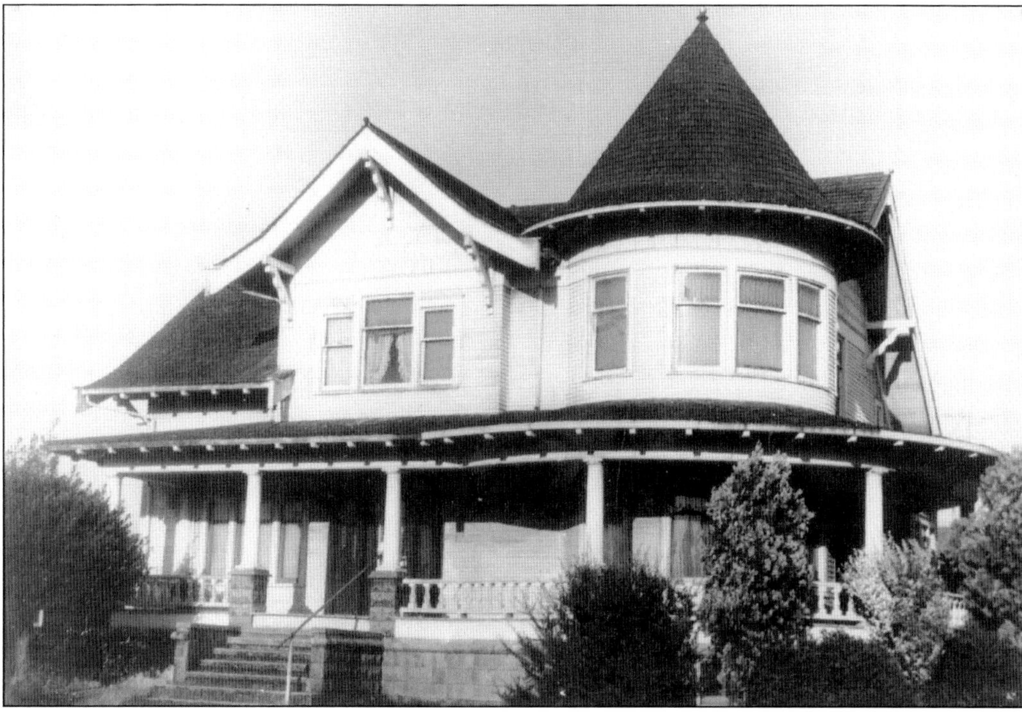

The Spanish Influenza pandemic struck the area in 1918, on the tail of World War I. With national resources depleted from the war, local communities had to pull together to care for the sick. Oscar Blomeen, a Borden employee, rented this house to self-appointed nurse Cora Stone in 1918 in order to house the sick citizens of Auburn.

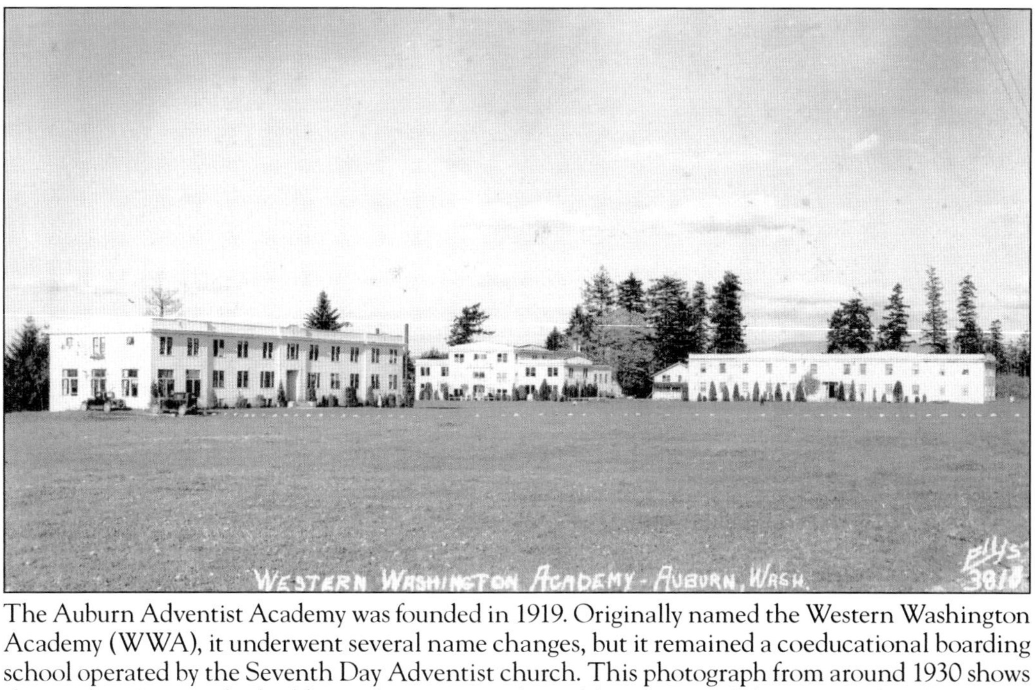

The Auburn Adventist Academy was founded in 1919. Originally named the Western Washington Academy (WWA), it underwent several name changes, but it remained a coeducational boarding school operated by the Seventh Day Adventist church. This photograph from around 1930 shows the academy's second rebuilding, after an unexplained fire destroyed the entire school in 1921.

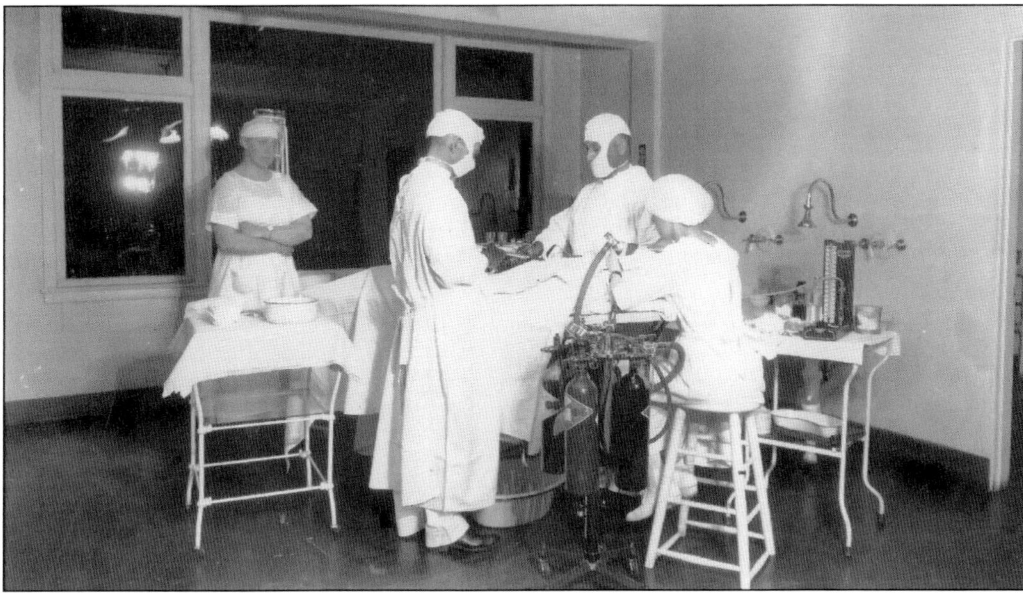

When Dr. Owen Taylor and Dr. Martin Lacey opened the first modern hospital in Auburn in 1921, everything inside was state-of-the-art. The operating room, seen here, had the most modern metal, glass, and rubber equipment available. Plastic equipment was not widely used in the medical profession until after World War II.

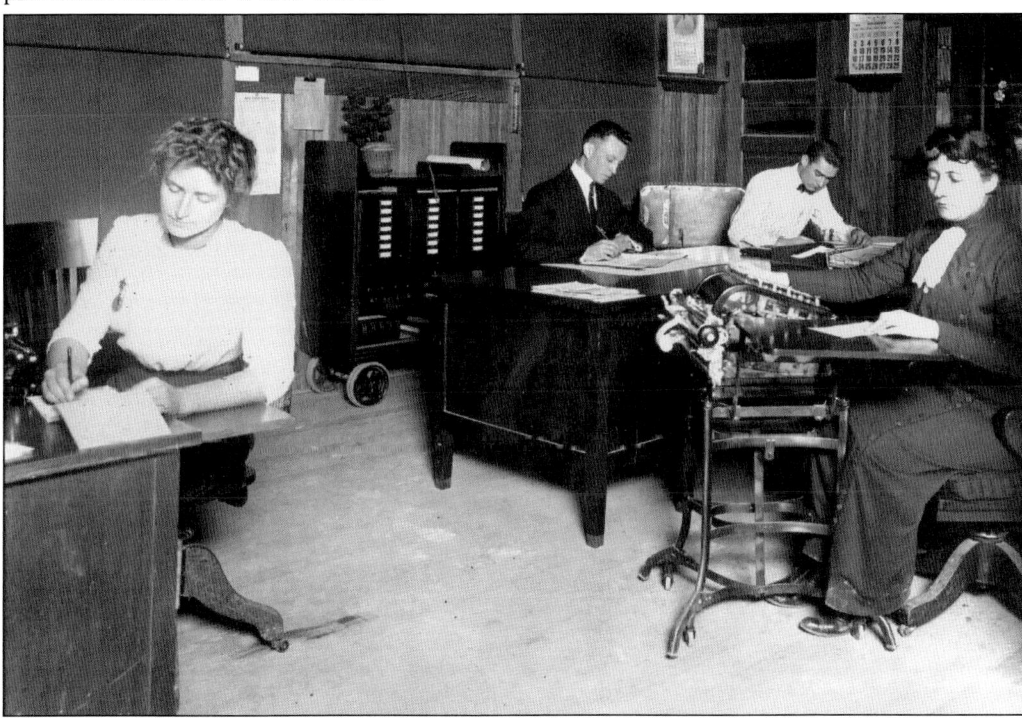

Thanks to the rich river clay deposits in the Auburn area, the Northern Clay Company opened in 1913. Located next to the railroad tracks on Third Street, the new office had all of the luxuries of a state-of-the-art business, including a telegraph machine, seen here being operated by the woman on the right.

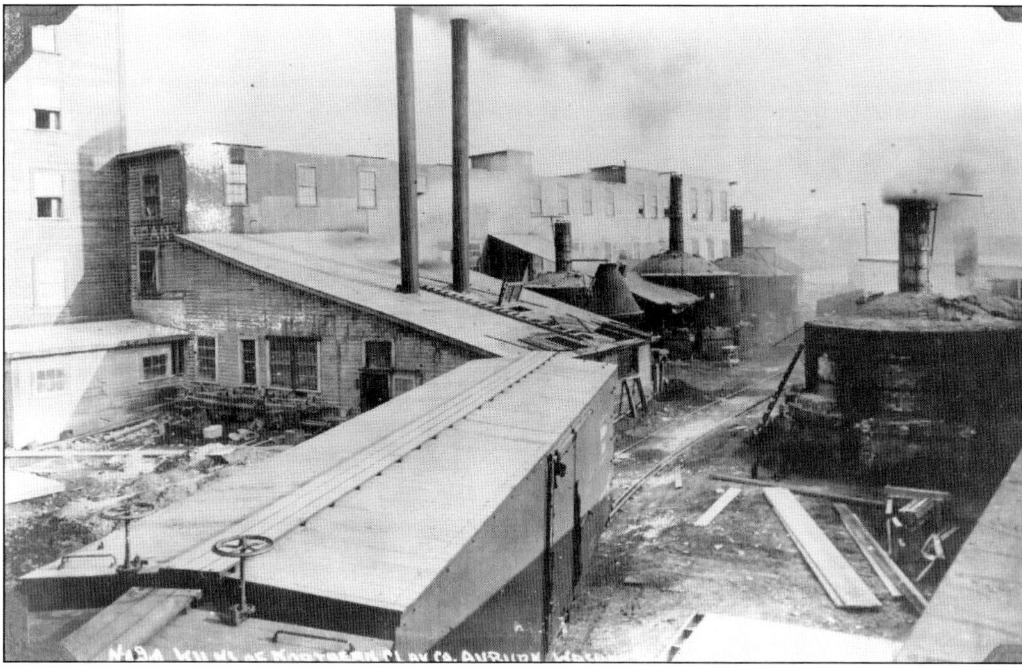

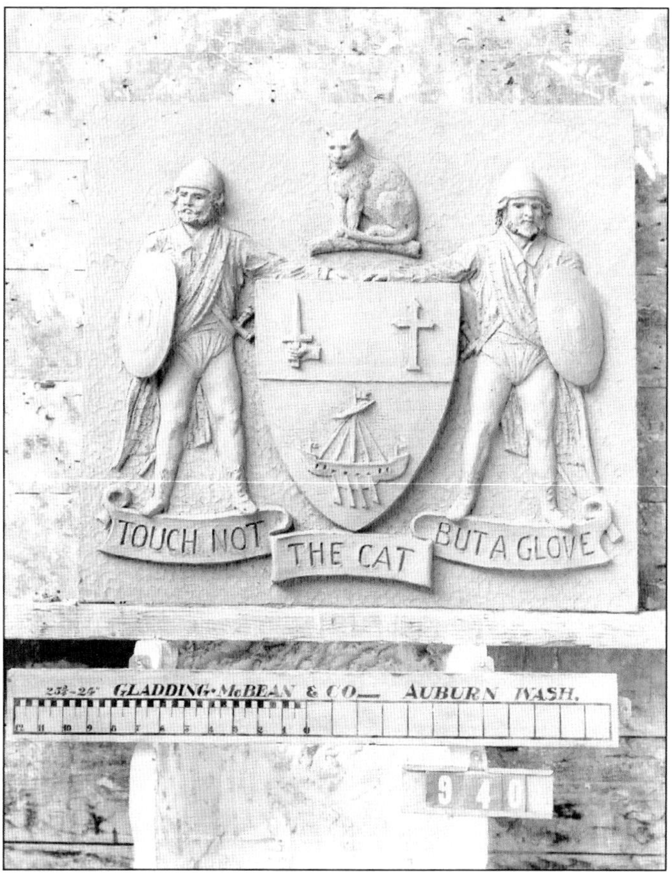

The Northern Clay Company factory was made up of offices and workrooms inside, with massive kilns for firing the finished terra-cotta pieces outside. The company was purchased in 1925 by Gladding-McBean, a terra-cotta company from California, and continued to operate in Auburn until the factory closed in 1932 because of the Great Depression.

The terra-cotta pieces produced by Northern Clay were used to decorate buildings around the state and the country, including the Pantages Theater in Tacoma, the Frederick & Nelson store in Seattle (now the Nordstrom flagship store), and the Wrigley Building in Chicago. This piece, showing the coat of arms of the Macpherson Clan of Scotland, was probably made for a private home.

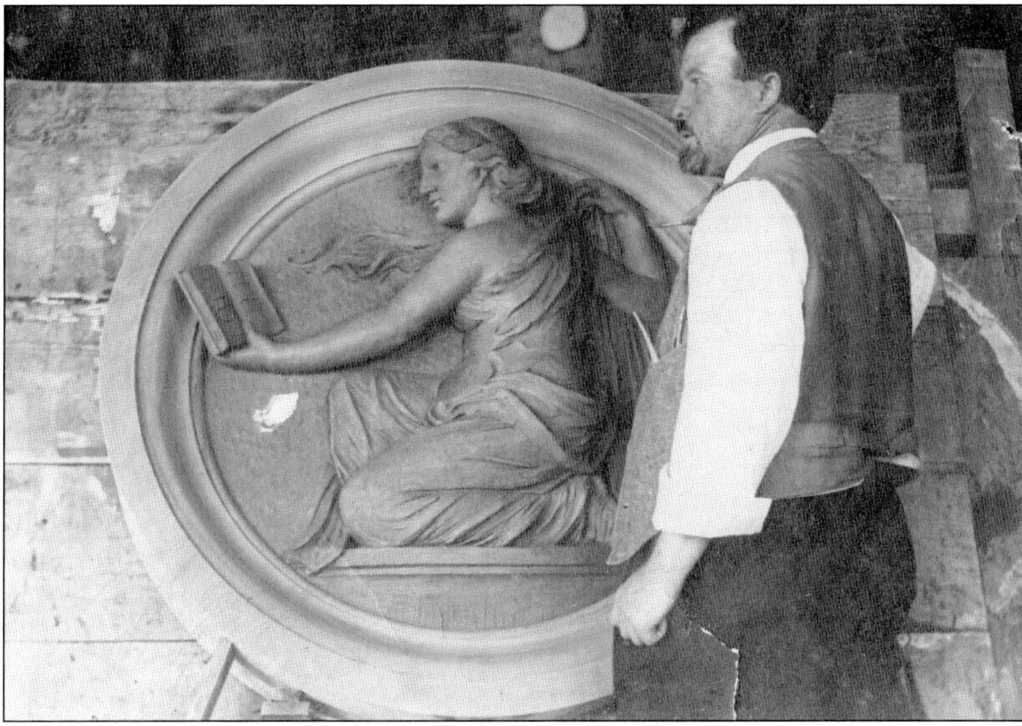

Louis Shubert was the head sculptor and artist at Gladding-McBean. He led a team of four other artists to create the detailed works of art produced by the company. Despite working for a company in Auburn, Shubert was actually a Seattle resident; he commuted to Auburn via the interurban every morning.

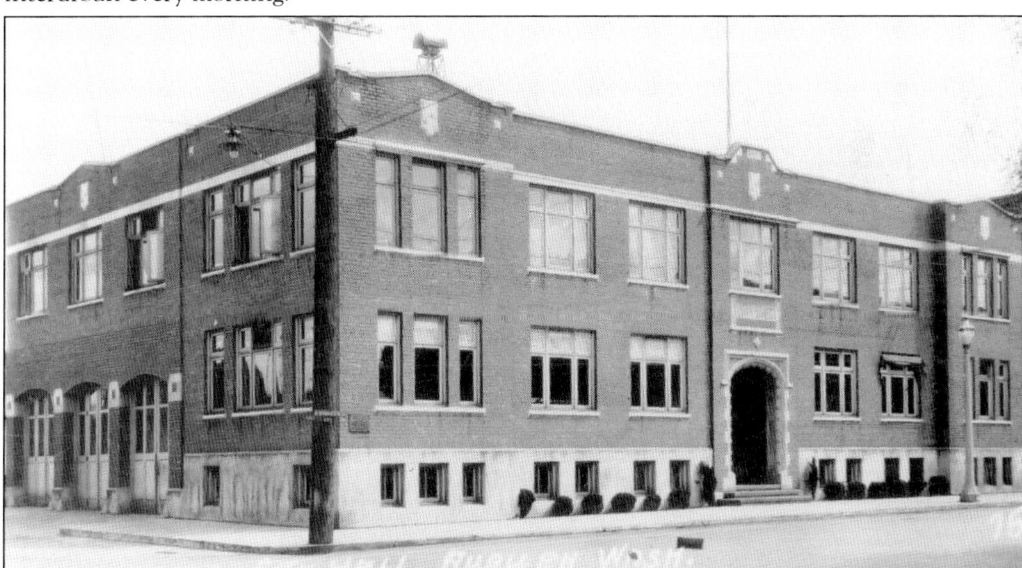

Auburn's second city hall building was constructed in 1923. The concrete and brick structure was styled similarly to other new buildings in Auburn, such as the brick library and post office. All city services were headquartered out of this building, including the fire department. The large garage doors for the fire engines can be seen on the left.

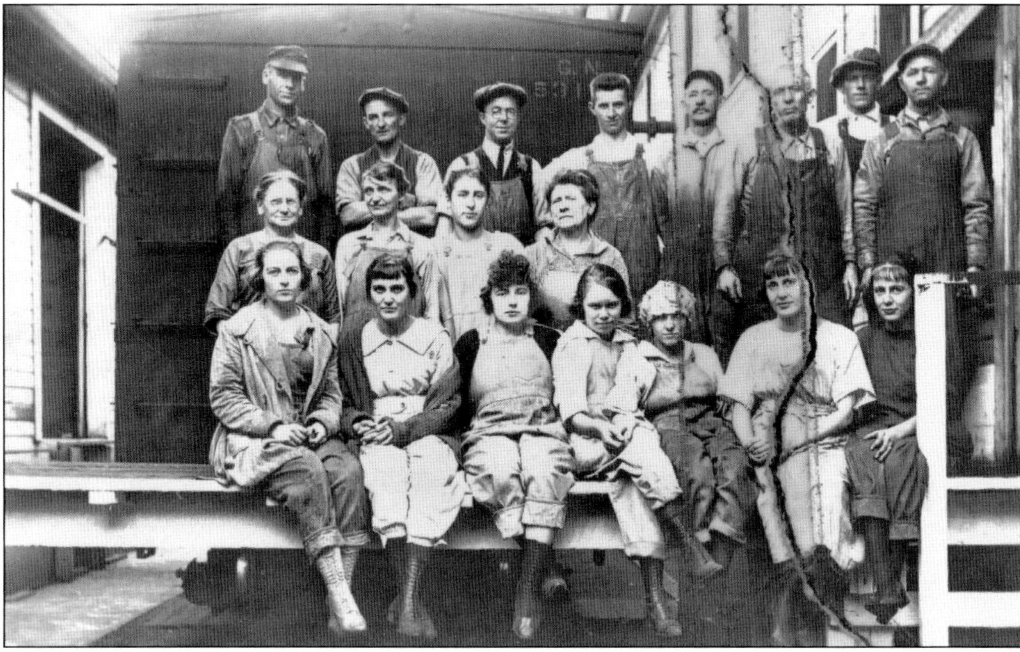

Railroads had been hiring female workers since the 1870s, but it was not until World War I that they became a significant portion of the workforce. These workers at the Northern Pacific roundhouse were mostly machinists and cleaners. After World War I, most women were laid off from these mechanical positions, but more were hired for clerical positions instead.

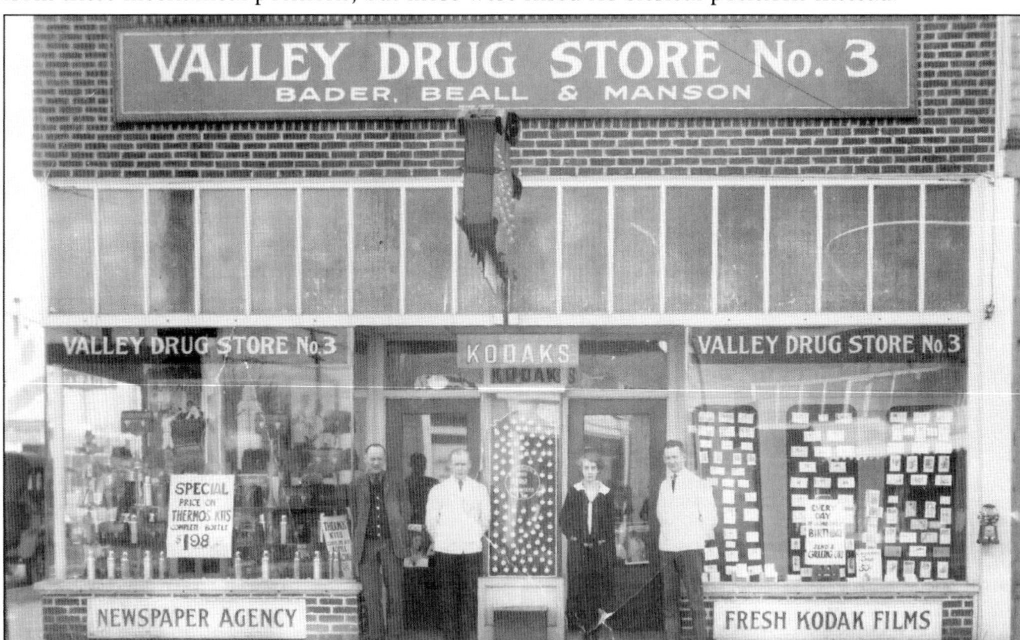

Auburn's population boom after World War I encouraged the growth and expansion of many local businesses. By 1924, Valley Drug Store No. 3, originally a simple pharmacy, was selling greeting cards, newspapers, and photography film. These products were intended as much for local Auburn residents as they were for people passing through town on the train.

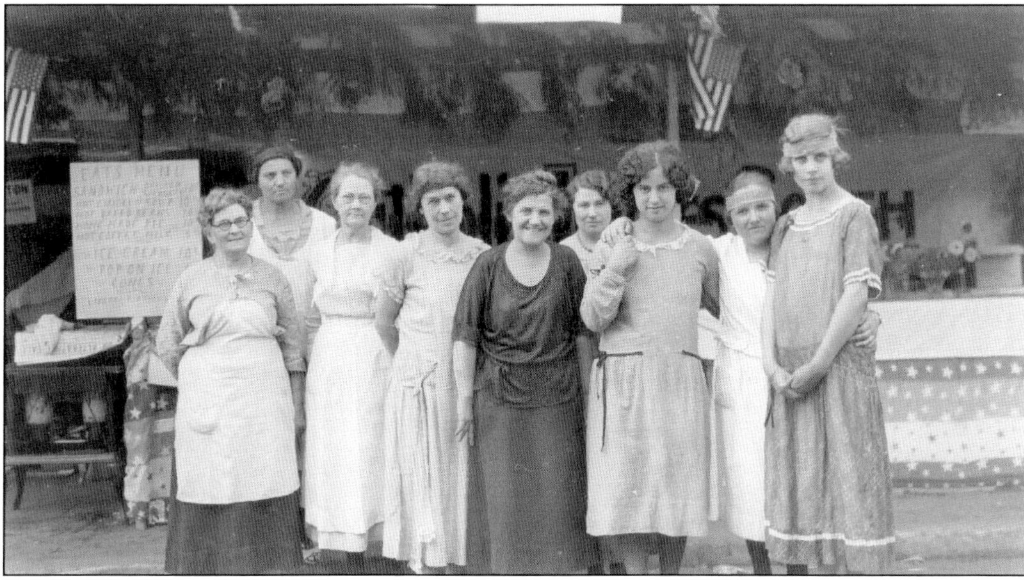

Auburn has always loved its parades. The Auburn Days parade, usually held in the early weeks of August, was a chance for clubs, churches, and other organizations to show off their abilities by arranging floats, booths, and entertainments for the parade. These ladies from Holy Family Church stand in front of their booth selling "Eats" and other treats to parade-goers in 1924.

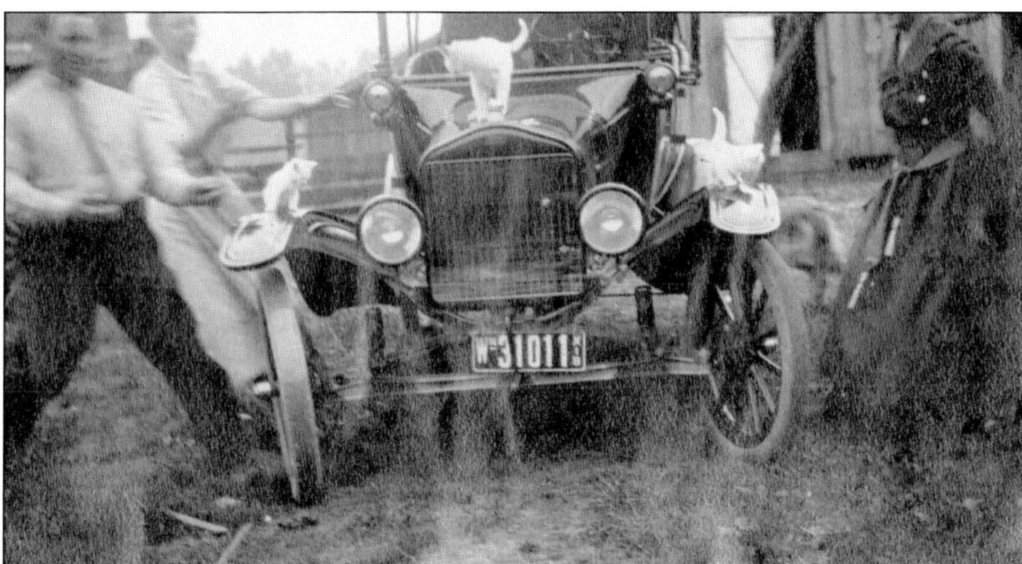

The growing popularity of personal film cameras in the early 1900s allowed people to take more casual snapshots, rather than the stiffly formal portraits of previous years. People began to photograph everyday occurrences, casual outings, and humorous events. In this 1917 snapshot, George Porter and his friends laugh while attempting to wrangle kittens on the hood of a Ford Model T.

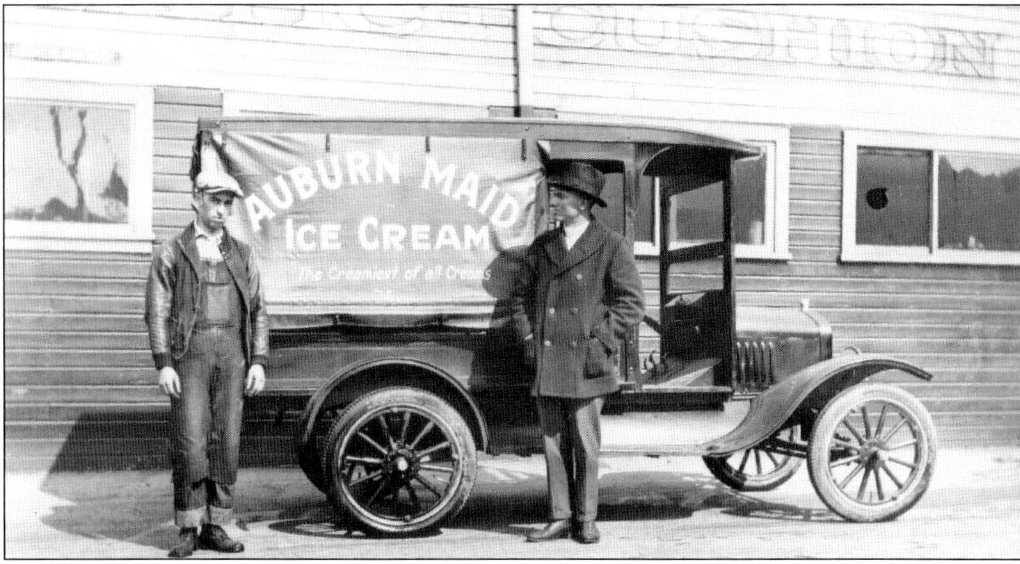

The popularity of dairy farming in Auburn led many dairy-related companies to set up shop in Auburn. Frank Fulmer (right) sold ice cream in Auburn and was well known for his friendly attitude, love of baseball, and kindness to children, to whom he often gave free ice cream. A park in Auburn was named for Fulmer in 1979.

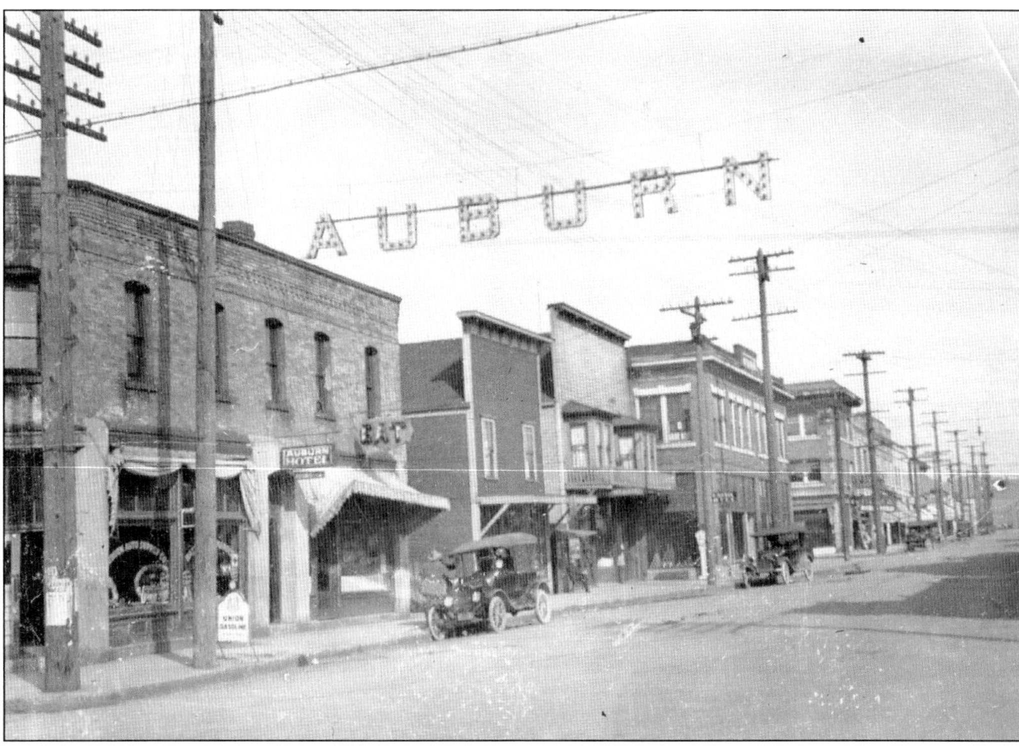

By 1920, most of the roads in downtown Auburn were paved and bordered by concrete sidewalks instead of wooden boardwalks, as seen here on Main Street. Automobiles were becoming the dominant form of transportation, and electrical lines crisscrossed the city to power new radios, electric lamps, and bulb-covered street signs.

Following World War I, women began entering the workforce in larger numbers than in previous generations. Most jobs for women were entry-level positions, since employers found they could pay women less than men for the same jobs. Genevieve Wendle, seen here around 1924, was a teller and bookkeeper at First National Bank in Auburn.

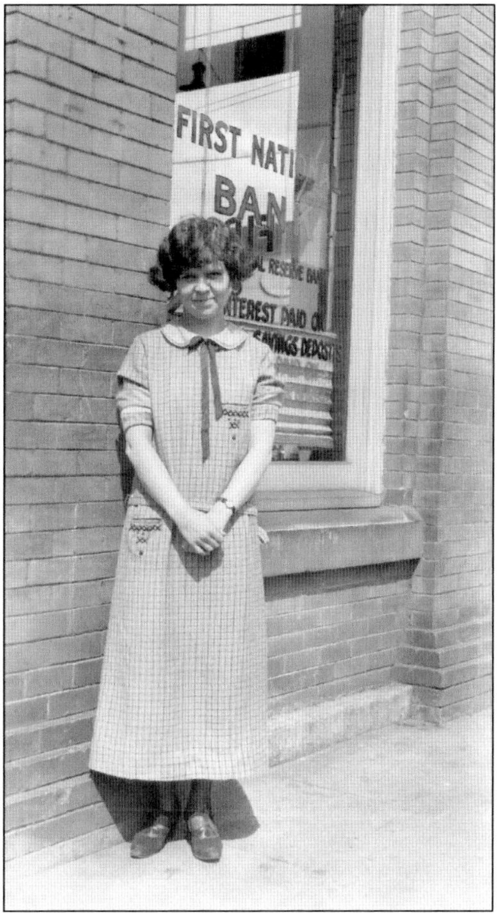

Masonic and other fraternal organizations enjoyed their heyday in Auburn in the 1920s, so much so that groups began fighting for limited meeting space. Auburn's King Solomon Lodge No. 60 decided to build their own Masonic temple in downtown Auburn on land donated by lodge member Aaron Neely, a prosperous farmer. Construction of the temple was completed in 1924.

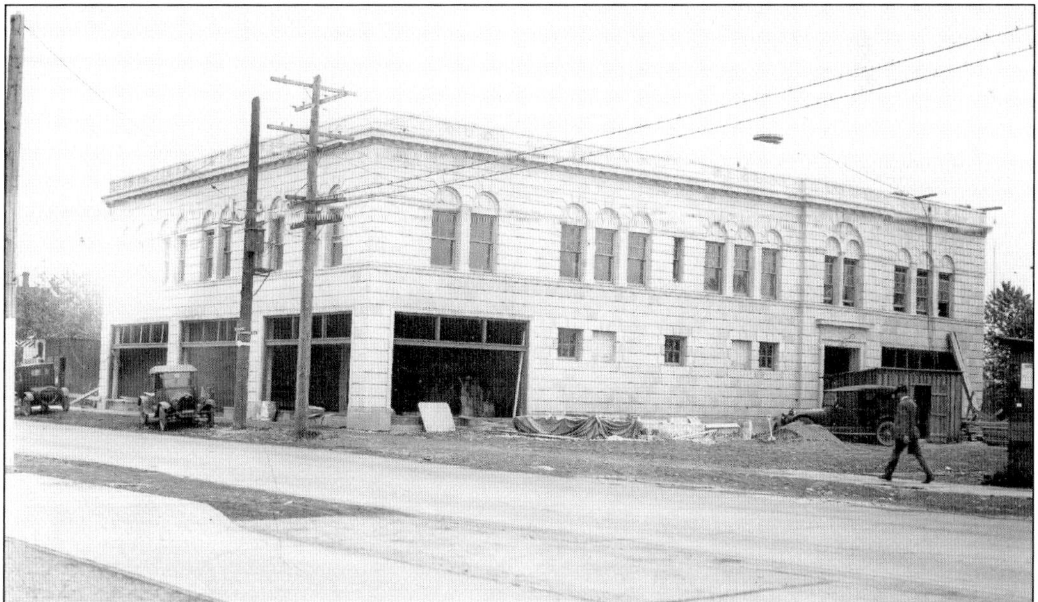

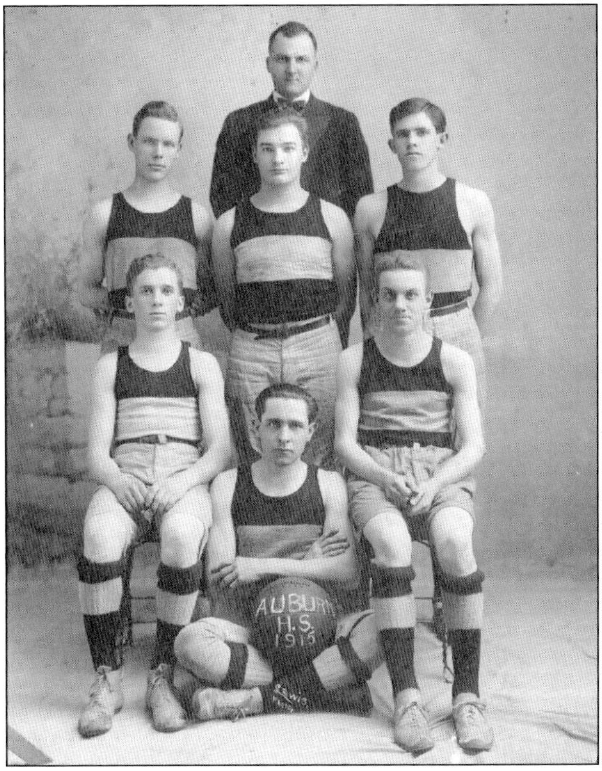

Basketball was one of the first organized school sports in Auburn, along with track, baseball, tennis, and football. Unlike those other sports, however, basketball in Auburn schools was organized first for girls, and then later for boys. The 1915 Auburn High School boys' basketball team poses left with their coach, while the 1924 girls' basketball team is seen below, surrounding their coach, Miss Mulhearn. Girls' basketball teams competed against each other throughout the 1910s and 1920s. However, by the late 1930s, most girls' athletics teams had dwindled, while boys' teams only gained in popularity. Girls' athletics would not experience the same level of popularity again until the 1980s.

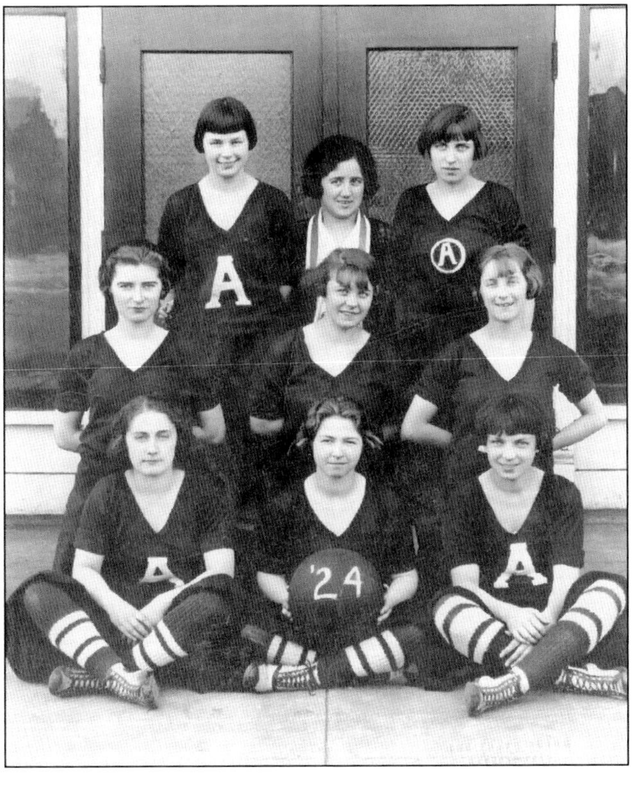

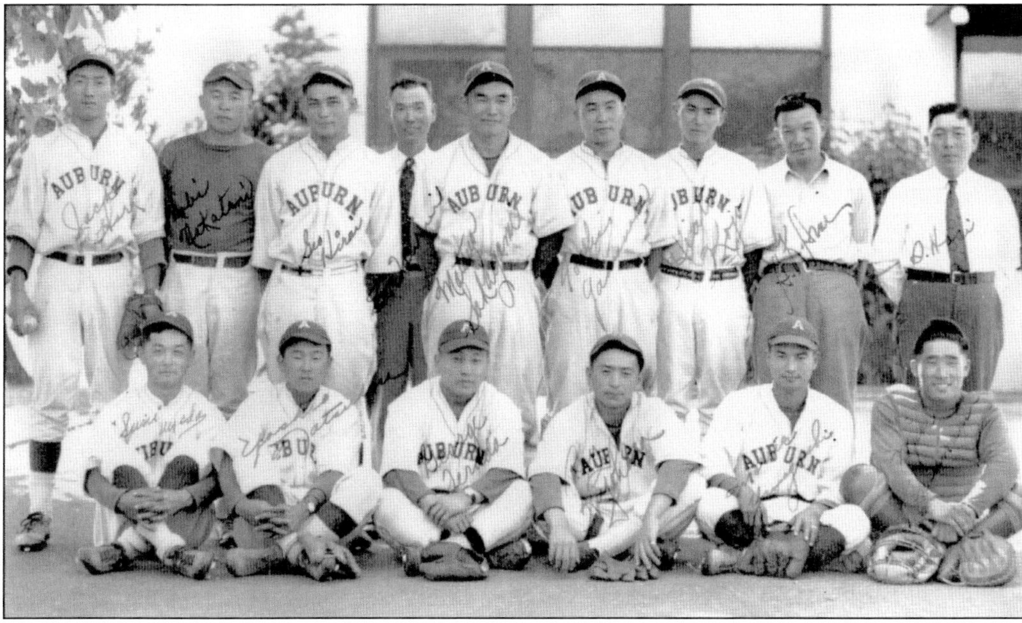

Sports teams, like most other institutions in America at this time, were often segregated, especially when adults were playing. The Auburn Japanese baseball team, seen here around 1929, played against other Japanese American teams in Washington State. There was a national Japanese American baseball league that organized tournaments and all-star games for Japanese American players.

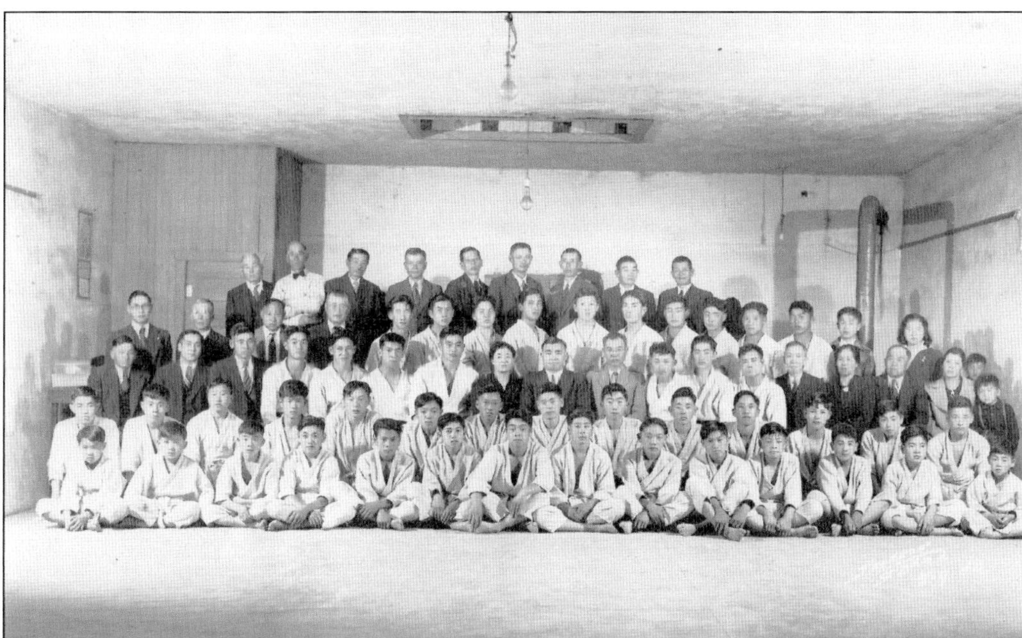

Schools were not the only organizations that sponsored organized sports. Churches, veterans' groups, and local businesses sponsored several athletic leagues in the Auburn area. This judo group, seen around 1928, was sponsored by the White River Buddhist Temple. They practiced in a hall next to the first White River Buddhist Temple, located in north Auburn.

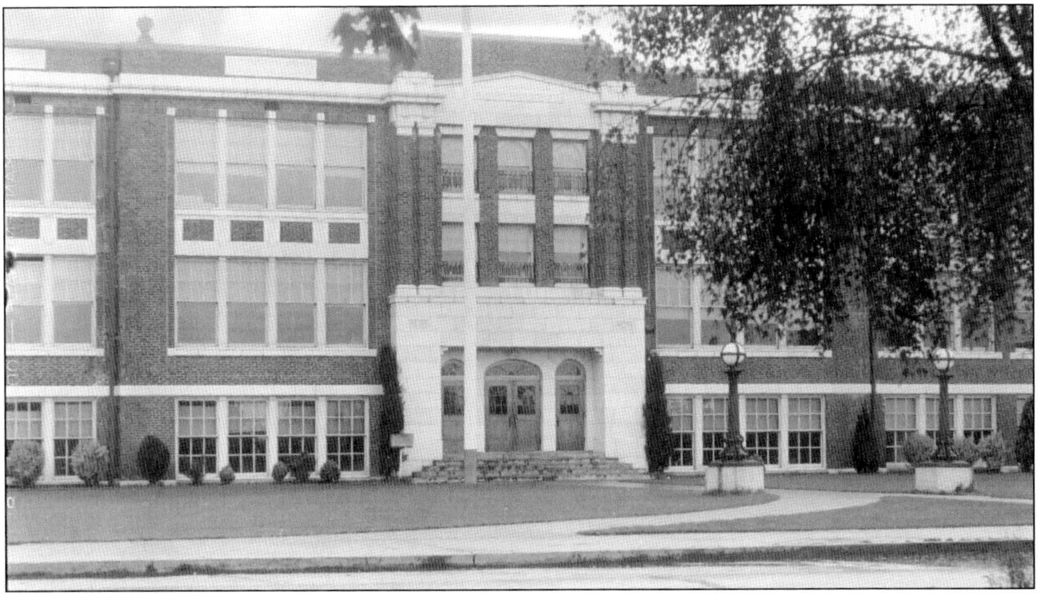

Auburn High School was built in 1927 close to the corner of J Street Northeast and Fourth Street Northeast. The new school was built using brick and masonry, like most of the other new buildings in Auburn in the 1920s, and replaced an earlier wooden high school building. In 1929, the Japanese Association of Auburn donated two ornate streetlamps to the school, as seen in the rainy November photograph below. The lights can also be seen in the 1934 image of the high school above, and they continued to grace the school's grounds until the building was demolished in 1981.

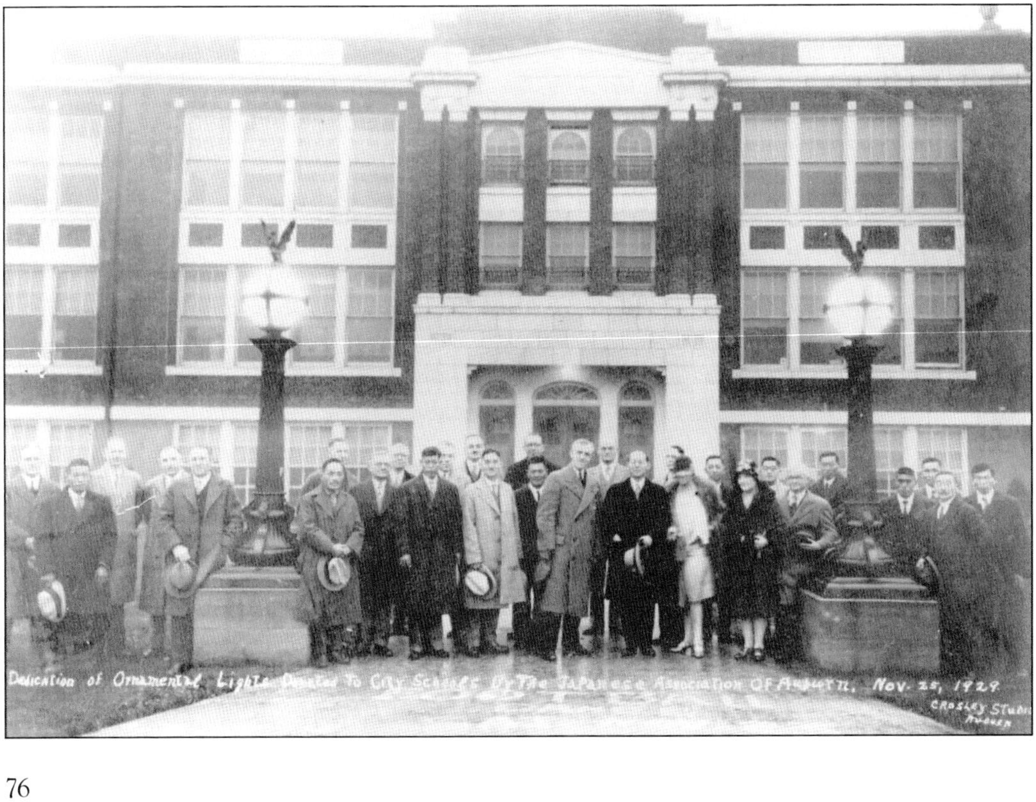

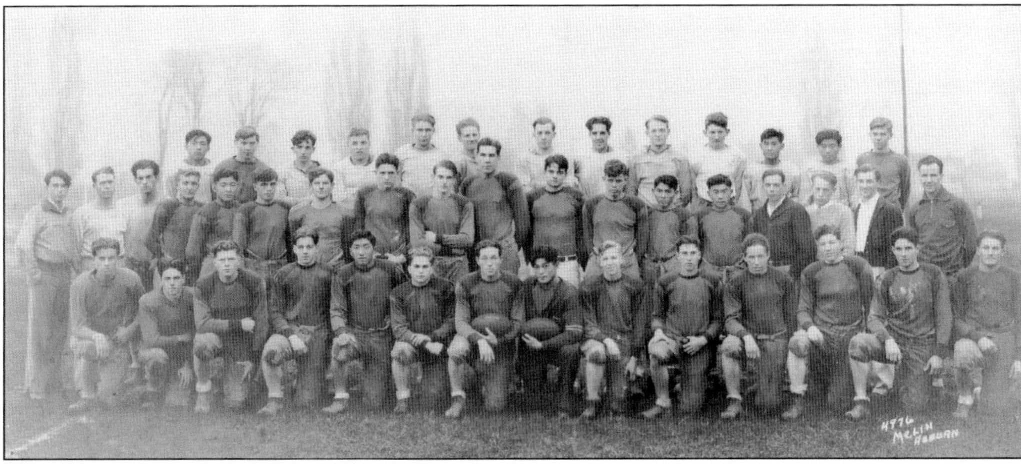

The 1933 Auburn High School football team was made up of children who had been born in the Auburn area to immigrant parents. The two boys holding footballs, Roy Calkins (captain, right) and George Hirai (quarterback), exemplify this: the Calkins family was from Iowa and Denmark and arrived in Washington in 1907, while the Hirai family emigrated from Japan around 1911.

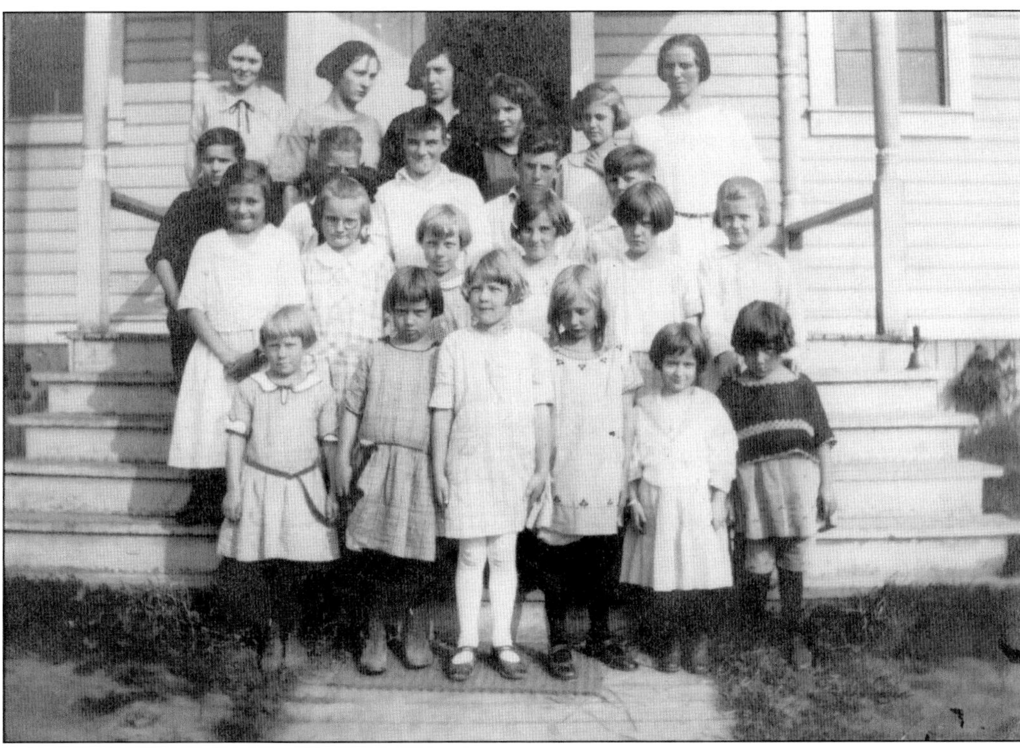

Many small communities surrounded Auburn in the early 1900s. This school group was from the town of Hazelwood, located on Lea Hill, now a small neighborhood on the eastern edge of Auburn on the border with Kent. The school building they are standing in front of eventually became the Hazelwood Community Center.

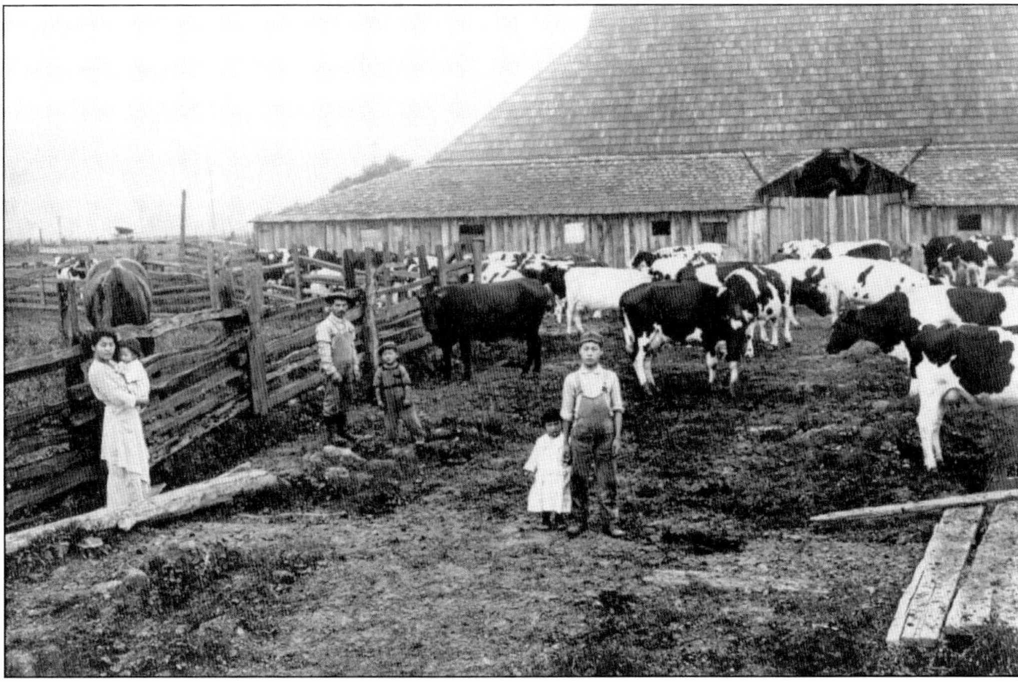

Dairy farming was popular in the Auburn area, and many Japanese immigrants learned the trade while working as laborers on other peoples' farms. Unfortunately, Washington's discriminatory Alien Land Laws prevented Japanese American farmers from purchasing their own farms or dairies. The Arima family, seen here around 1919, leased their land from the Berner family.

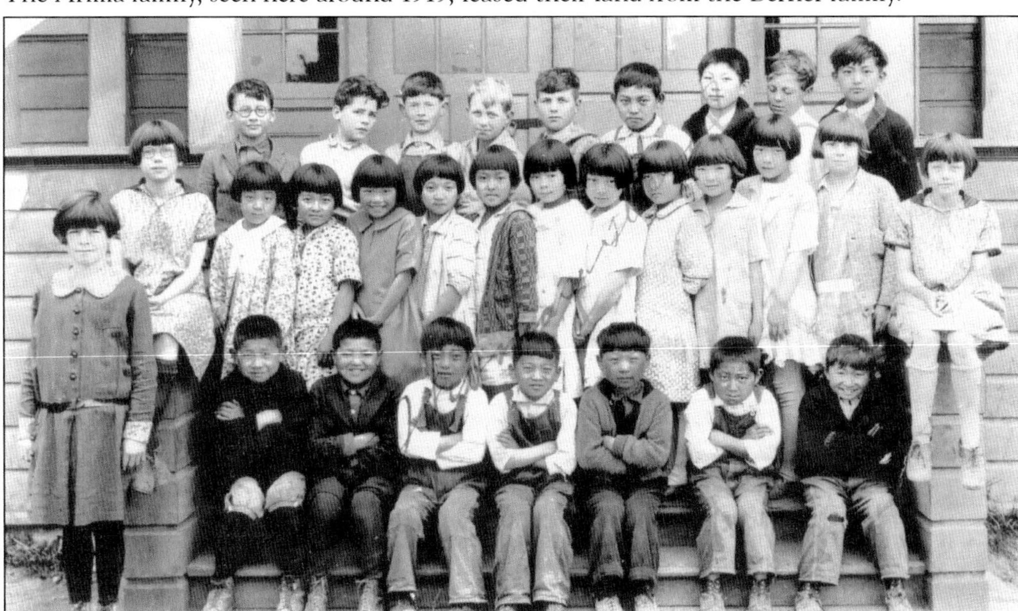

The majority of Auburn's Japanese American population lived in north Auburn and Thomas. This population difference can be seen in school photographs of the era, including this 1926 class photograph from the Thomas School. Seated third from the right in the first row is a young Gordon Hirabayashi, who would go on to play an important role in protesting Japanese internment.

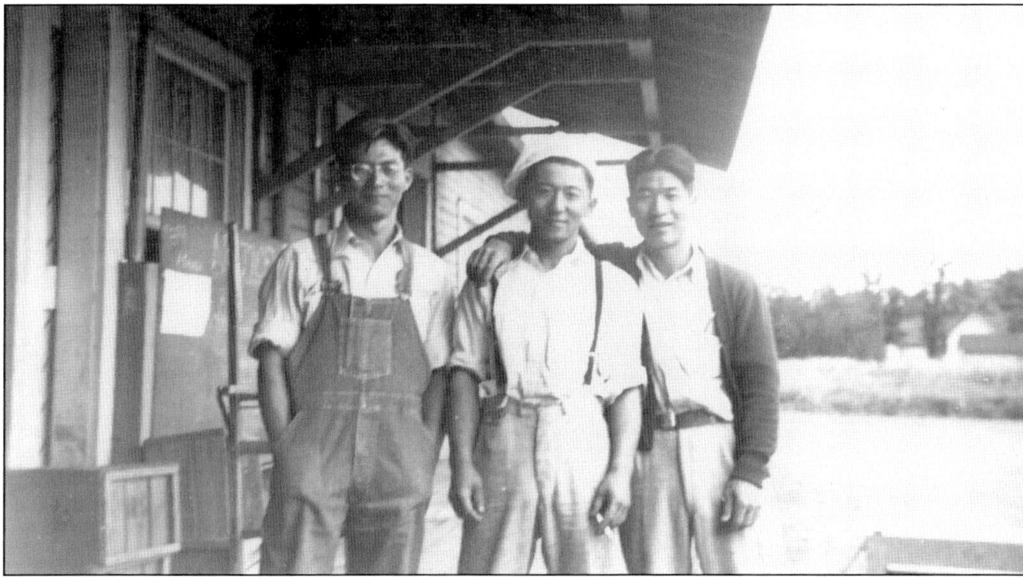

In the late 1910s and 1920s, several large produce companies were founded in Auburn, Thomas, and Kent by Japanese American residents. Many of these companies thrived, becoming the vital lifeline between large city markets and local growers of commercial crops like lettuce and strawberries. This photograph from around 1935 shows three local farmers standing in front of the Auburn Produce packing plant.

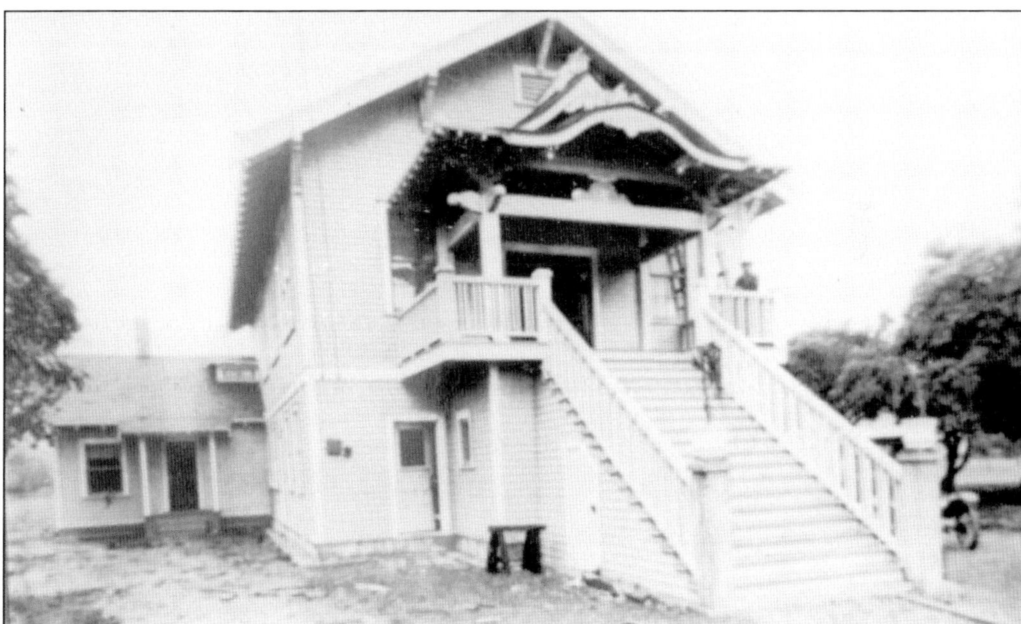

The White River Buddhist Church (now known as the White River Buddhist Temple) was established in Thomas in 1912. By 1925, it had grown so much that it built the Auburn Buddhist Church and Language Center, seen here shortly after opening. The Buddhist churches were gathering places for Japanese immigrants to Auburn, 90 percent of whom were adherents of Shin Buddhism.

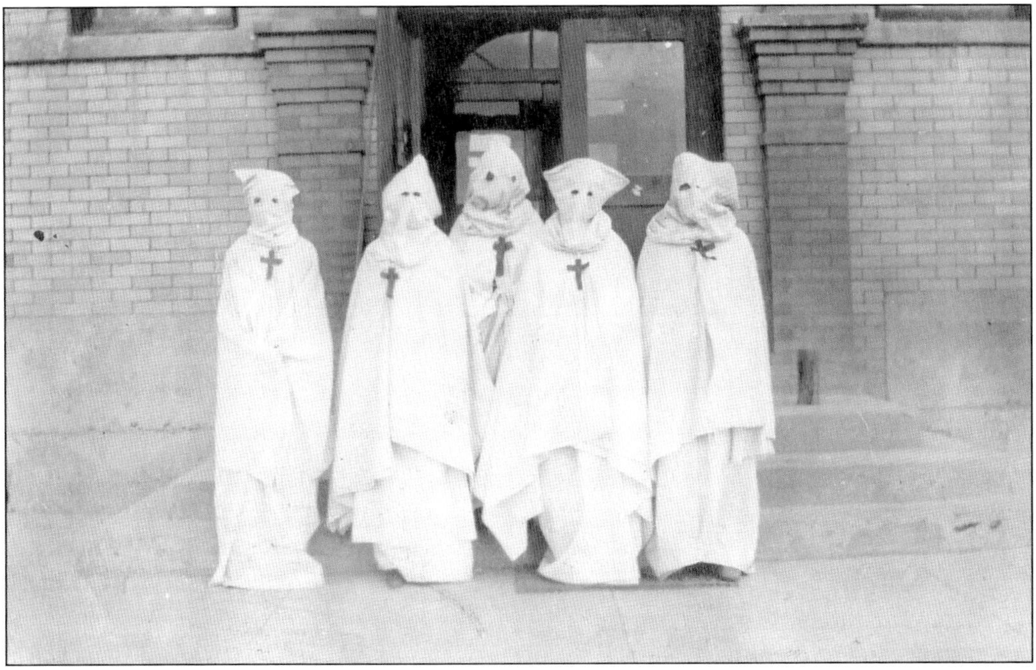

The Ku Klux Klan experienced a revival in the 1920s and held several meetings in Auburn in Fraternity Hall, which was located above the J.C. Penney building. In Washington State, they mostly focused their efforts on spreading hatred of the Catholic Church and, through association, hatred of the immigrant groups that had Catholic majorities, such as Irish and Italians.

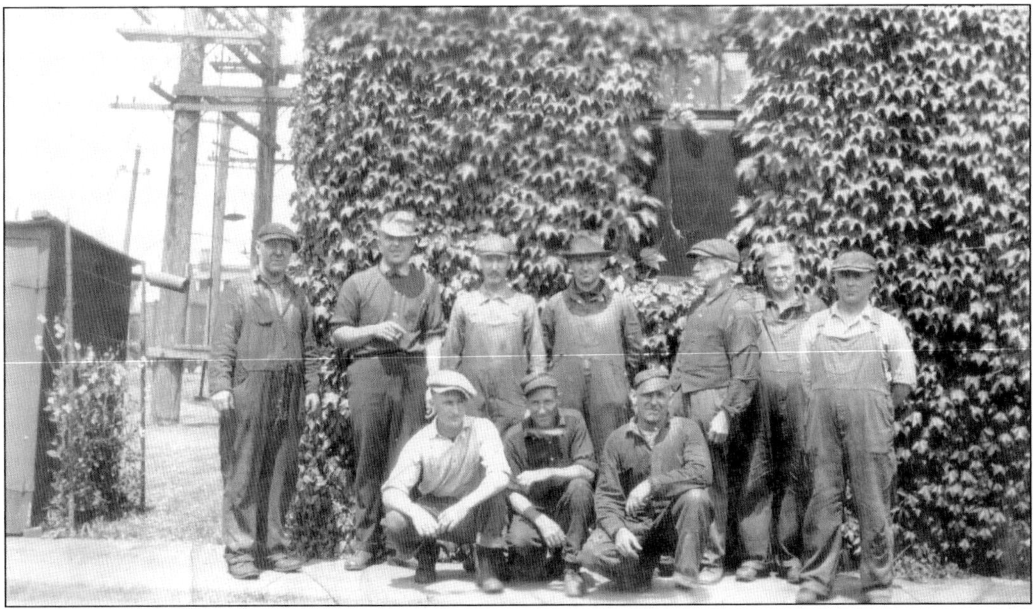

The interurban brought new workers and residents to Auburn, but it also opened up new job opportunities for Auburn's citizens. Railroads provided steady, reliable work with a good chance for advancement and, eventually, even pensions and other benefits. Workers, like this interurban trolley crew around 1915, often picked up their families and moved rather than losing their job with a railroad.

The interurban supported the Auburn economy in several ways. Aside from allowing workers and goods to easily move between Auburn and other cities on the rail line, businesses like the Interurban Confectionary, owned by entrepreneur William "Ferge" Ferguson, were opened to support the many commuters and railway workers traveling through Auburn.

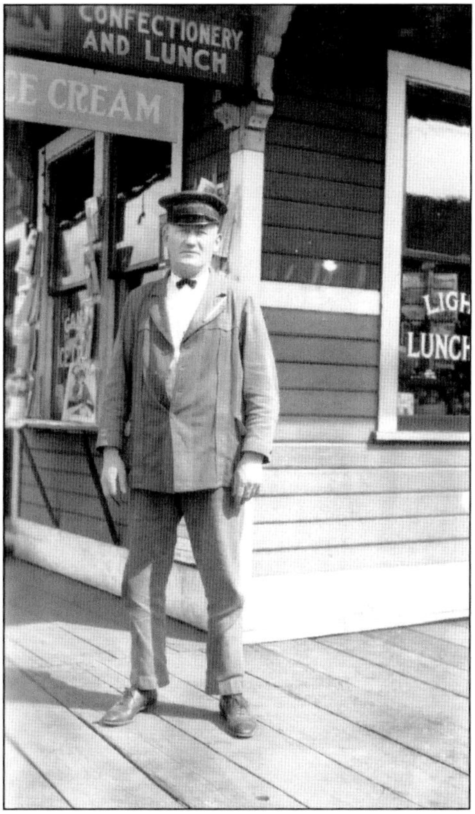

The interurban stopped running between Seattle and Tacoma in 1928. A combination of poor financial decisions and competition from the automobile and the slowly growing highway system caused the line to cease being profitable for the Puget Sound Traction, Light & Power Company, despite its popularity among the residents of Auburn.

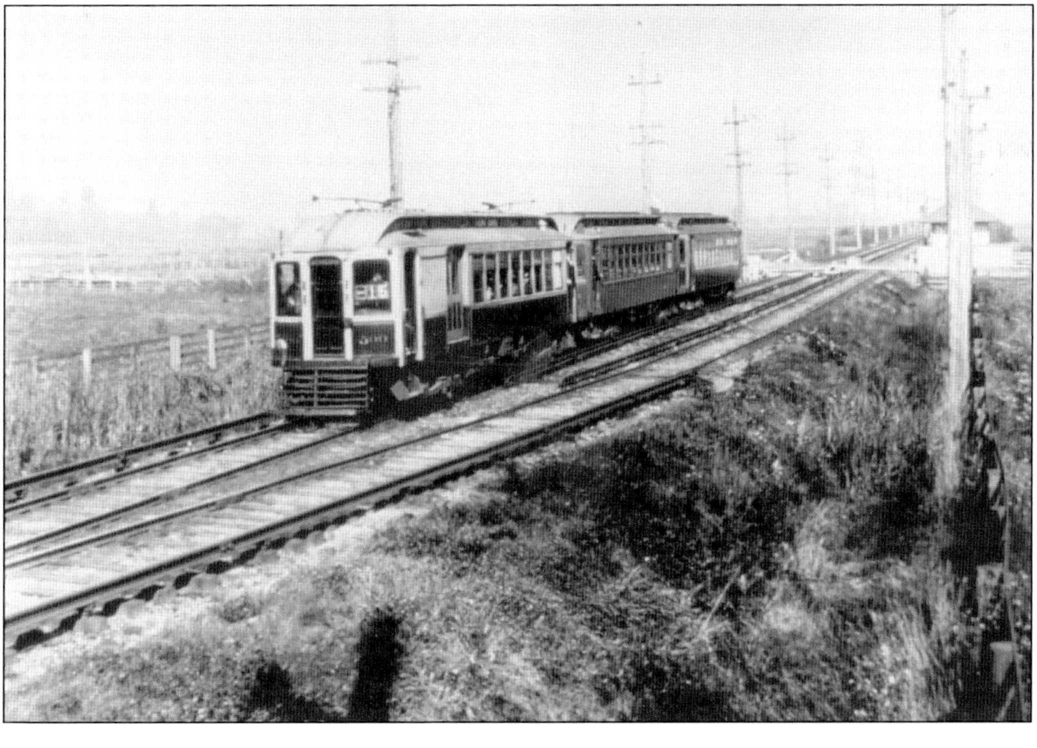

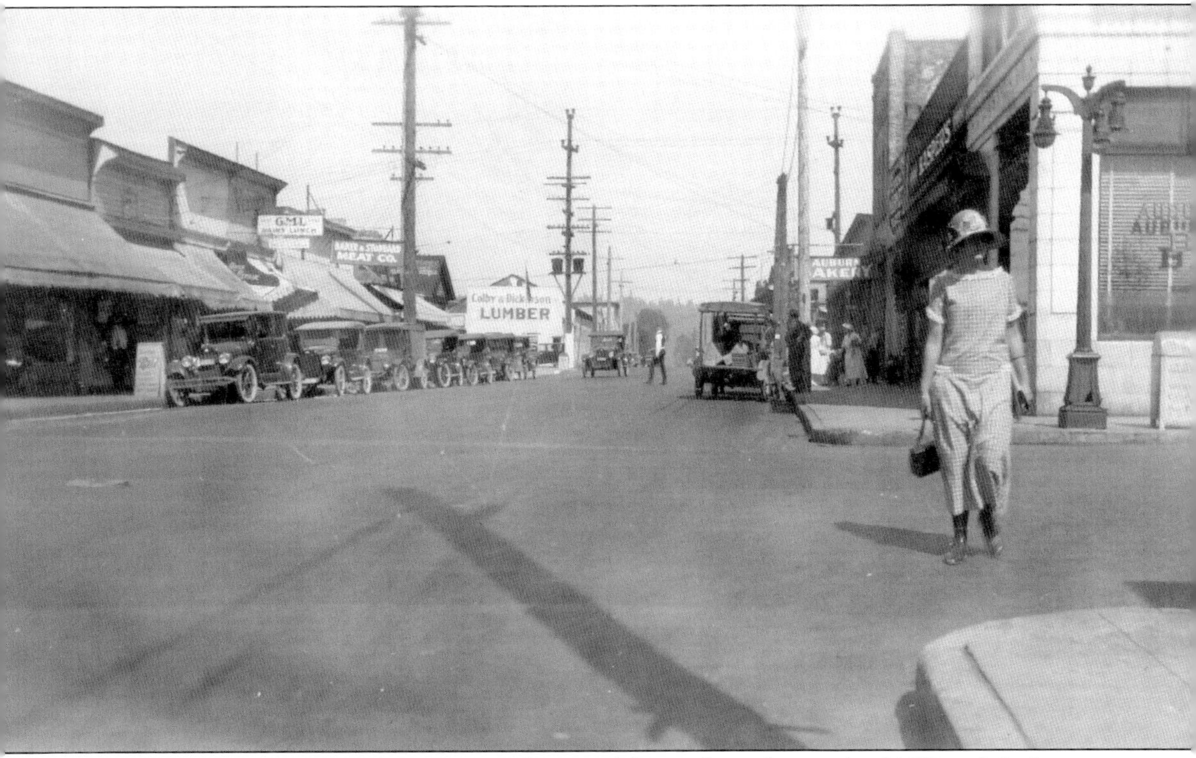

The closure of the interurban came on the eve of the stock market crash of 1929 and the beginning of the Great Depression. Despite Auburn's strong economic position as an agricultural town on a well-used railway line, the Depression hit the city hard; many businesses closed or downsized, and unemployment skyrocketed. The clay and terra-cotta industry completely left Auburn, as the demand for decorative architectural pieces on new buildings completely dried up. Many Main Street businesses were forced to close, including the Auburn National Bank, seen on the far right in this 1930 image. Banks and financial institutions essentially vanished in Auburn until after World War II, which made it increasingly difficult for business owners and entrepreneurs to access financing for new business ventures. Most retailers who sold expensive or luxury goods were forced to close or change their business models. At the same time, affordable forms of entertainment like movies gained in popularity, and Depression-era Auburn supported multiple movie theaters.

William T. Behne was the president of First National Bank in Auburn for most of the 1920s. When First National Bank and Auburn National Bank merged in 1929, he became the president of the new, larger organization. Shortly after the merger, the stock market crashed, causing bank activities to freeze across America.

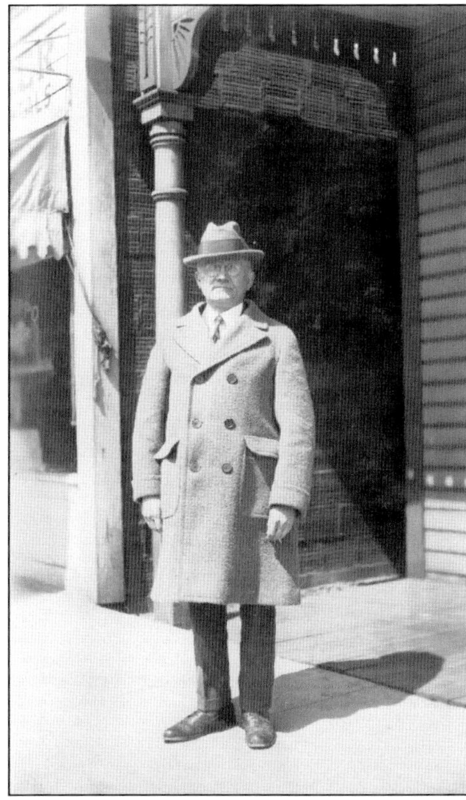

Bankers and other white-collar workers in the financial field were largely blamed for the 1929 stock market crash and the resulting unemployment and poverty in the United States. This group of homeless workers set up a shelter in the Union Pacific stockyards, naming it "Behne's Hotel" after the Auburn banker.

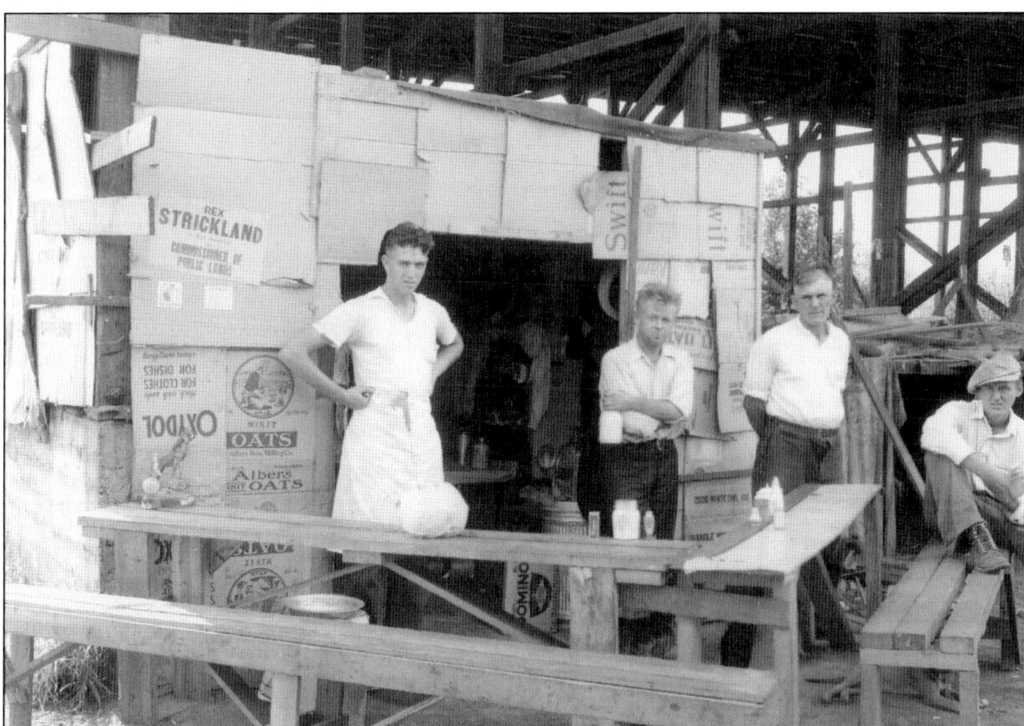

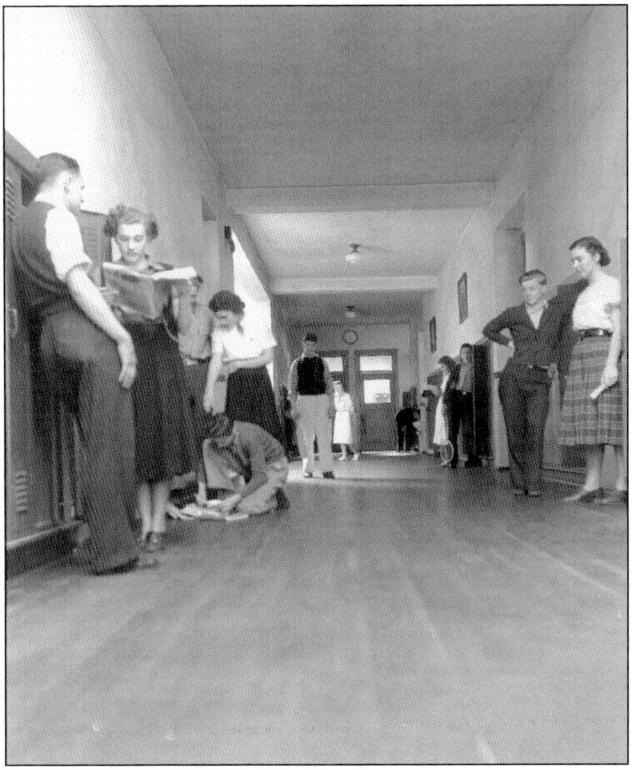

The Great Depression caused jobs to become scarce. Teenagers who might have planned to leave school after eighth grade to work now had no jobs to go to, and instead, they began attending high school in record numbers. This 1934 photograph shows the main hallway of Auburn High School. In 1936, a total of 124 students graduated the 12th grade, up from 65 in 1926.

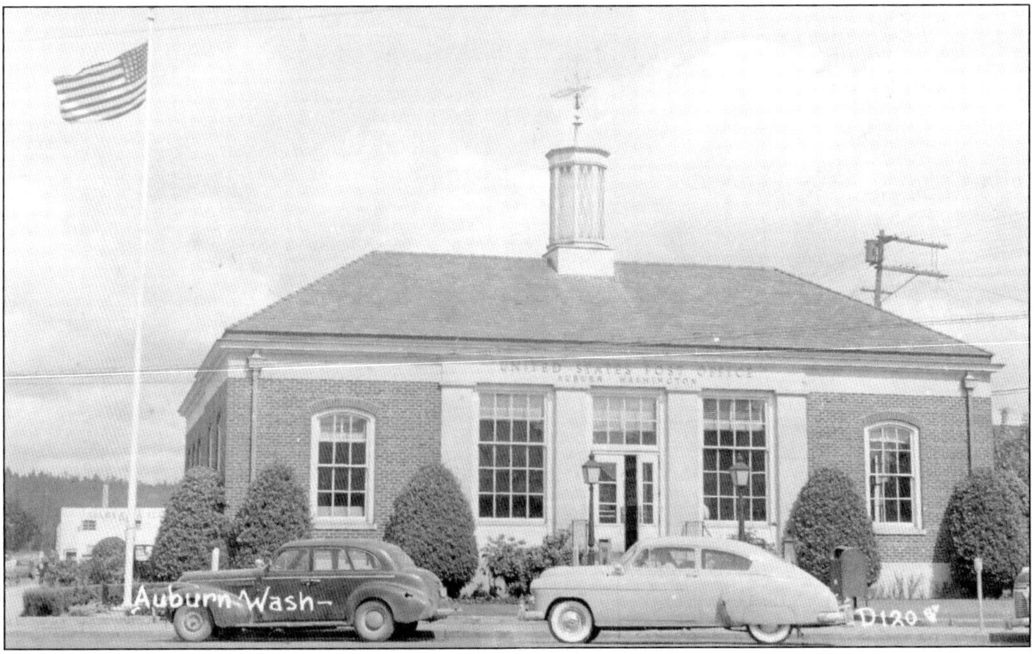

The Works Progress Administration (WPA) was a federal agency established in 1935 to hire unemployed laborers to complete public works projects like roads and public buildings. In 1937, WPA workers constructed the Auburn post office, which was used until the 1960s. Today, the post office building is listed in the National Register of Historic Places.

Five

Auburn and World War II 1941–1945

When the United States entered World War II in 1941, it significantly affected Auburn, both culturally and economically. Young men joined the military or were drafted for service, leaving many farms and businesses without adequate labor. Women stepped up to the plate, taking positions in manufacturing and retail that had previously been reserved for men, while teens and older children were conscripted out of school to assist in bringing in the harvest. The economy was still recovering from the effects of the Great Depression, but unemployment plummeted during the war years thanks to a surge in government spending on supplies and transportation for the military.

Despite the general spirit of cooperativeness fostered by the war effort in Auburn, an act of wartime injustice had the most lasting impact on the city. In February 1942, with anti-Japanese sentiment still high after the attacks on Pearl Harbor, Pres. Franklin Roosevelt issued Executive Order 9066, a law that led to the US government forcibly removing and imprisoning approximately 110,000 Japanese Americans from states on the West Coast under the guise of protecting national security. These Japanese American citizens were incarcerated in internment camps across the country; most of the Auburn-area residents were sent to Tule Lake Detention Center in California or Minidoka Detention Center in Idaho.

Internment had a devastating effect on the Japanese American community in Auburn. Incarcerated families were forced to sell their homes and businesses at a huge loss, if not completely abandon them. Students were forced out of school, not knowing how long it would be before they could return to their classes and friends. Perhaps worst of all, Japanese Americans family had to endure the shame of being imprisoned and labeled traitors to their country simply for having Japanese ancestry.

After internment legally ended in 1945, very few of the incarcerated Japanese families returned to Auburn. The city's population went from being approximately 10 percent Japanese American to barely 1 percent, and postwar racism against Japanese Americans was still rampant. The labor shortage caused by the absence of Japanese American farmers would not be filled until new immigrant groups began settling in Auburn in the 1950s.

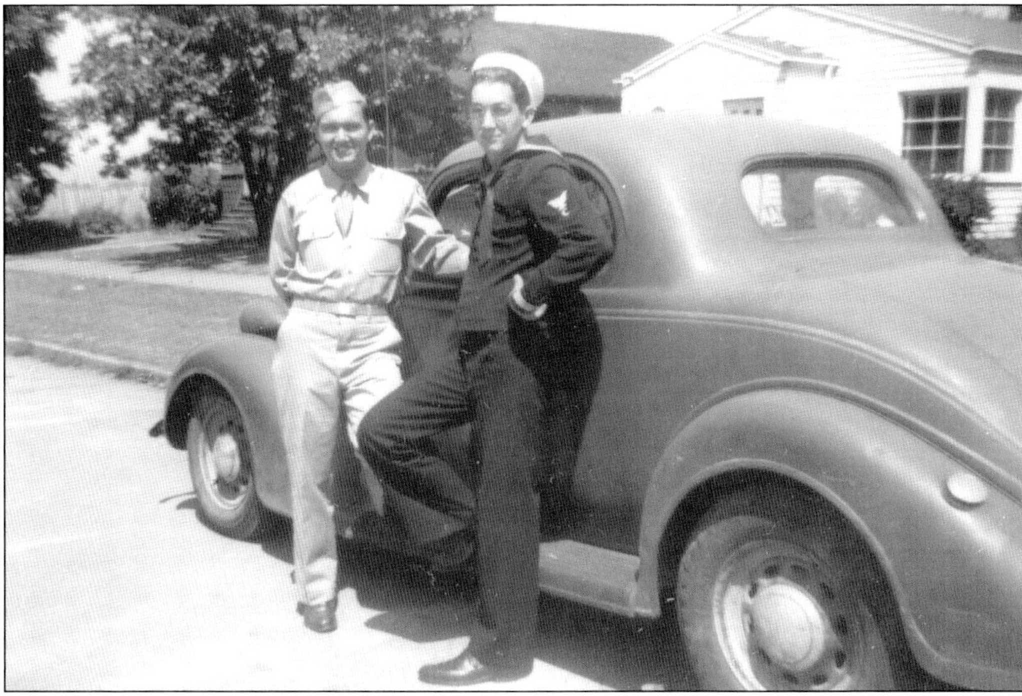

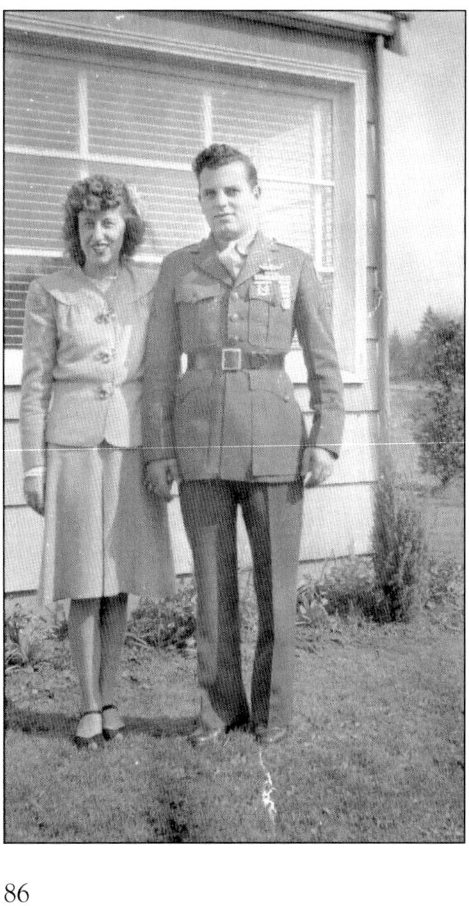

After the 1941 attack on Pearl Harbor, young men flocked to military recruitment centers to join the armed forces. Many of those who did not volunteer were later drafted. In this 1943 photograph, Auburn brothers Thomas and James Chapman pose in their new uniforms. Thomas (left) fought with the Army in Europe, while James joined the Navy and fought in the Pacific.

Johnny Porter was a well-known high school athlete in Auburn before he joined the military. Like many young soldiers at this time, he took advantage of his leave in 1944 to marry his sweetheart, Isabelle Zafforini. Porter never made it back home to his young bride; however, he died nearly a year later during the Battle of Iwo Jima.

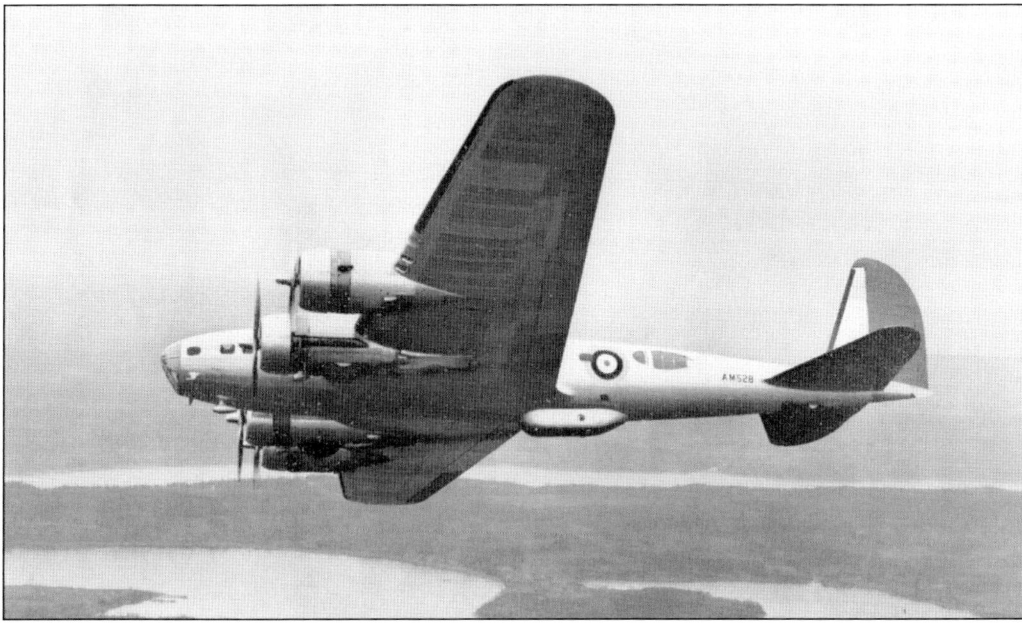

World War II caused a massive surge in manufacturing in the United States, especially in the production of vehicles and materials for the overseas war effort. The Boeing Company shifted its entire production capacity to manufacture military airplanes like this B-17 Flying Fortress, a bomber plane. Many laborers from Auburn flocked to Boeing factories in Renton and other nearby cities.

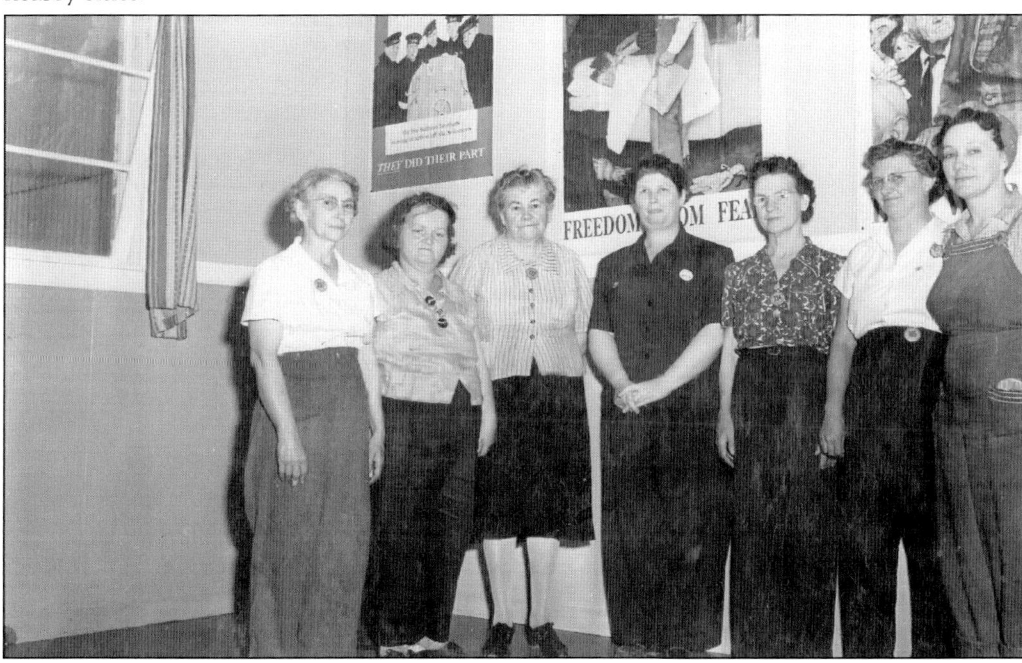

With so many men occupied overseas during the war, women once again took up jobs traditionally reserved for men. This group of Kent and Auburn residents were photographed at their place of employment, Northwest Metal Products, in 1944. Behind them are a series of propaganda posters encouraging women to take jobs as an act of patriotism.

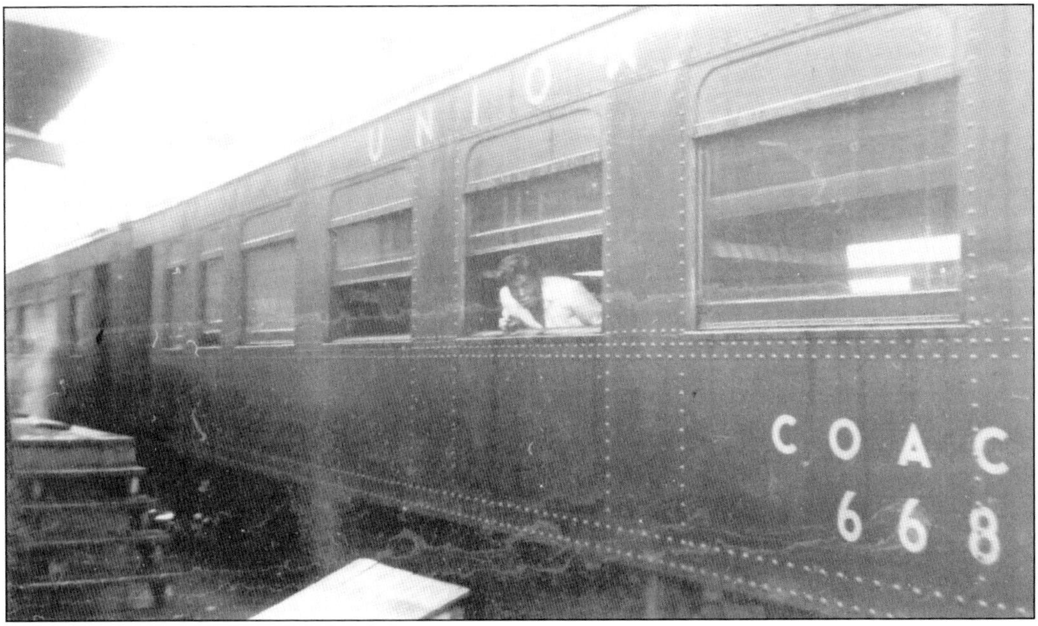

Japanese Americans were forced to sell or abandon their homes in order to be "evacuated," a euphemism for the forced removal and imprisonment of 110,000 legal immigrants and American citizens of Japanese descent. In Auburn, evacuees were allowed a few pieces of luggage before loading onto trains going south, as seen in these two 1942 images. They spent their first few weeks of evacuation at Camp Harmony, located on the Puyallup fairgrounds. After being processed, they were sent on to larger internment centers. Most Auburn residents were first sent to Tule Lake Detention Center in California. After Tule Lake was converted to a camp for those of "questionable loyalty," those who were transferred out were largely sent to Minidoka Detention Center in Idaho.

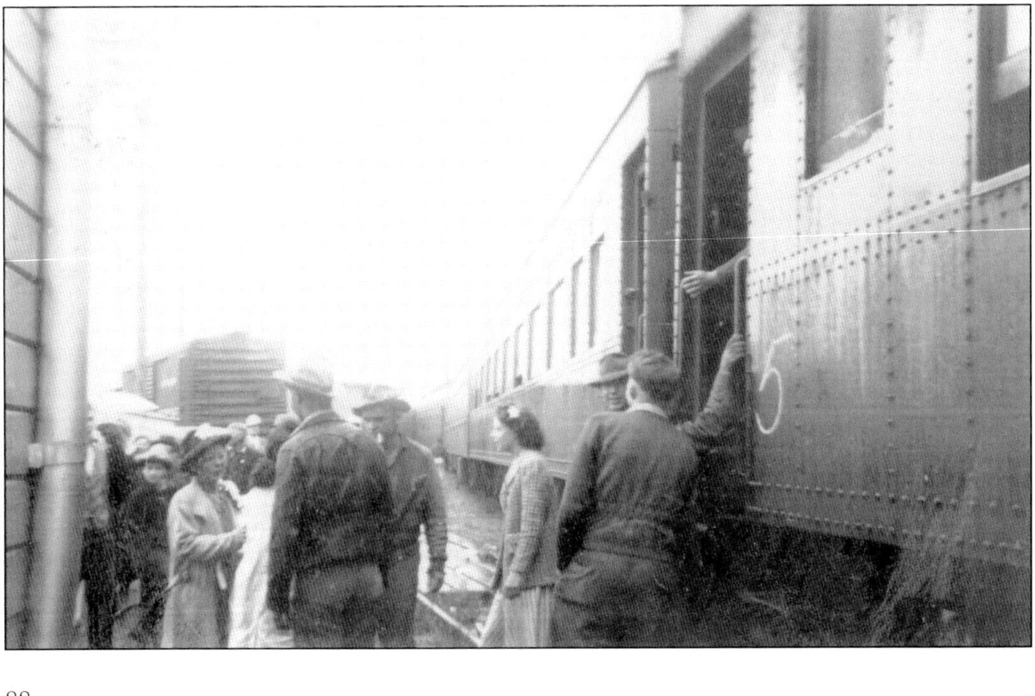

Sam Iseri was one of the several Auburn residents imprisoned at Tule Lake Detention Center in 1942. Detainees attempted to have normal lives while in the camp, and they found creative ways to hold classes, religious services, and even birthday parties. Despite the pretense of normality, a watchtower and a barbed-wire fence can be seen behind Iseri.

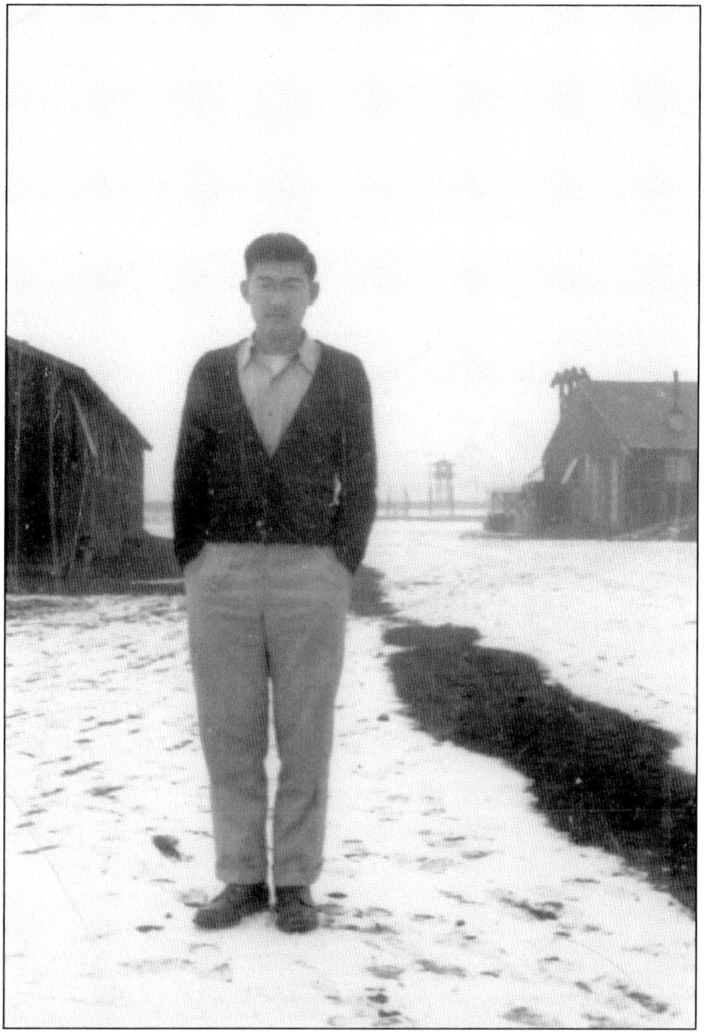

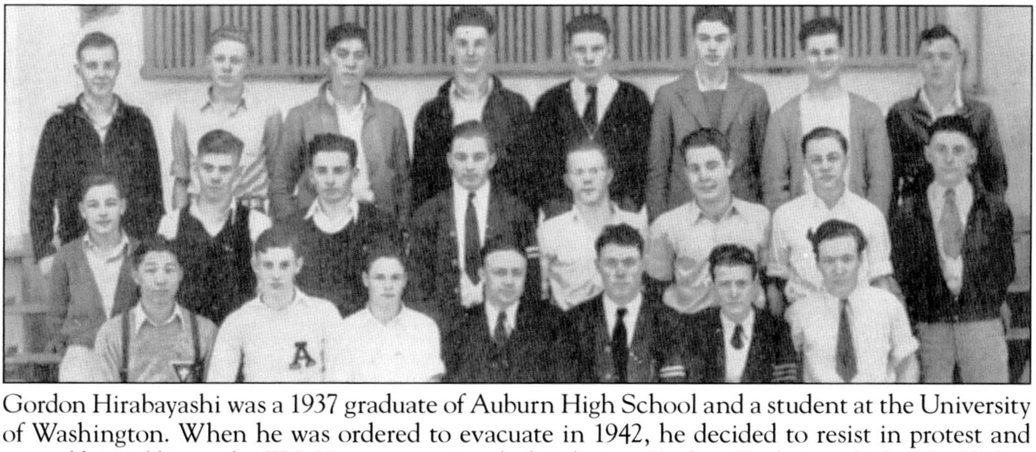

Gordon Hirabayashi was a 1937 graduate of Auburn High School and a student at the University of Washington. When he was ordered to evacuate in 1942, he decided to resist in protest and turned himself in to the FBI. He was convicted of violating Civilian Exclusion Order No. 57, but he appealed the constitutionality of his conviction all the way to the Supreme Court.

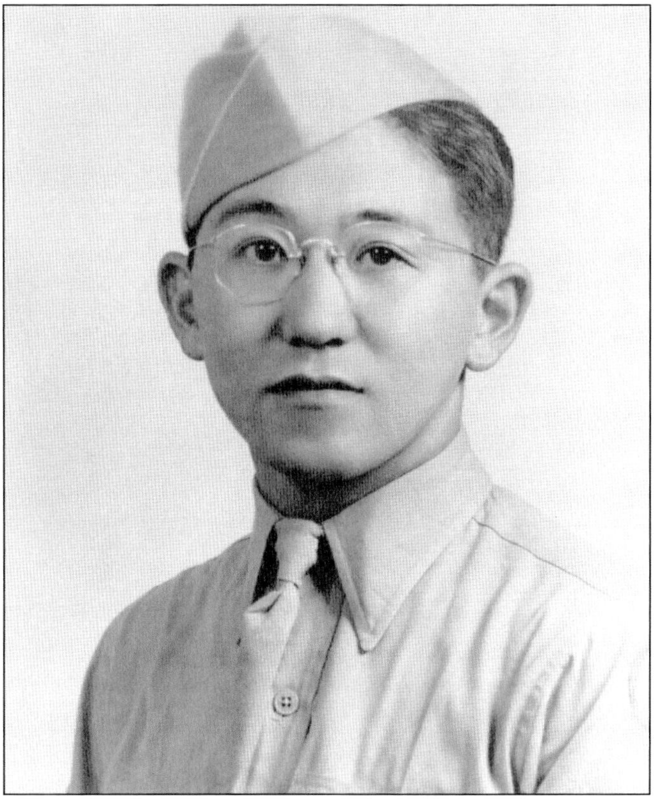

Mitsuo "Mike" Iseri volunteered for military service in 1942, ultimately joining the all-Japanese 442nd Infantry Regimental Combat Team. Despite having their families imprisoned in internment camps, the 442nd served with distinction, becoming the most decorated unit in the history of US armed forces. Mike Iseri died in France in 1944, one of 680 members of the 442nd to die in combat.

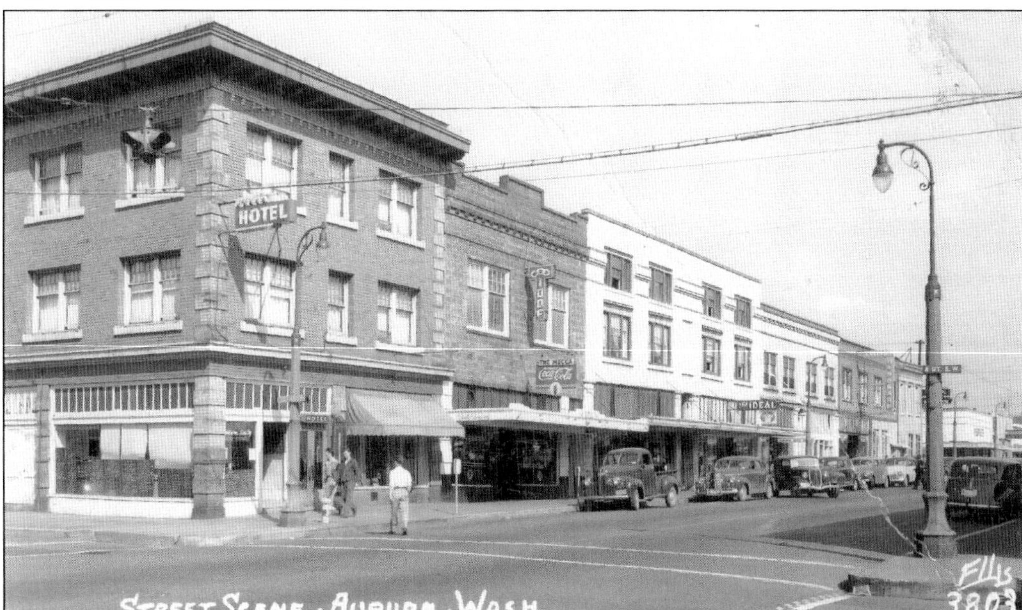

Despite rationing, the draft, internment, and other hardships, Auburn was able to make a significant economic leap forward at the end of World War II. This image of the intersection of Main and A Streets from around 1945 is filled with automobiles, which were now officially the preferred method of travel for most Auburnites.

Six

Auburn, Little Detroit of the West 1946–1961

Postwar Auburn was a booming center of commerce in the White River Valley. Thanks to the economic lift from World War II manufacturing, jobs were plentiful, and improvements to the local highway system made transportation and shipping around the region increasingly easy. Businesses rushed to cater to the needs of a growing group of middle-class workers who were moving to Auburn to escape the perceived crime and crowding of larger cities.

Returning veterans came back to Auburn with new skills and good discipline. Many of them were married and wanted to settle down and raise a family, resulting in the same baby boom trend seen across the United States in the 1950s. The energy brought to Auburn by returning veterans and other newly transplanted families encouraged citizens to open new businesses, fund charitable causes, and organize and open new facilities for recreation and education in the city, including a state-of-the-art new high school building.

Car dealerships were especially successful in Auburn in the decades after World War II. Land was both available and affordable in Auburn, unlike in the traditional hubs of automobile sales, Tacoma and Seattle. Former farmlands were converted into car lots on the outskirts of town, beginning with the Ford dealership. Soon, other Auburn dealerships were following suit and moving away from downtown, creating a cluster of car dealerships to lure buyers from out of town. An advertising slogan billed Auburn as "the Little Detroit of the West" in newspaper and radio advertisements.

As in previous decades, new groups of immigrants added new dimensions to Auburn's population. The Filipino community, already established in Seattle since the 1930s, began to settle in the Auburn and Algona region after the Philippines gained their independence in 1946.

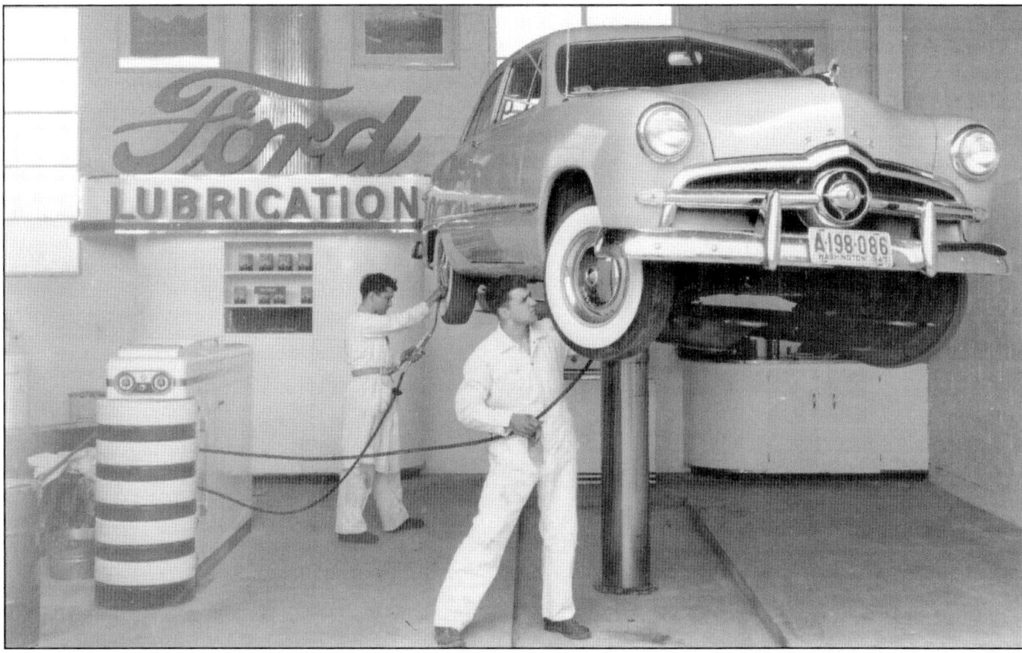

In 1948, Scarff Motors became the first Auburn dealership to move to what was then the outskirts of town, at 501 Auburn Way South. The move was initially seen as too risky, but within a few years, several other dealerships followed Scarff's lead, including Roberts Oldsmobile. Soon, dealerships were moving out of larger cities to join the crowd in Auburn.

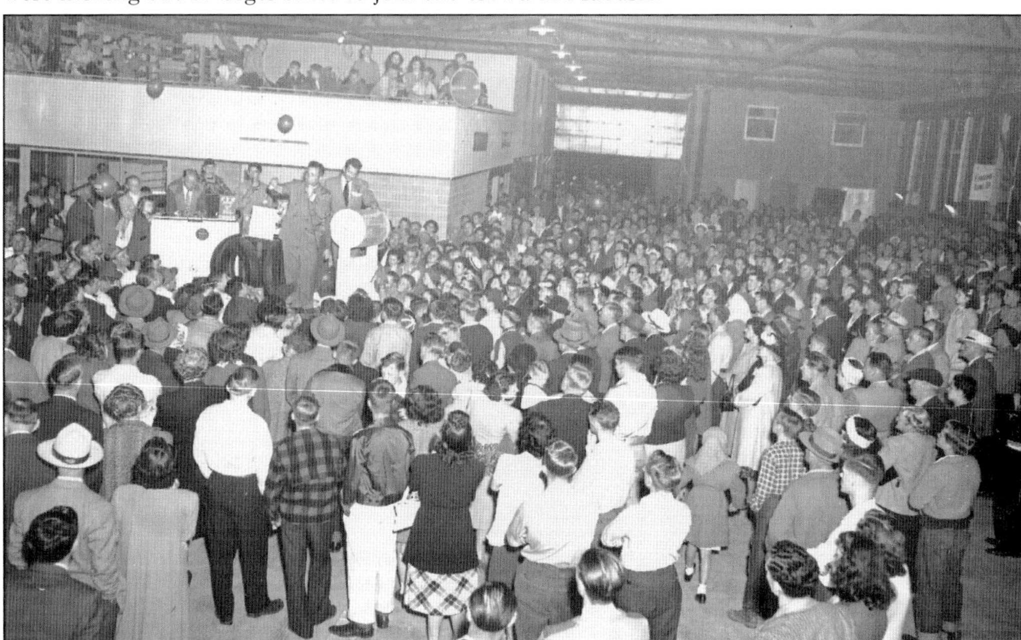

In June 1948, a crowd of 10,000 came to see the grand opening of the new Scarff Motors building. Contests and drawings for tires, furniture, and home appliances were held throughout the day. Visitors also had a chance to view the brand-new 1949 Ford models, which had been glamorously debuted in New York City only a few weeks earlier.

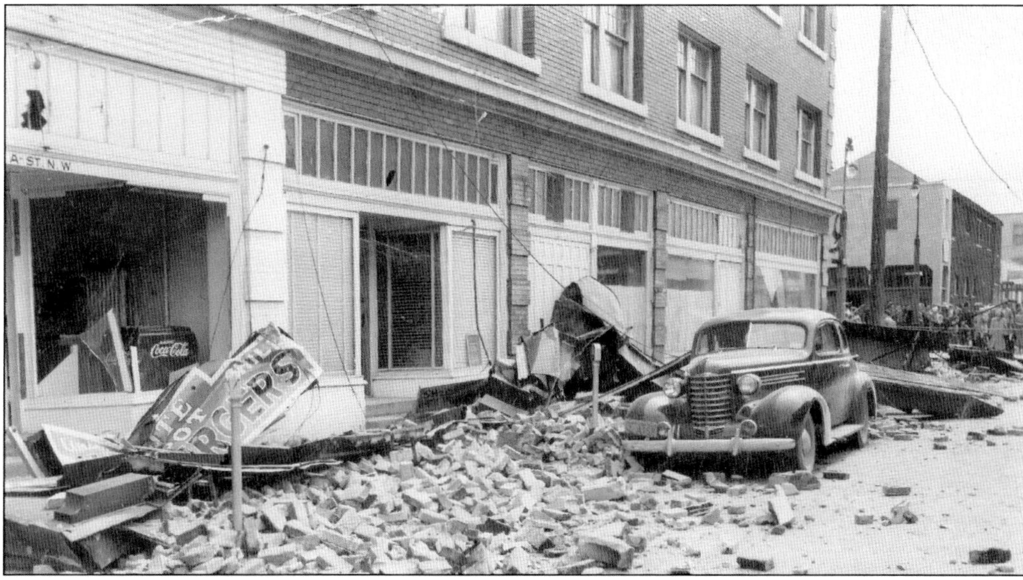

A 7.1 earthquake shook Auburn and the rest of King County on April 13, 1949. Auburn sustained some of the worst damage in the county, as seen in this photograph of A Street taken shortly after the quake. Many brick and masonry buildings lost their facades and chimneys and were rebuilt in a more modern style.

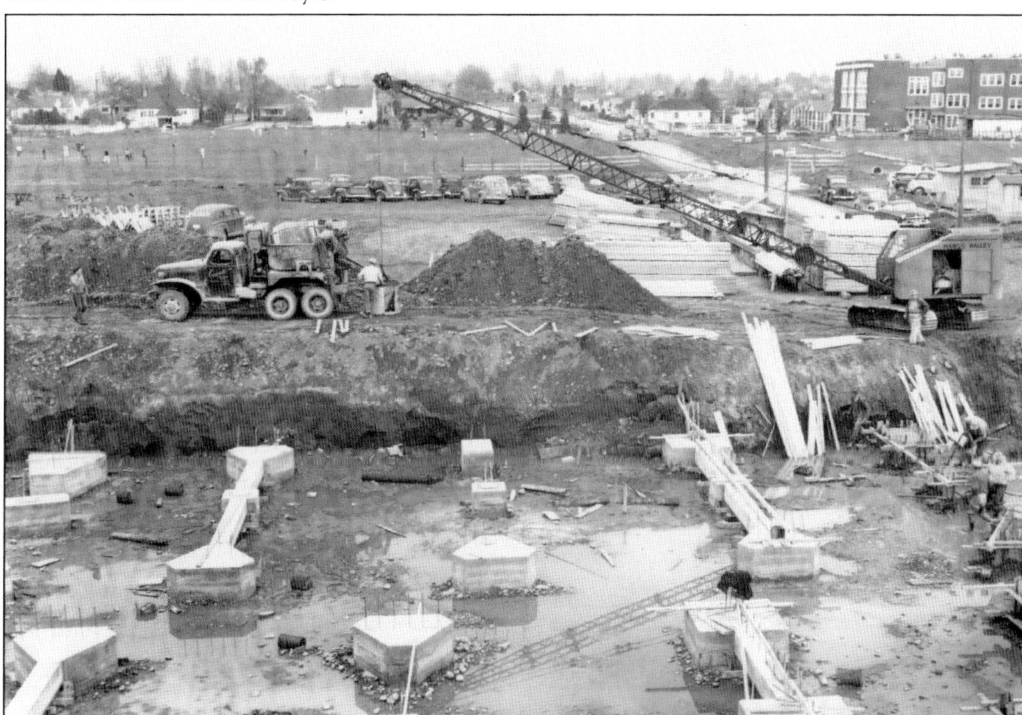

As Auburn's overall population expanded, so did its population of children. A new high school building was built in 1950, boasting state-of-the-art chemistry labs and other specialized equipment to help train students in the sciences. The older high school building can be seen in the upper right corner of this 1949 photograph of the new high school's construction.

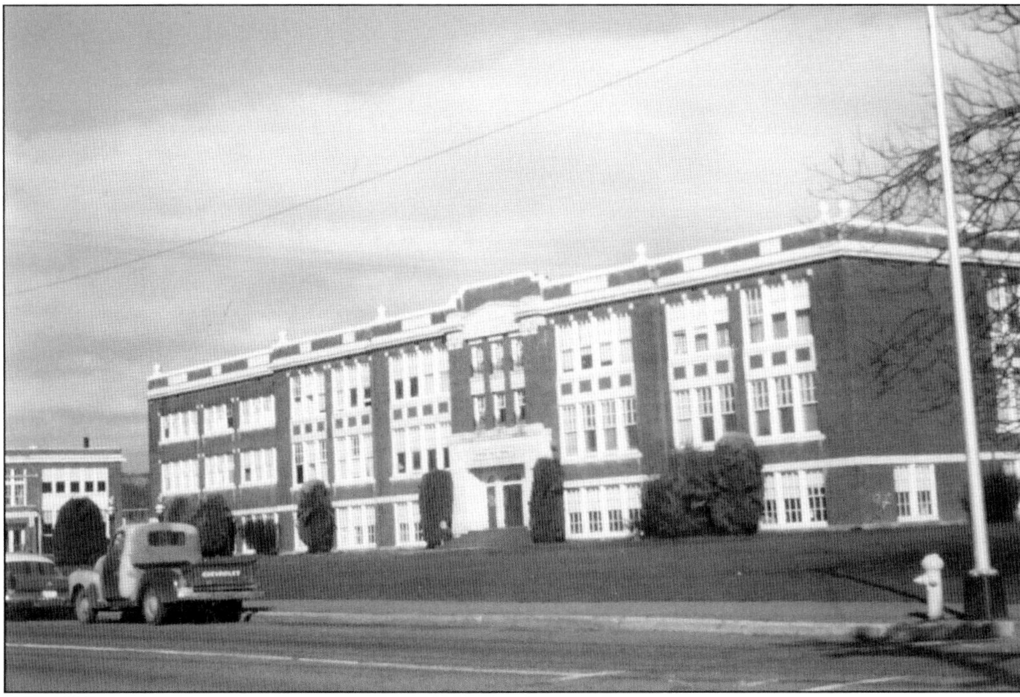

In 1949, Auburn High School became the very crowded home to both Auburn Junior High and Auburn High School students after the junior high school building was severely damaged in the 1949 earthquake. After the new high school opened in 1951, the building continued to serve as Auburn Junior High School until 1978 and was torn down three years later.

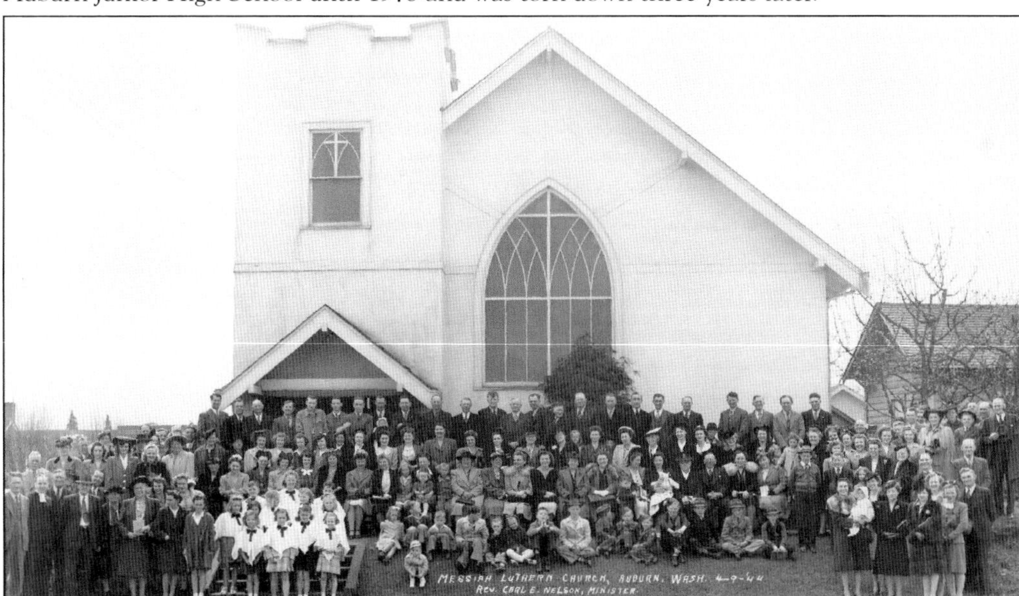

Messiah Lutheran Church, located directly across the street from Auburn High School, served as an auditorium and performance center for high school–sponsored activities throughout a large portion of the 1900s. The original church building and its congregation are seen here on a chilly Easter Sunday in 1944.

By 1952, when this photograph was taken, Auburn was becoming a larger city. Housing developments and businesses were crowded in between the Northern Pacific tracks and the foot of Lea Hill, while farms were slowly pushed farther and farther away from downtown. On the left, a new automobile overpass crossing the railroad tracks can be seen. This overpass is now a part of Highway 18.

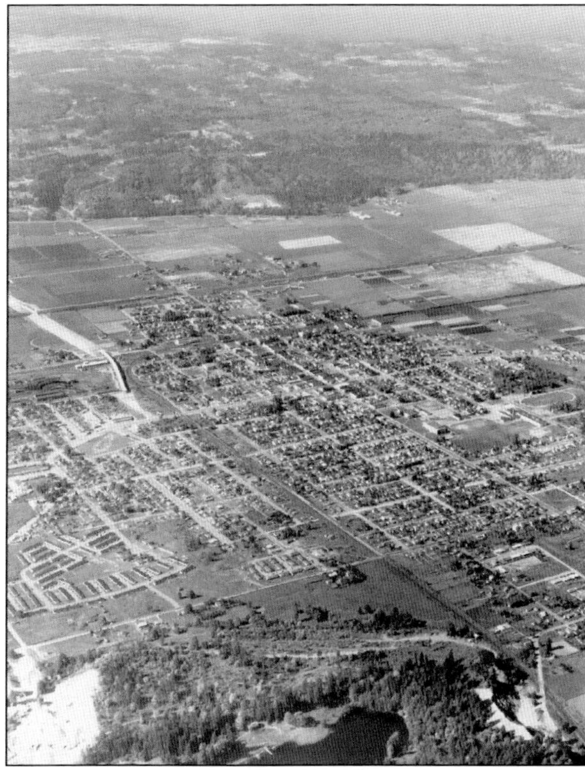

Three Auburn police officers pose with their motorcycles in front of their new police department building around 1960. This new building was the first separate headquarters the police department had. Previously, they had shared space with other city employees at city hall. The building was also one of the city's fallout shelters—note the sign in the upper left corner.

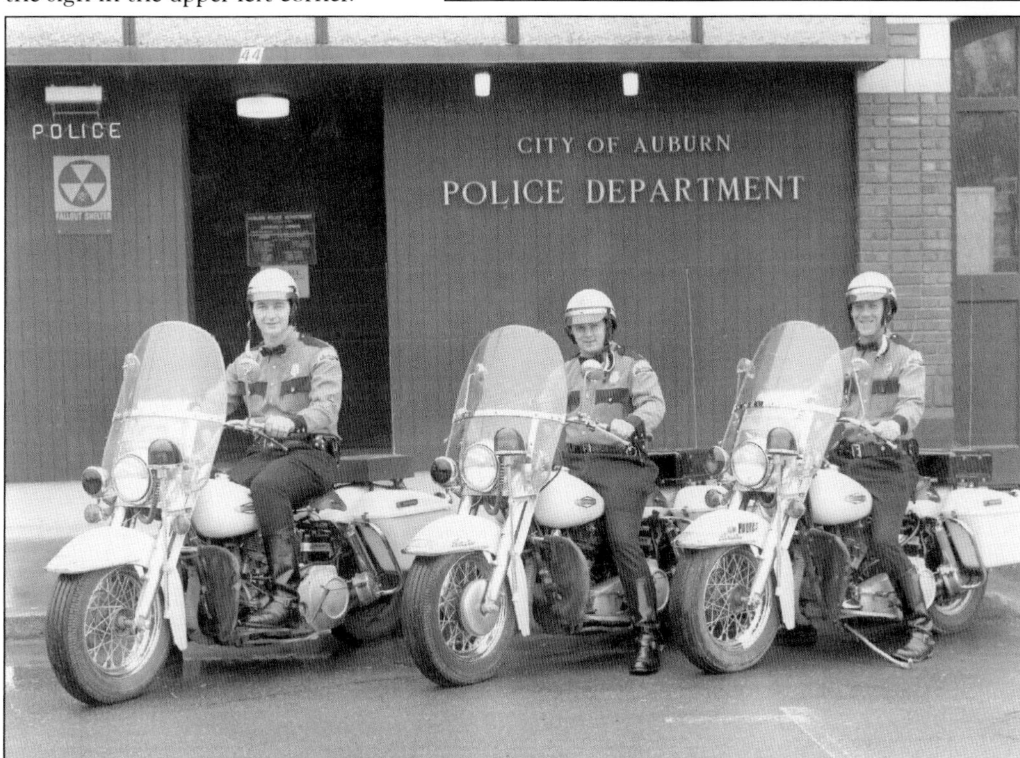

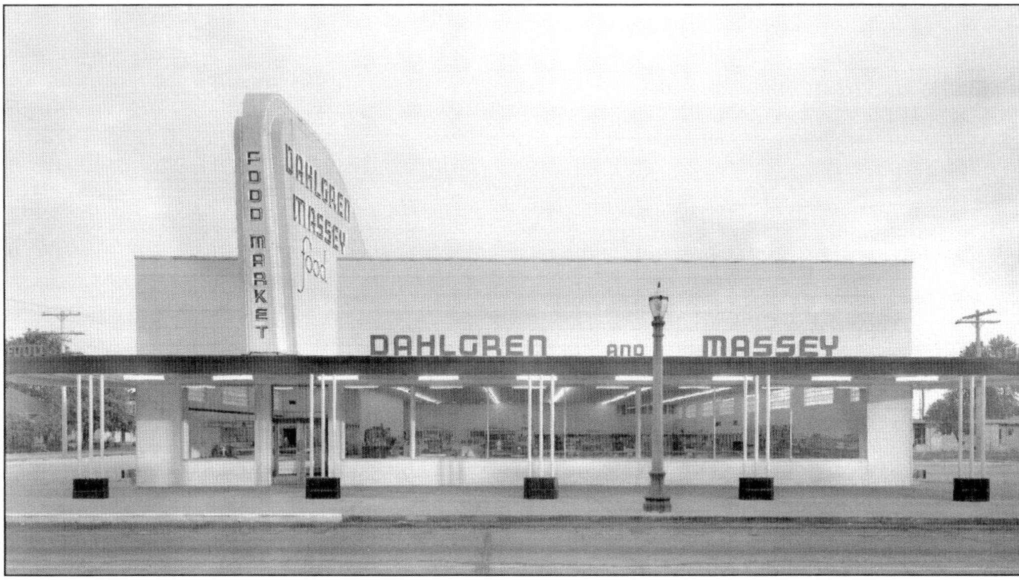

The Dahlgren & Massey grocery store opened for business in 1946. It was a very modern grocery store for its time and was one of the largest on the West Coast. The market also had the very first paved parking lot in Auburn, a luxury for businesses of the era. Today, this building houses the Auburn Police Department.

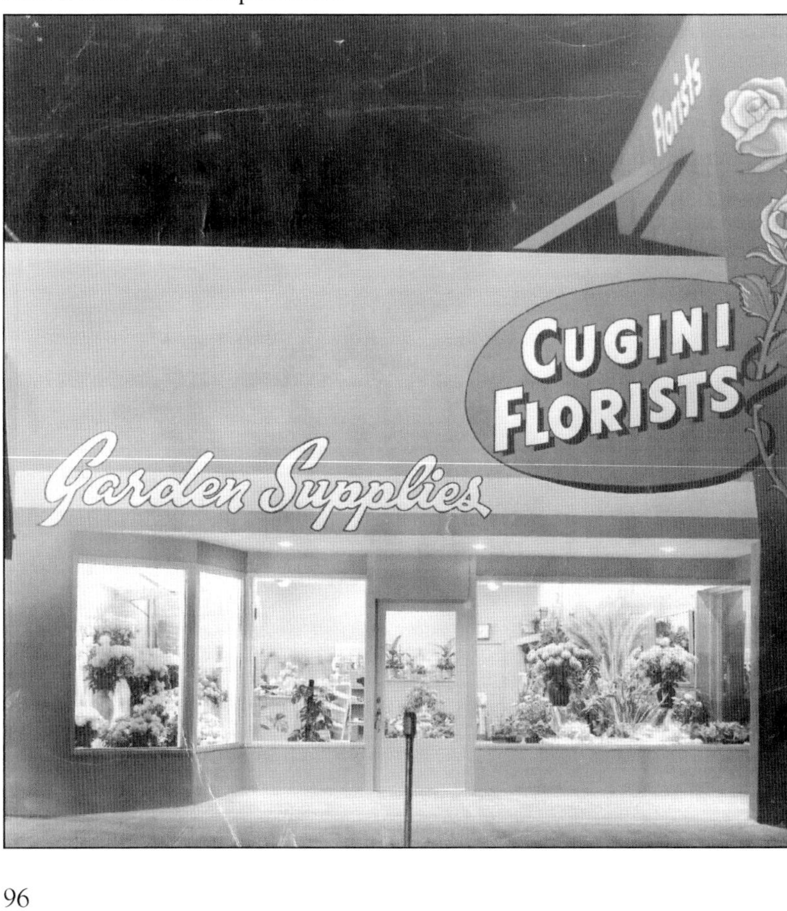

Cugini Florists, previously known as the Cugini Shurefine Store, began as an Italian immigrant–owned grocery store with a small side business in flowers. By the 1950s, the floral business had outpaced the grocery business, and the Main Street store was remodeled and reopened as Cugini Florists & Garden Supplies in 1954.

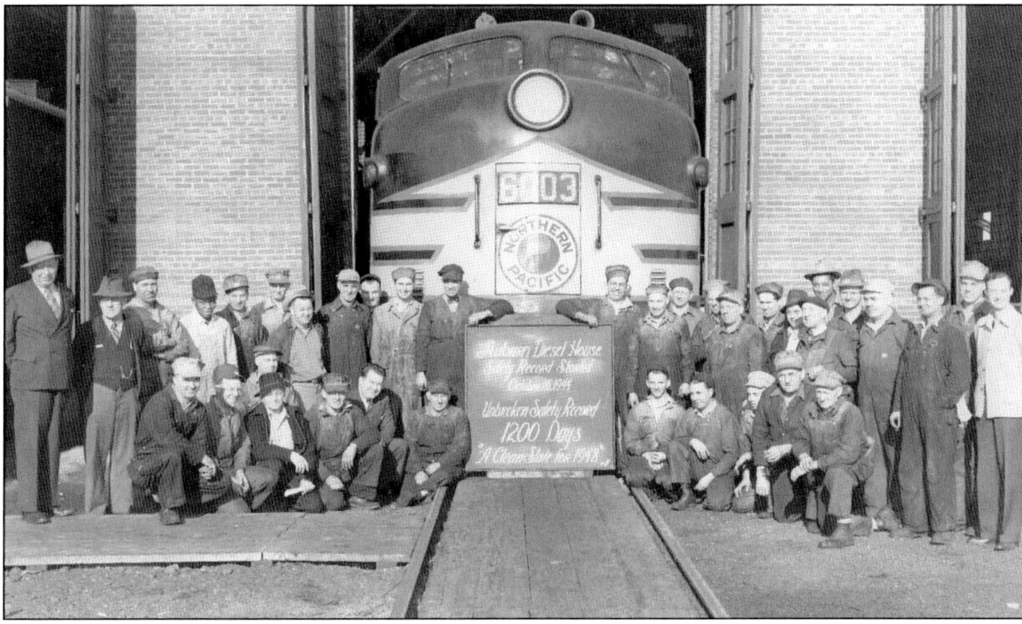

The Northern Pacific Railroad opened its first diesel repair shop in Auburn in 1944. The shop was designed for working on the new diesel and diesel-electric locomotives that were quickly replacing the coal-powered steam engines that had once made up the Northern Pacific fleet. Three large bays allowed for engines to easily enter the brick shop.

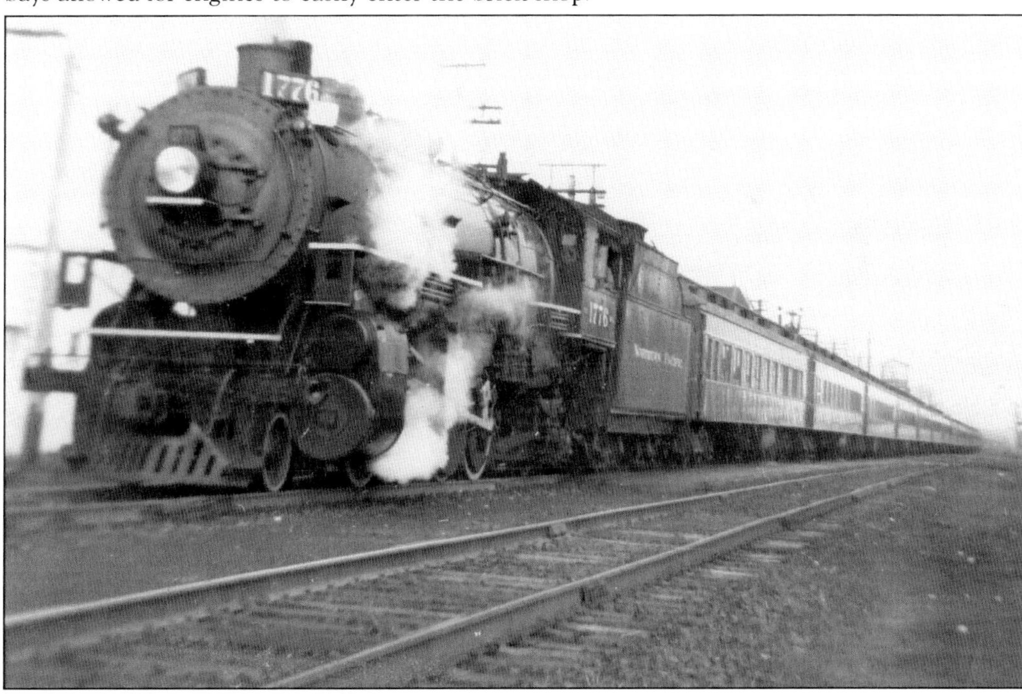

Engine 1776 was the last steam engine to pass through Auburn in 1957. The transition from steam locomotives to diesel and diesel-electric locomotives along the Northern Pacific Railroad lines was one of many signals that the railroad industry in Auburn was about to undergo significant changes as the 1960s approached.

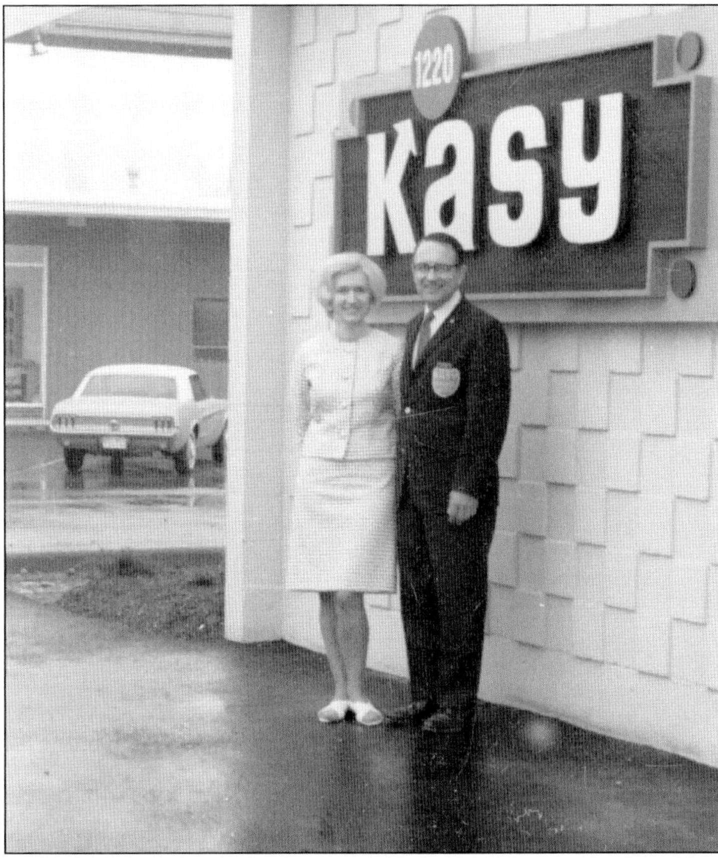

Radio KASY was Auburn's only local radio station from 1958 to 1989. KASY played mostly jazz and instrumental music, but also broadcast local news and events from around Auburn. Ed and June Garre, seen left in front of the KASY studios in 1969, owned the station and acted as the head announcers. The station was completely analog, as seen in the 1959 photograph below of the station studio. Virgil Swanson, an announcer, sits in front of his control board and plays individual songs from records. A phone to his left allowed Auburn residents to call in and request songs.

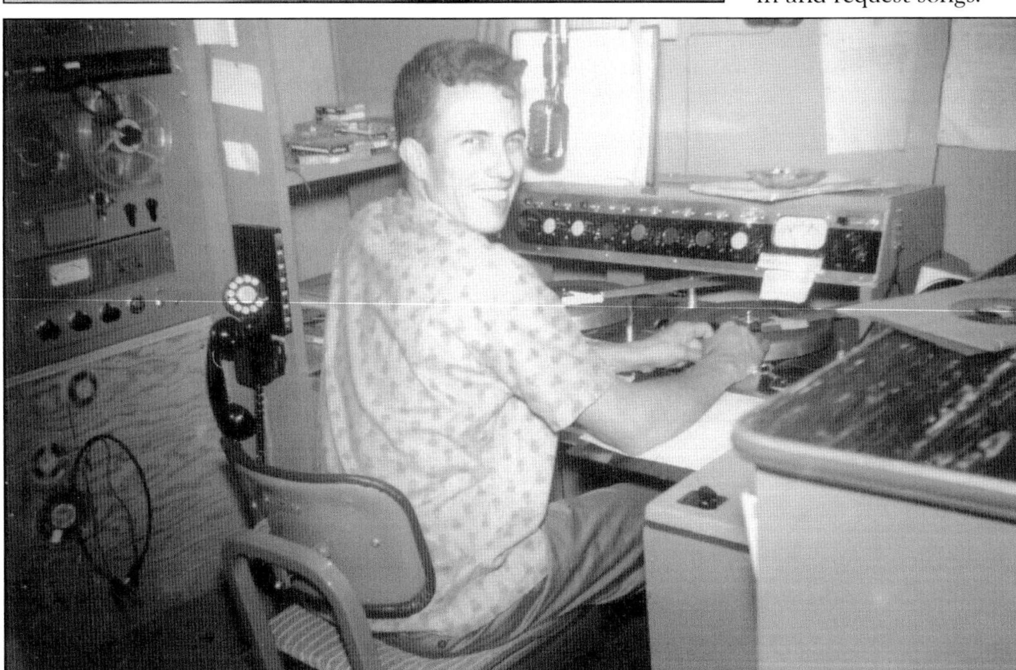

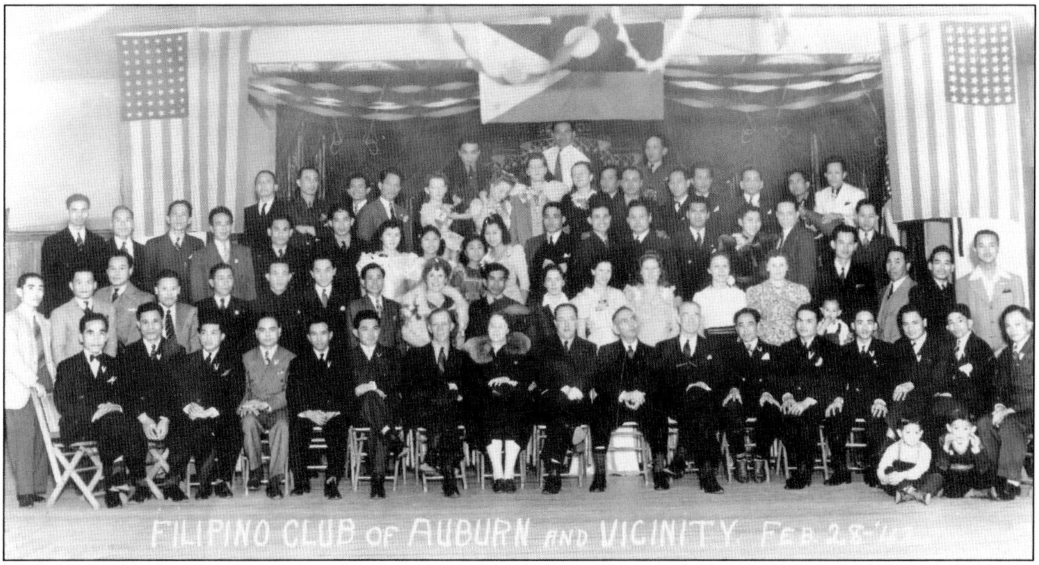

Filipino immigrants began moving into the Auburn and Algona areas in the 1940s and 1950s. Filipino workers had been moving to the United States since the beginning of the American occupation of the Philippines in 1898, after the Spanish-American War. Those that came to the Pacific Northwest mostly congregated in Seattle until after the Philippines gained their independence following World War II. The photograph above shows the members of the Filipino Club of Auburn and Vicinity in 1942. Just 14 years later, the Filipino American Community of Puget Sound had built a community center, seen below, and was holding community events.

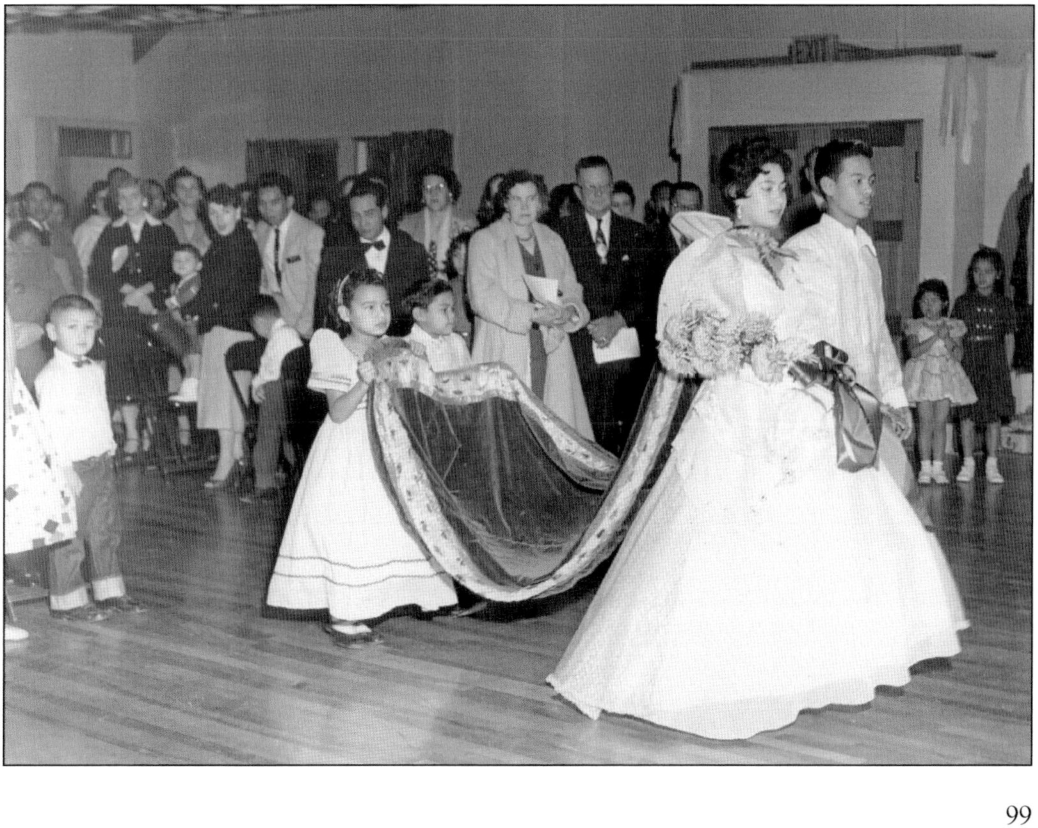

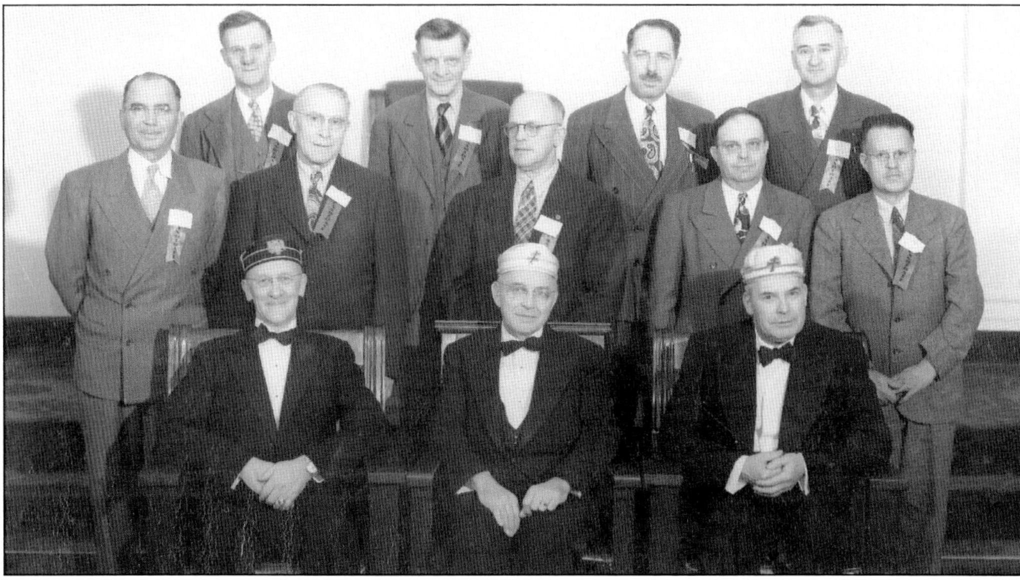

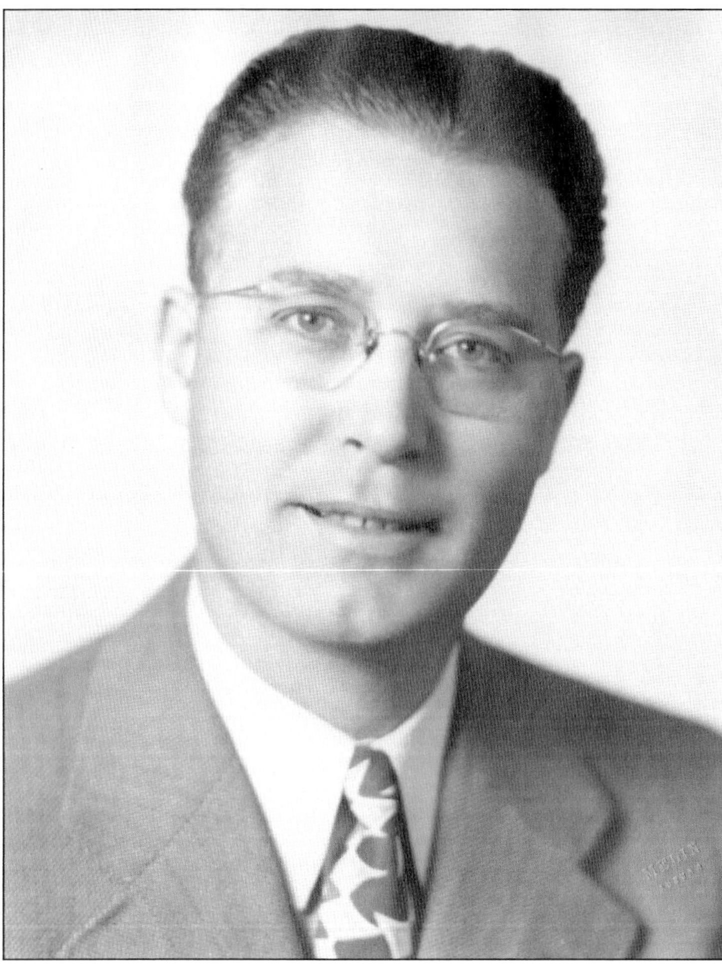

In the 1950s, fraternal orders began to see a significant shift in membership patterns in Auburn. Many older, more traditional fraternal groups, like the Knights of Pythias, saw membership plummet. Some groups, like the 1947 delegation of Masons seen above at a conference in Tacoma, were able to hold their membership levels steady through the 1970s before eventually seeing a decline. Many of the relatively newer, less outwardly religious civic clubs, like the Kiwanis, gained membership in the 1950s, mostly thanks to a generation of veterans and their families who wished to improve their new suburban communities. Seen left is Don Glenn, an Auburn-area businessman and the Kiwanis president in 1946.

Seven

Auburn, Aerospace Center 1962–1989

From the 1960s to the 1980s, Auburn shifted from a commercial center to an industrial one. The largest example of this change was the opening of a new Boeing commercial aviation factory in 1966, which manufactured components of Boeing commercial jets, including parts for the brand-new 747 jumbo jet. Other local industrial companies supported the Boeing plant both directly and indirectly, together bringing hundreds of new jobs to the city.

A statewide initiative for the building and improvement of Washington's freeways brought a full-fledged highway, Route 18, through the heart of Auburn in 1964. Increasingly easy access to the highway system was good news for manufacturers as well as for workers, as it allowed for shorter commutes for workers and lower transportation and shipping costs for businesses. At the same time, railroad service in Auburn began to decline, eventually leading to the closure of many Burlington Northern Railway facilities in the late 1970s.

Boeing was only one segment of the aerospace boom in Auburn in the second half of the 20th century. The Federal Aviation Administration opened an air traffic control center in Auburn in 1962, Auburn Municipal Airport opened for general aviation use in 1969, and the 1962 World's Fair in Seattle brought tourists from across the country to the Puget Sound area to see the new, futuristic technologies promised by air and space technologies.

Not everything in Auburn was about business during this period. Auburn's rapidly growing population required updated civil services, and the city government was looking for opportunities to expand its revenue options to meet the challenges of a growing city. The Auburn Golf Course was purchased by the city and added to its growing list of public parks and recreational facilities. A new city hall was built with modern facilities, and city utilities were upgraded. The Howard Hanson Dam was completed in 1962, finally giving residents and businesses security from flooding. New grade schools were built by the Auburn school district, and Green River Community College was established to provide training opportunities to students throughout southern King County.

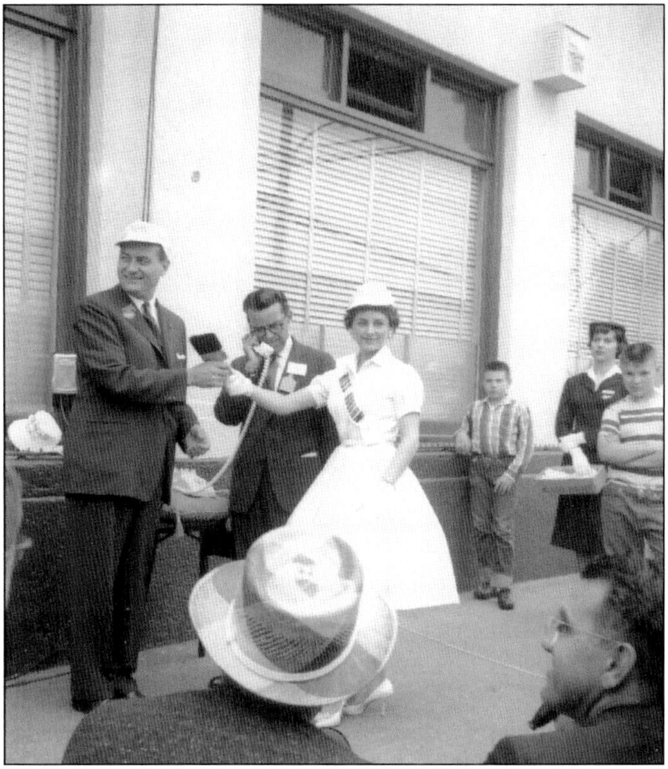

The 1962 Century 21 World's Fair in Seattle had an economic impact on the entire Puget Sound region. Towns across the area, including Auburn, participated in the Century 21 Beautification Project, cleaning up the commercial areas of cities to make them more scenic for visiting tourists and business leaders. Left, Washington State governor Albert Rosellini (left) poses with an unidentified Miss Auburn to ceremonially begin repainting the National Bank of Washington, located on Main Street. On the other side of the bank (below), a National Ladies Paint Derby painting contest was held. The cleanup occurred throughout town, and culminated in a festive parade.

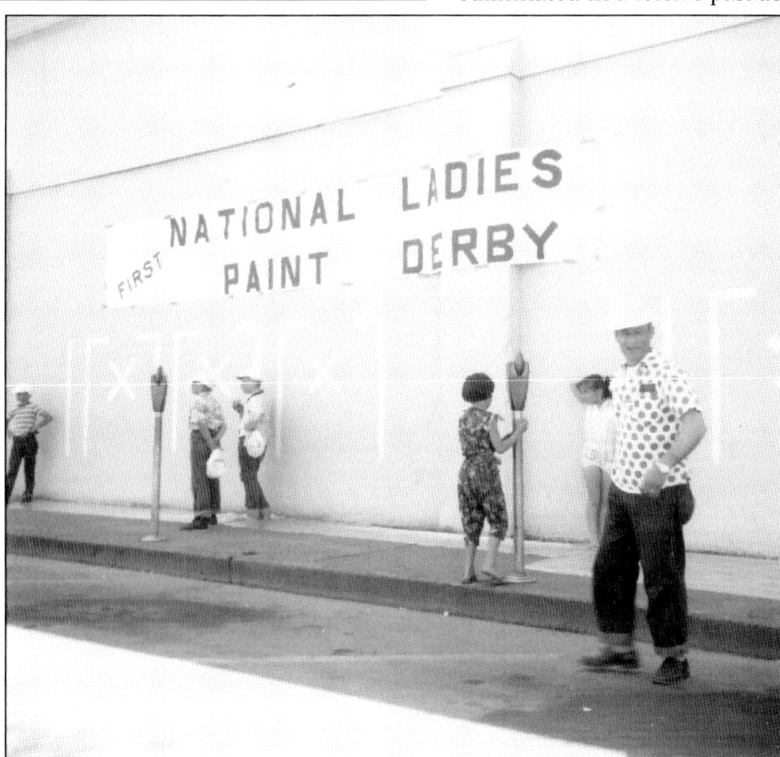

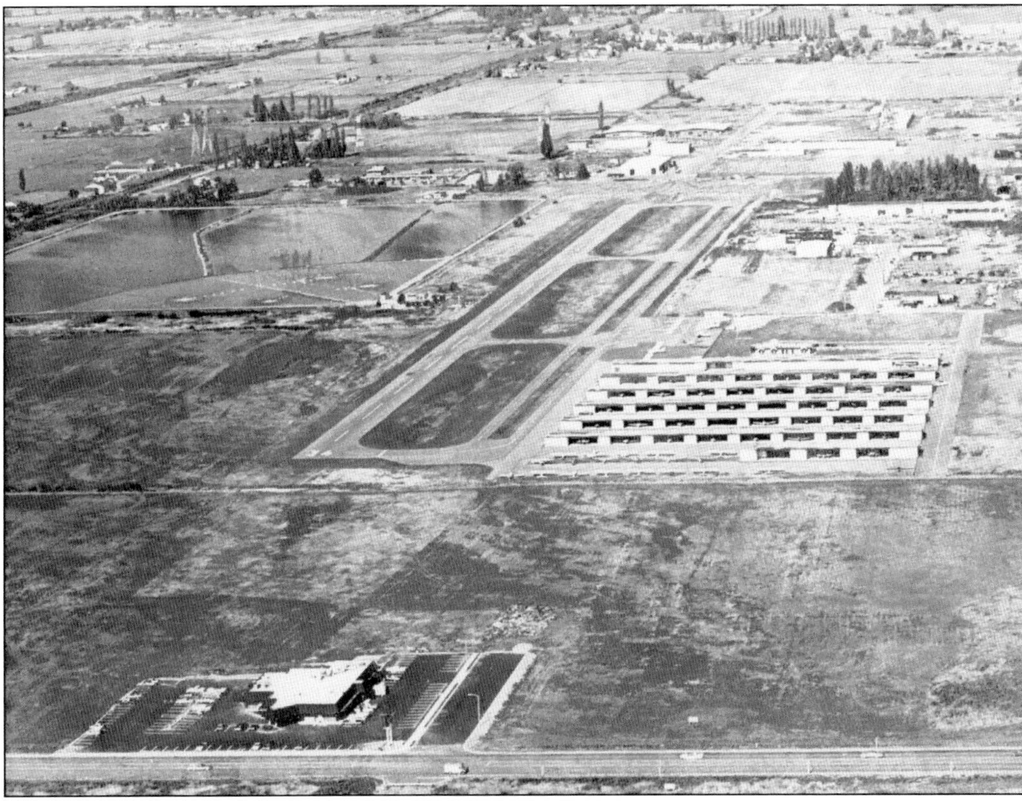

Auburn Municipal Airport opened for business in September 1969 after seven years of political wrangling and heated debate. The entire airport can be seen in the 1971 photograph above, taken shortly after the completion of the airport's hangers. Mayor Robert Gaines and the city council members that served with him were largely responsible for the ultimate creation of the airport, even in the face of intense public outcry about the priorities of the city government. The airport became a hub of general aviation in the valley and supported several flight-related businesses, including Auburn Flight Service, seen below in 1971.

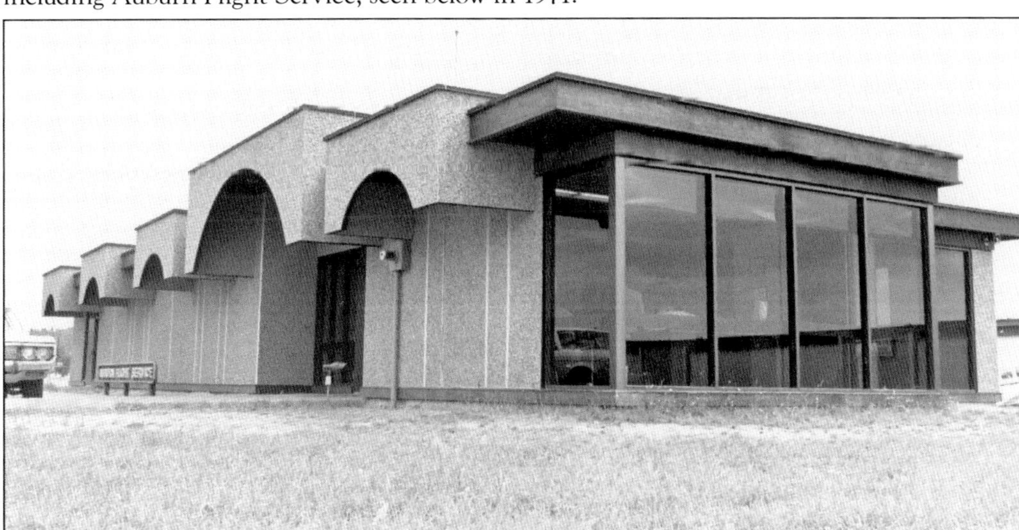

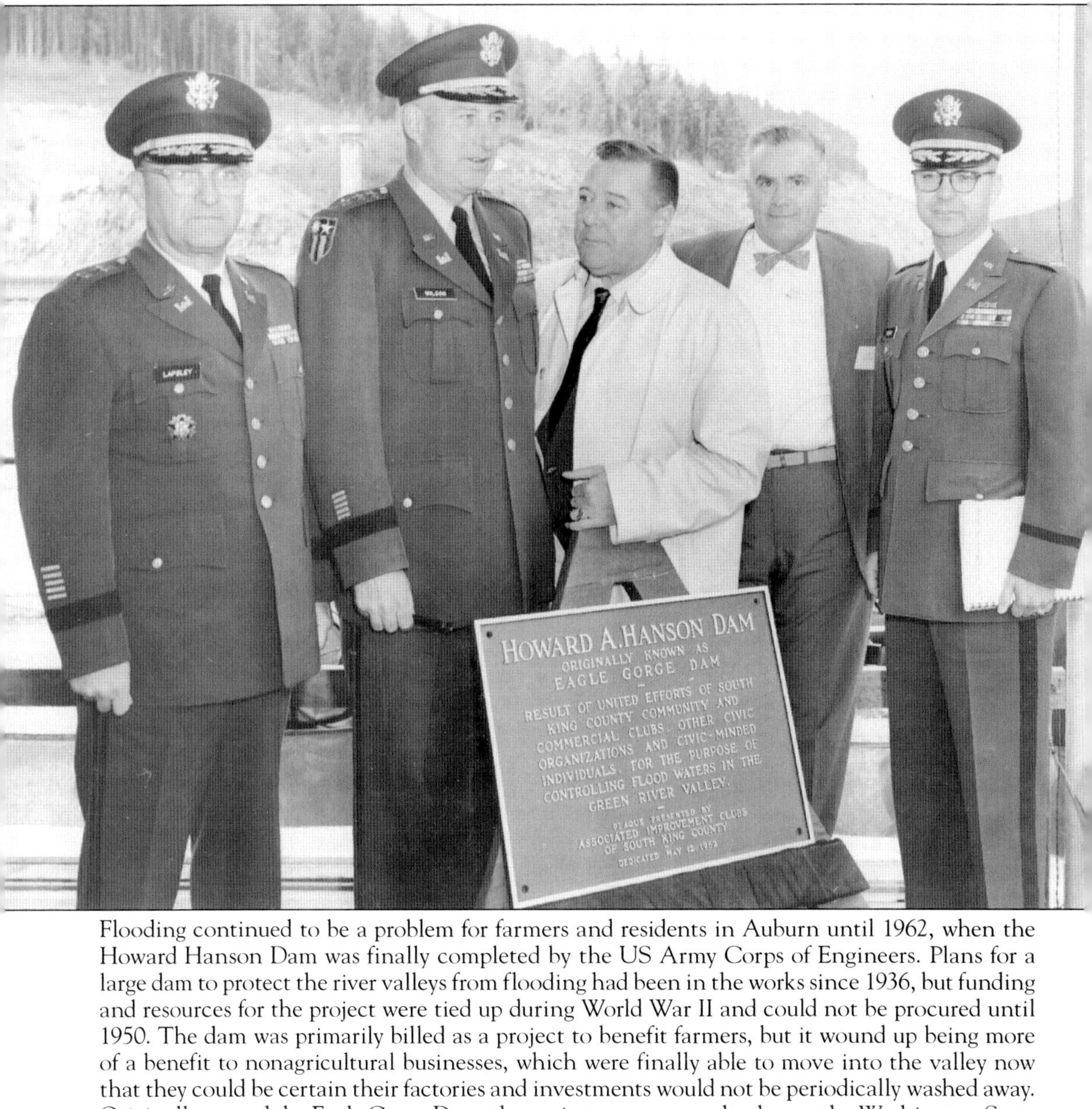

Flooding continued to be a problem for farmers and residents in Auburn until 1962, when the Howard Hanson Dam was finally completed by the US Army Corps of Engineers. Plans for a large dam to protect the river valleys from flooding had been in the works since 1936, but funding and resources for the project were tied up during World War II and could not be procured until 1950. The dam was primarily billed as a project to benefit farmers, but it wound up being more of a benefit to nonagricultural businesses, which were finally able to move into the valley now that they could be certain their factories and investments would not be periodically washed away. Originally named the Eagle Gorge Dam, the project was renamed to honor the Washington State legislator who had championed the dam since its inception.

The regional headquarters for the Federal Aviation Administration opened in Auburn in 1972, with KASY radio personality Ed Garre serving as the master of ceremonies. The center, formally called the Seattle Air Route Traffic Control Center, is in charge of managing air traffic for the entire Pacific Northwest region and some portions of the Pacific Ocean.

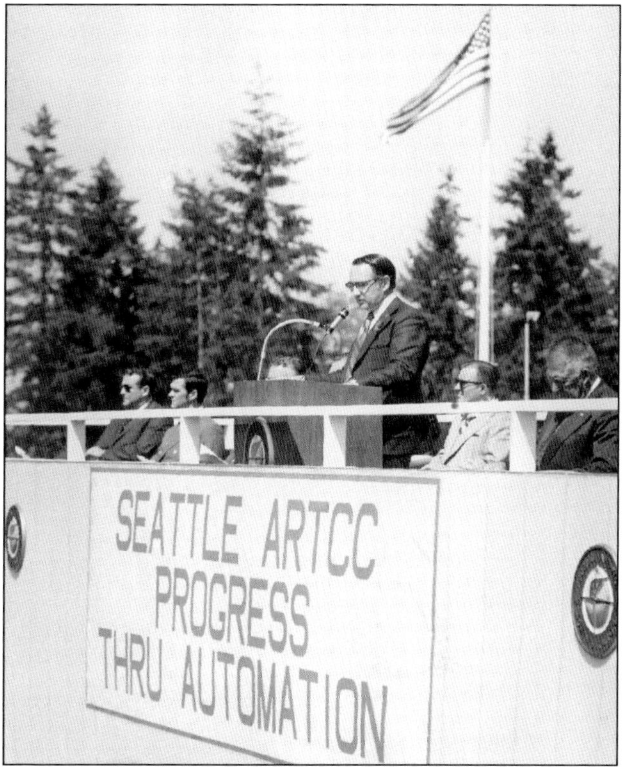

The Rohr Aircraft Company, later renamed Rohr Industries, was one of several companies that supported Boeing and the aerospace industry in Auburn. Seen here around 1970, Rohr produced specialized jet airplane components. Other manufacturers followed suit, providing Boeing with everything from tools and vehicles for workers to highly specialized plastics.

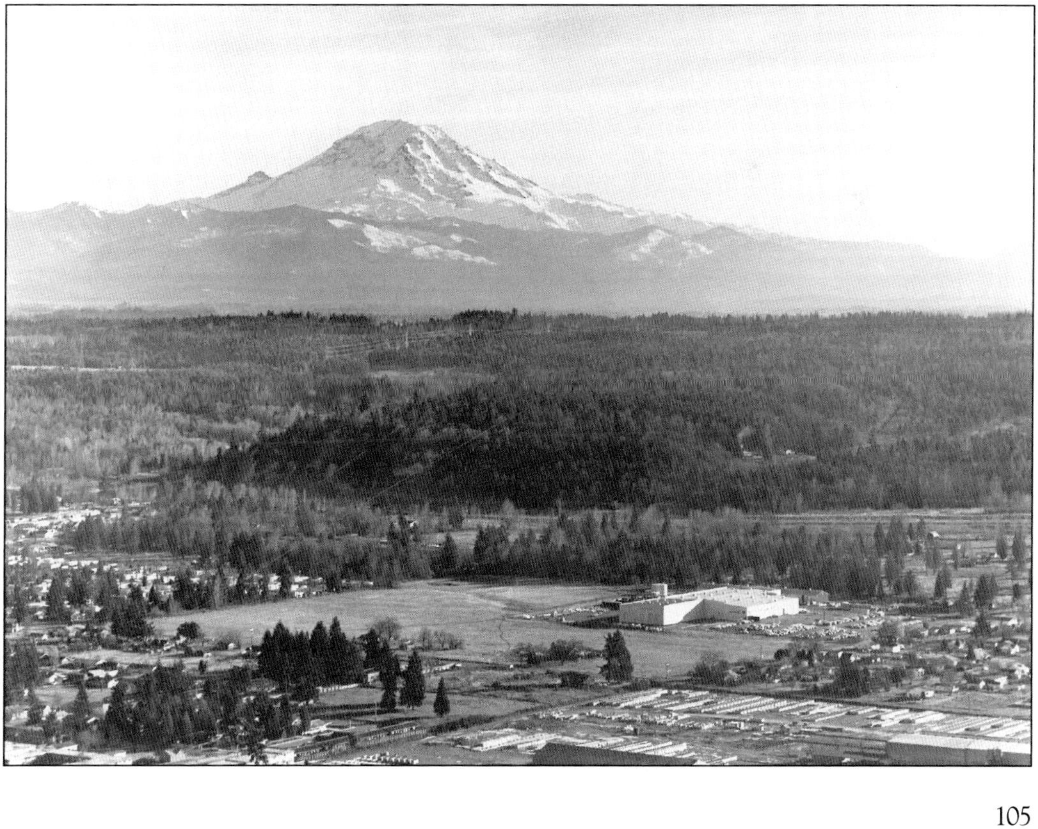

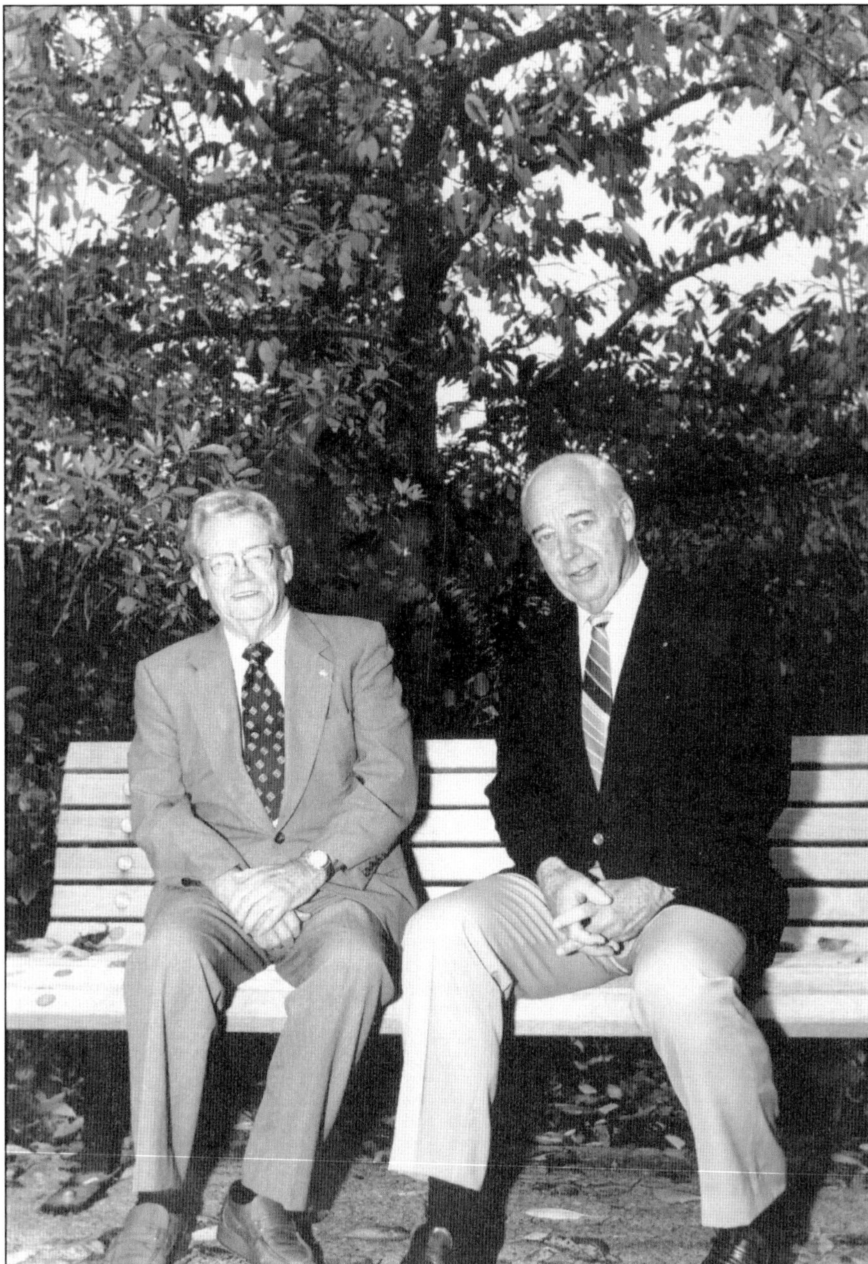

Green River Community College first opened its campus on Lea Hill in 1965 with total of 840 students. The college began as an adult education program run through the Auburn school district in the late 1940s, but the exploding population of Auburn in the 1950s and 1960s meant a higher demand for adult education programs that were not connected to major academic universities, especially vocational training and college preparation tracks. Mel Lindboom and Hayes Holman, seen here on campus in 1965, were instrumental in the creation of the college and helped shape its unique character. Defining features of the college included a particular devotion to preserving the natural environment and the thick forests of the campus and not segregating vocational training programs from traditional academic class work. In 2012, Green River served 10,000 students.

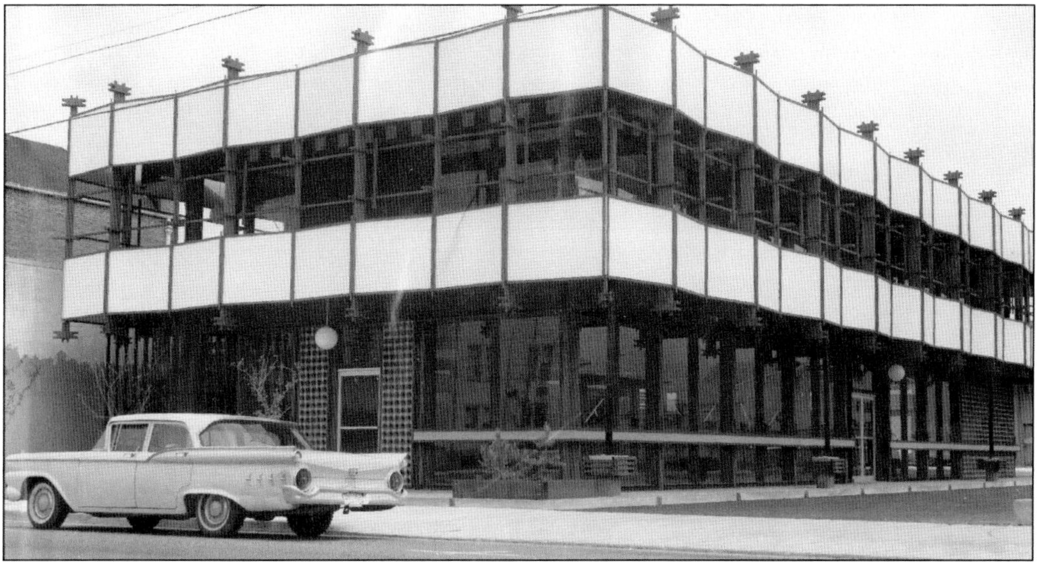

After Highway 18 opened in 1964, Auburn Way became an even more frequently traveled road than Main Street. Cugini Florists took advantage of this trend and moved from their original location on Main Street to this new, very modern building on Auburn Way in 1964. The building still stands today.

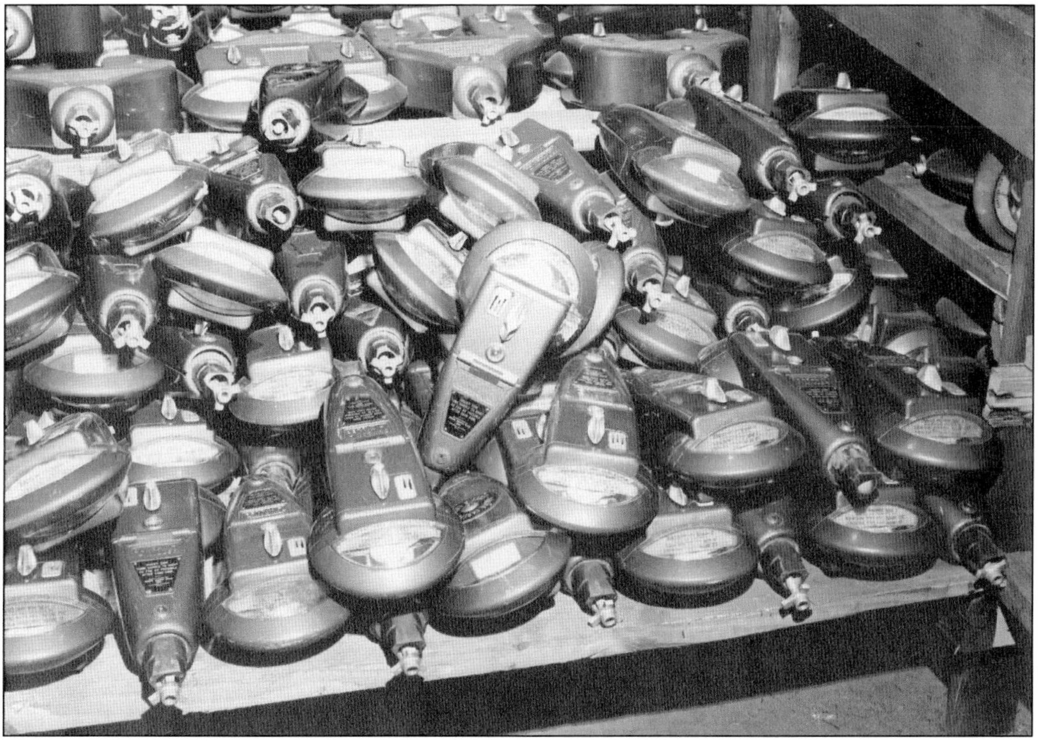

Auburn removed its parking meters in 1965. Most cities, including Auburn, installed parking meters as a way to fund street improvements and other municipal projects. When transportation became easier and merchants had to compete with businesses from other towns, Auburn business leaders asked for the meters to be removed to make shopping in Auburn more attractive.

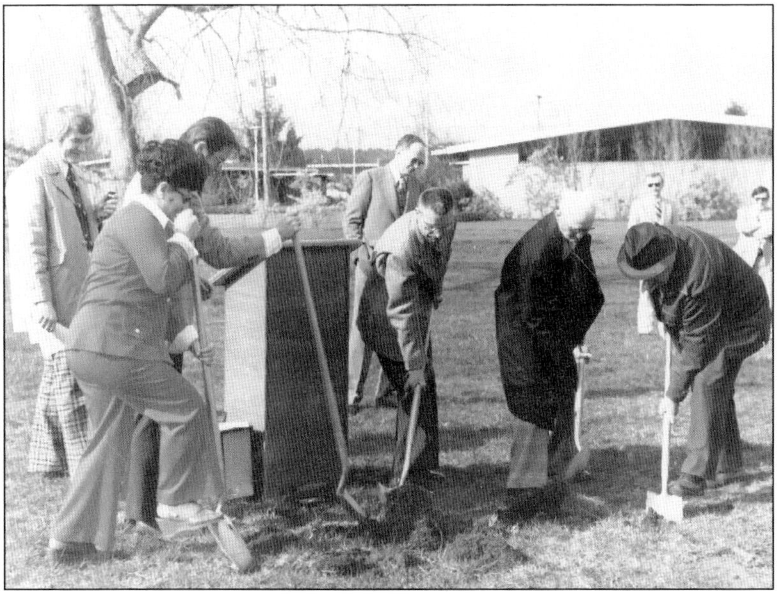

The passage of the Older Americans Act of 1965 was the beginning of a wave of new services and facilities focused on the needs of the elderly, including medical centers and senior centers. Auburn's first senior center was built in 1977. Here, city leaders stand together with senior citizens at the ground breaking of the senior center.

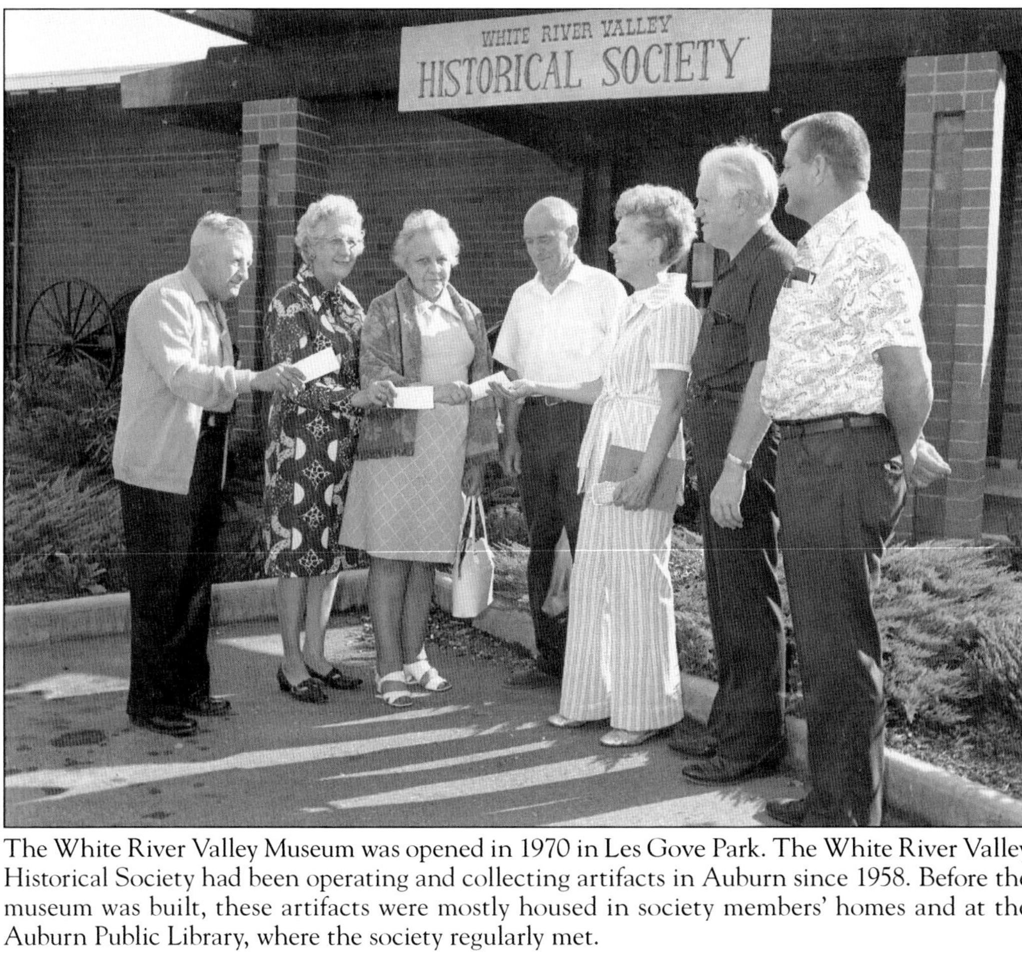

The White River Valley Museum was opened in 1970 in Les Gove Park. The White River Valley Historical Society had been operating and collecting artifacts in Auburn since 1958. Before the museum was built, these artifacts were mostly housed in society members' homes and at the Auburn Public Library, where the society regularly met.

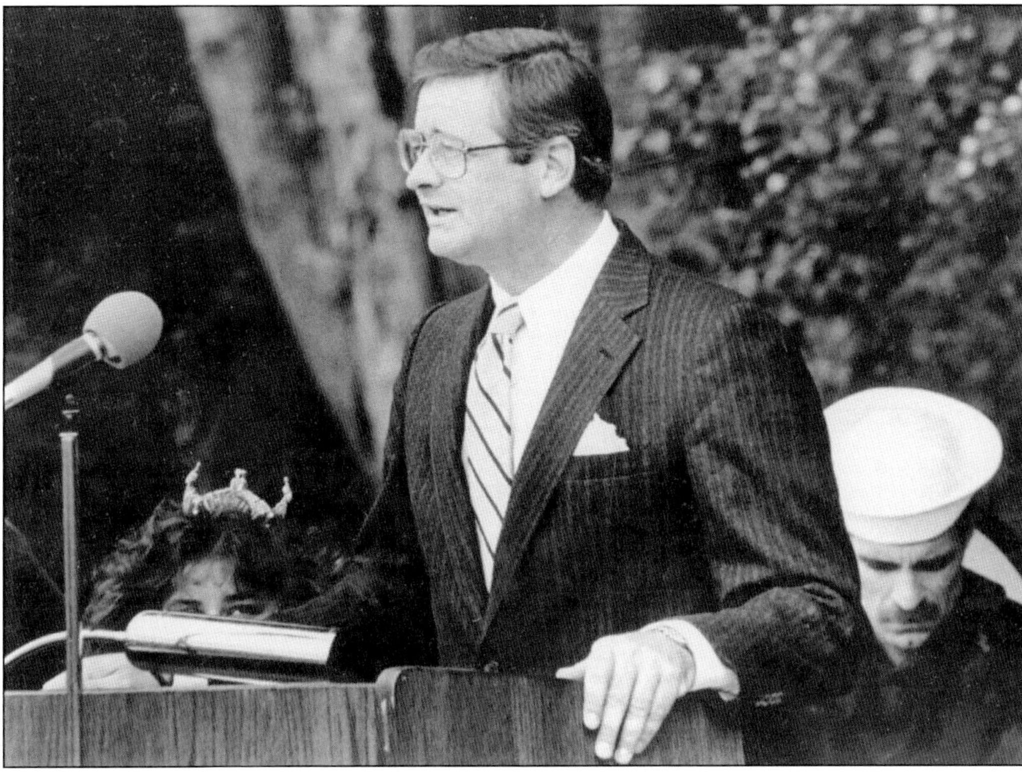

Game Farm Park had a presence in Auburn long before it became a part of the city's park system. Originally a true game farm, the site was used for hunting imported game birds like pheasants, quail, and partridge. One of the few visible portions of the White River diversion dam can be found in Game Farm Park. It eventually passed from state ownership to the City of Auburn in 1984 and was formally dedicated in 1988. Above, Auburn mayor Bob Roegner speaks at the park dedication. Below, dignitaries release balloons at the opening of the park. A year later, 10 acres of the park were set aside as a wilderness area for environmental purposes.

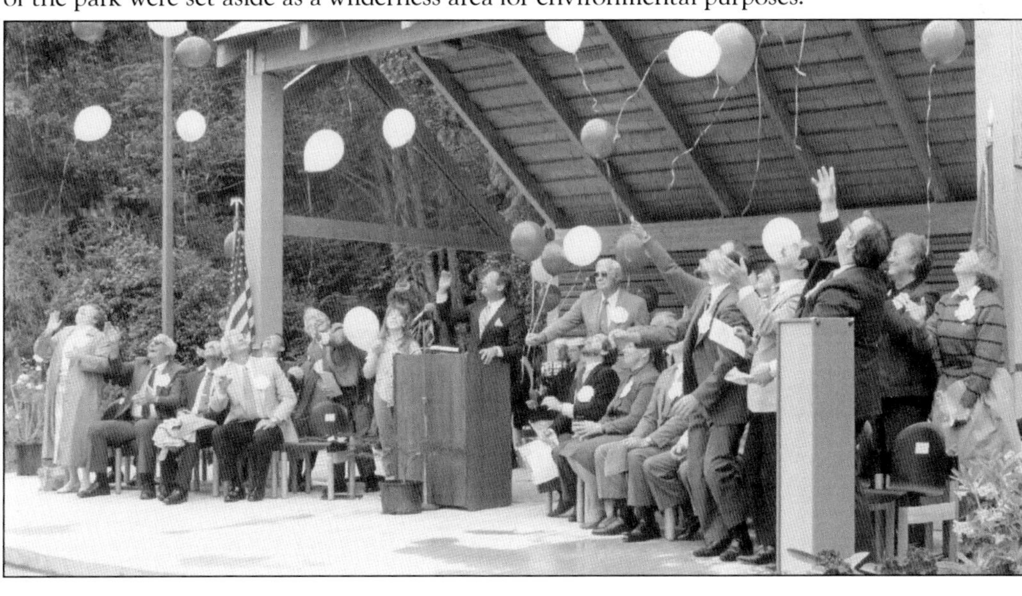

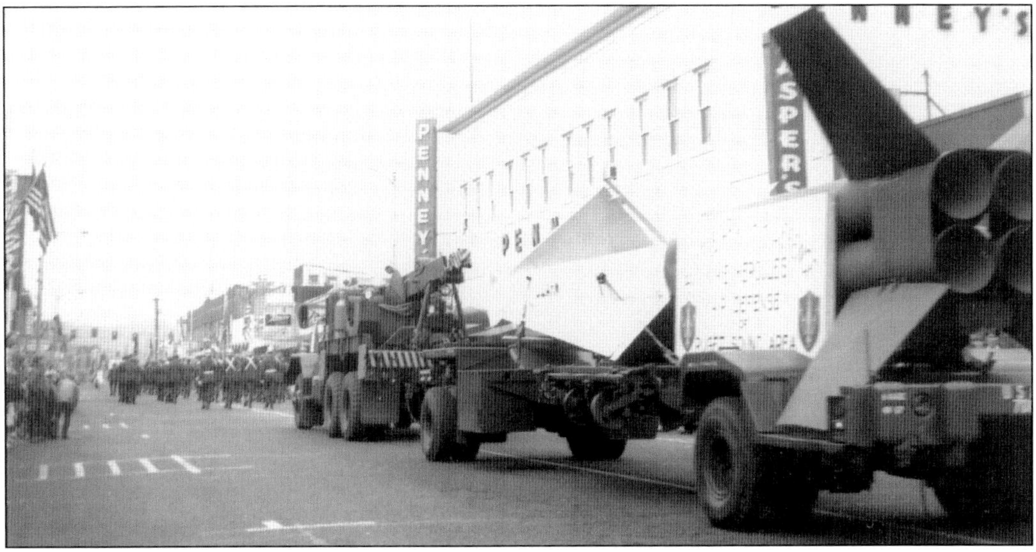

Auburn has always honored its veterans, but it was not until 1965 that it began honoring them with a parade. Today, the Auburn Veterans Day Parade is one of the largest Veterans Day parades in the United States and the official regional Veterans Day Parade for the Puget Sound area. These two photographs show the 1969 parade as it travels up Main Street. Above, military equipment, including massive missiles, is displayed for parade-goers in front of the J.C. Penney building. Below, the Auburn High School girls' drill team crosses the intersection of Main Street and Auburn Way, in front of the Federated Order of Eagles building.

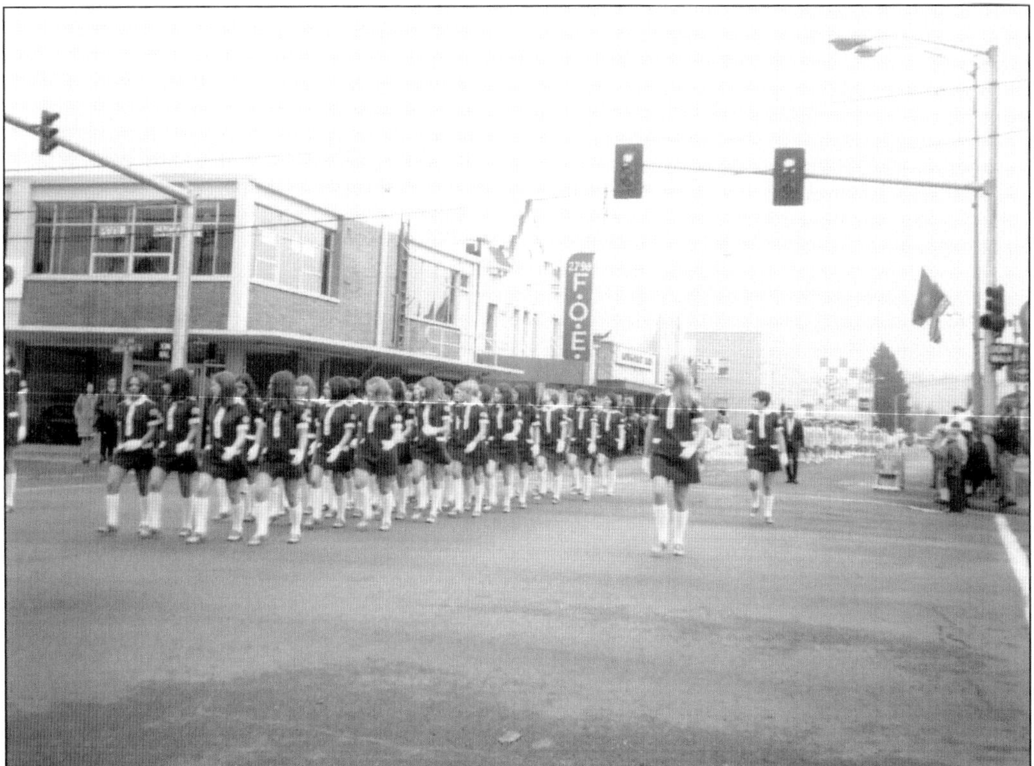

Auburn's new identity as a growing industrial powerhouse and population center brought it attention from government dignitaries and commercial and industry leaders around the state. At this event around 1965, Auburn mayor Robert "Bob" Gaines (left) chats with powerful Washington State senator Henry "Scoop" Jackson (center) and Washington State lieutenant governor Johnny Cherberg.

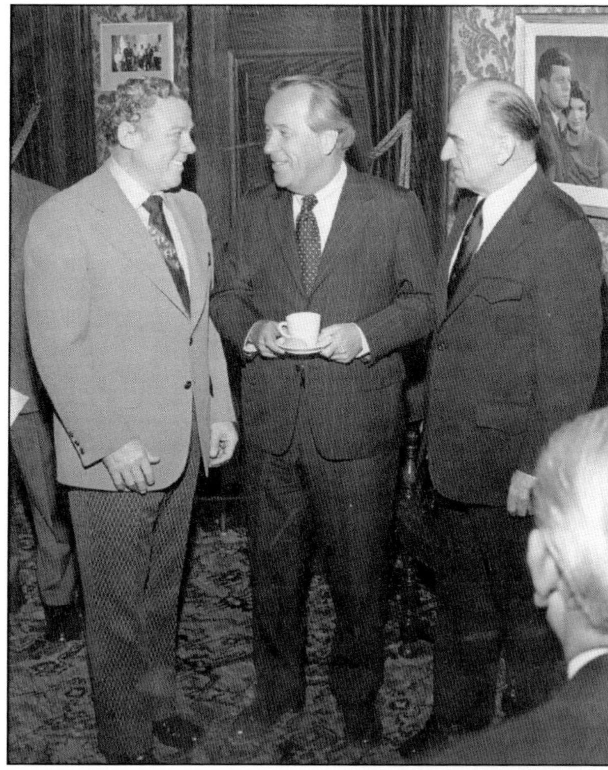

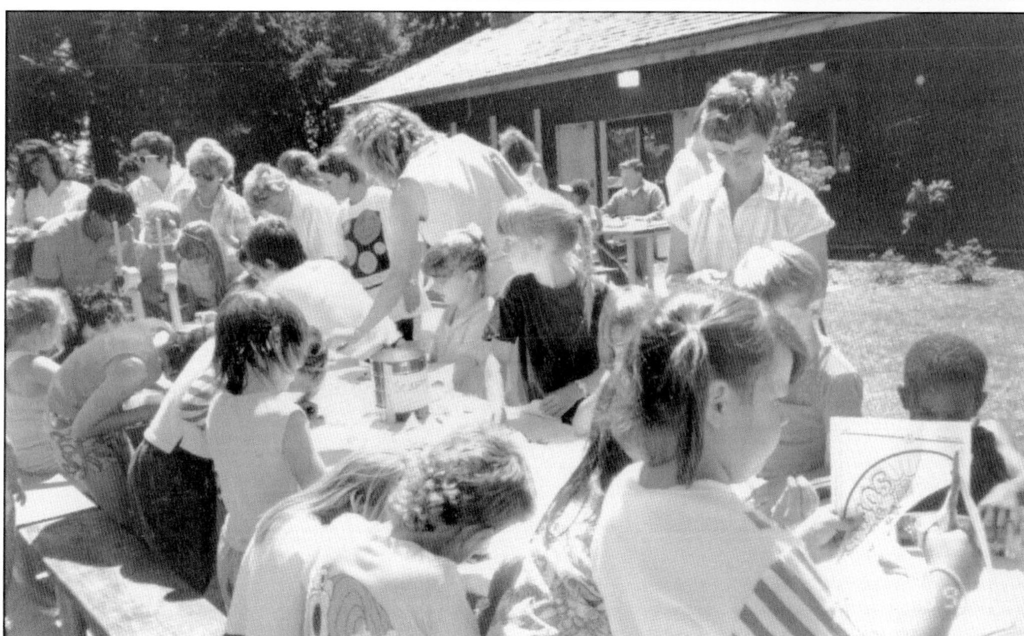

Fairs and festivals have always been popular in Auburn, and the growth of the city during this period provided plenty of impetus for more public activities, especially for families. Kid's Day began as an event in Game Farm Park where kids freshly out of school for the summer could gather, as seen in this Kid's Day photograph from around 1970.

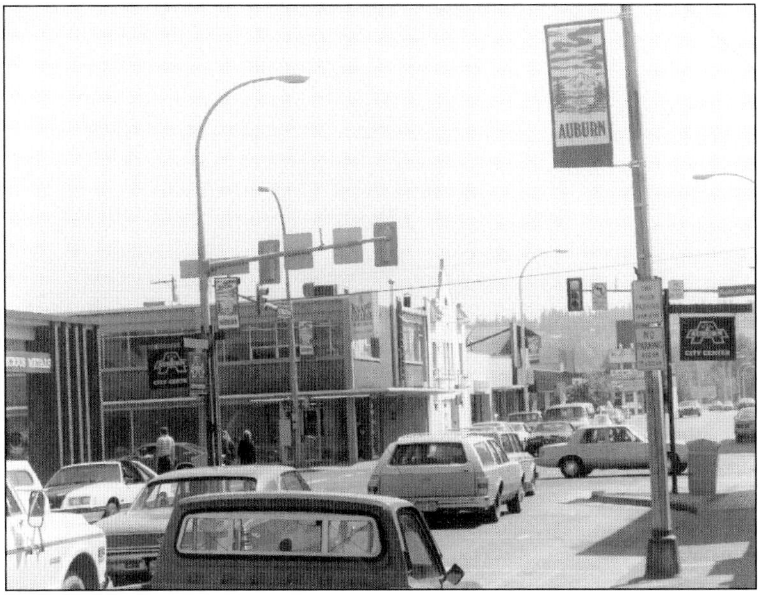

By the 1970s, Auburn had changed significantly from its railroad-town roots. This 1975 image of the intersection of Main Street and Auburn Way shows how busy this major intersection could be in the afternoons. Many of the building facades familiar to Auburnites today can be seen in images from the late 1960s and early 1970s.

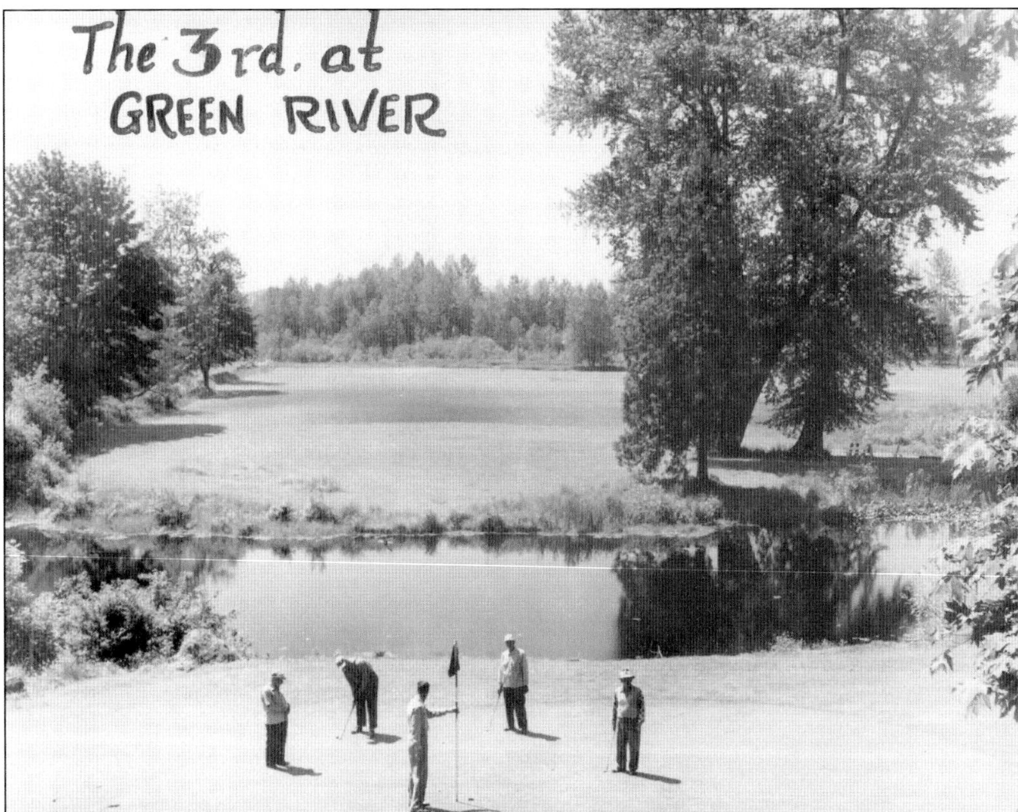

The Auburn Golf Course was first opened in 1949 as a private course by the Auburn Golf & Country Club. In 1970, the golf course was acquired by the City of Auburn and became a part of the parks department. In this photograph from around 1960, members play a round on the third hole.

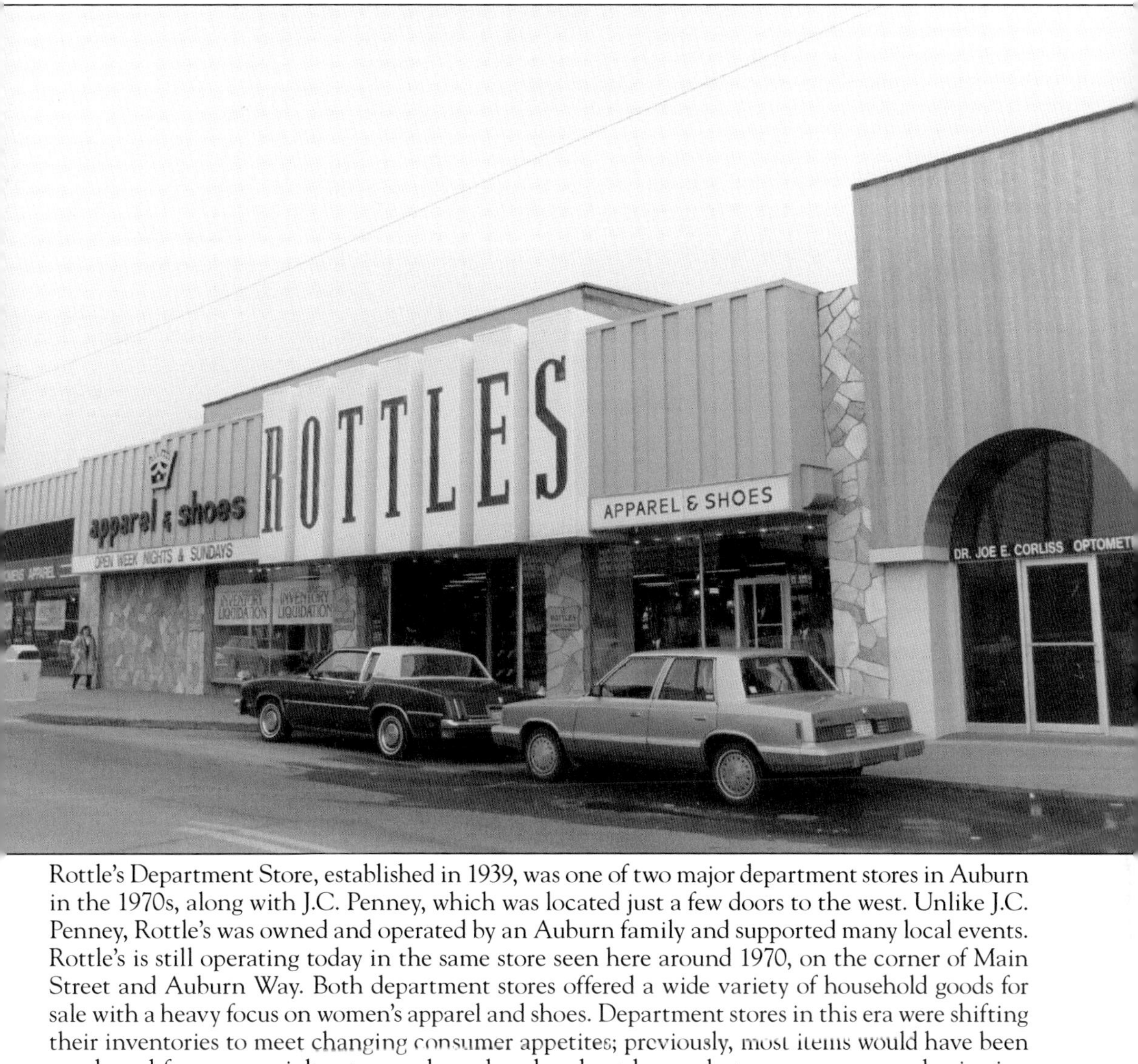

Rottle's Department Store, established in 1939, was one of two major department stores in Auburn in the 1970s, along with J.C. Penney, which was located just a few doors to the west. Unlike J.C. Penney, Rottle's was owned and operated by an Auburn family and supported many local events. Rottle's is still operating today in the same store seen here around 1970, on the corner of Main Street and Auburn Way. Both department stores offered a wide variety of household goods for sale with a heavy focus on women's apparel and shoes. Department stores in this era were shifting their inventories to meet changing consumer appetites; previously, most items would have been purchased from a specialty store or been handmade at home, but consumers were beginning to find it more cost-effective to purchase ready-made products in order to save their time for employment-related activities.

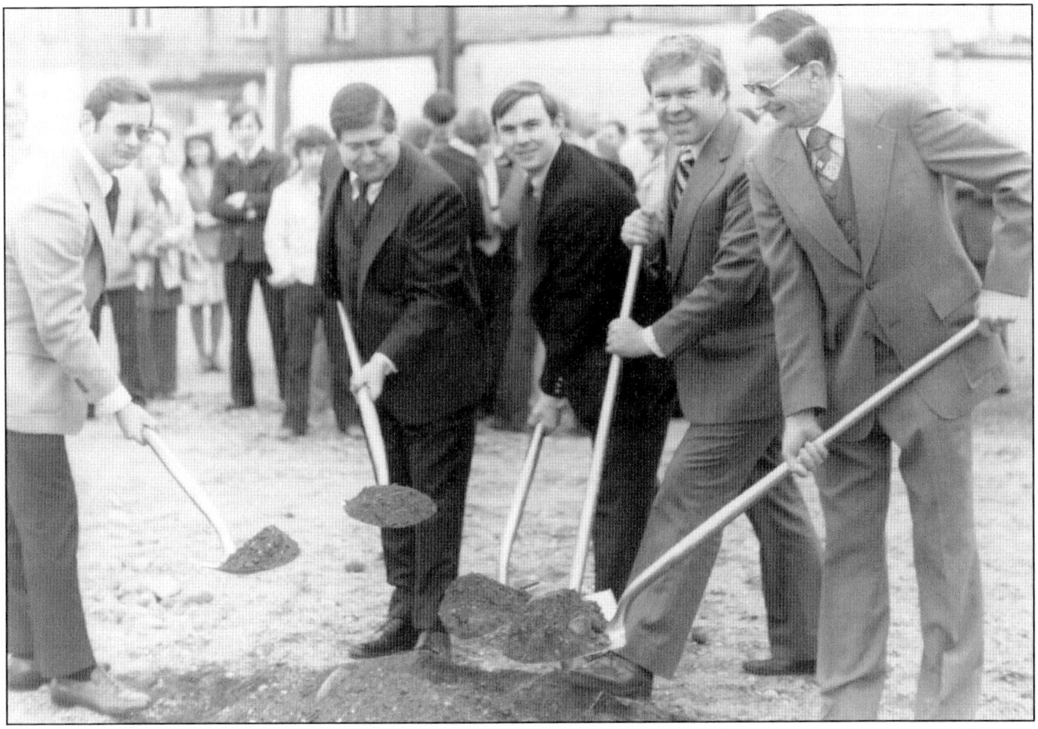

Auburn's second city hall building, situated near City Park, was quickly becoming too crowded for the expanding city government. Aside from the overcrowding problem, the building's basement and foundations were significantly damaged during a 1965 earthquake, and plans were made for a new building. After selecting a new site on Main Street, the ground breaking for the new city hall (above) took place with great ceremony in 1977. The city hall building included a front plaza and space for public art, as seen below. Today, the same city hall building is still in use, though with several renovations and the addition of an annex across the street.

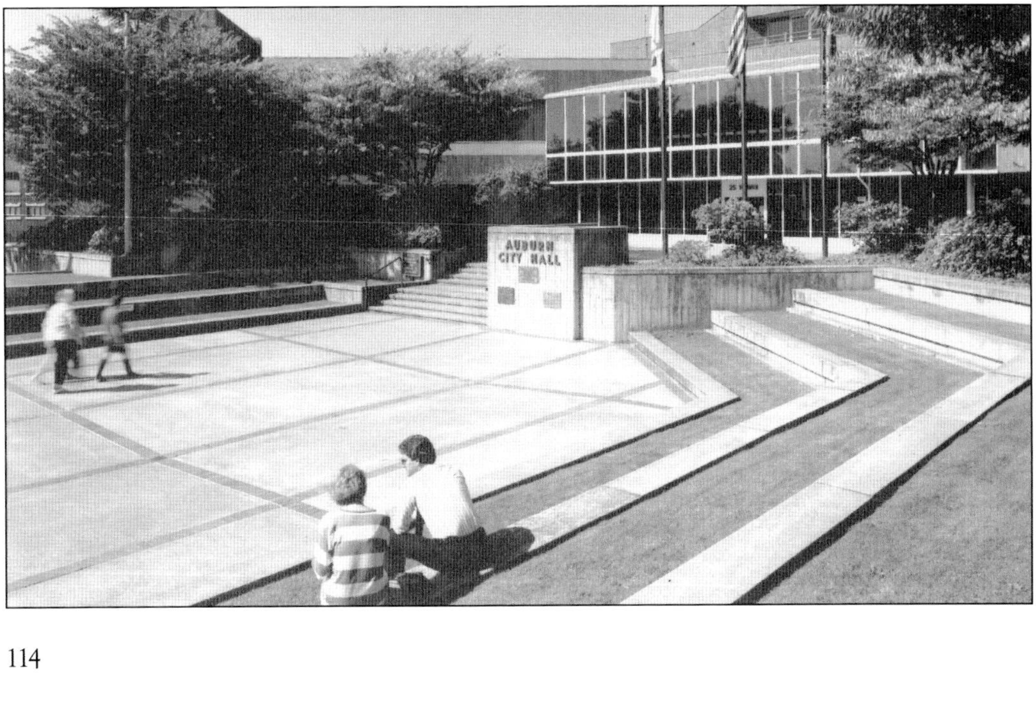

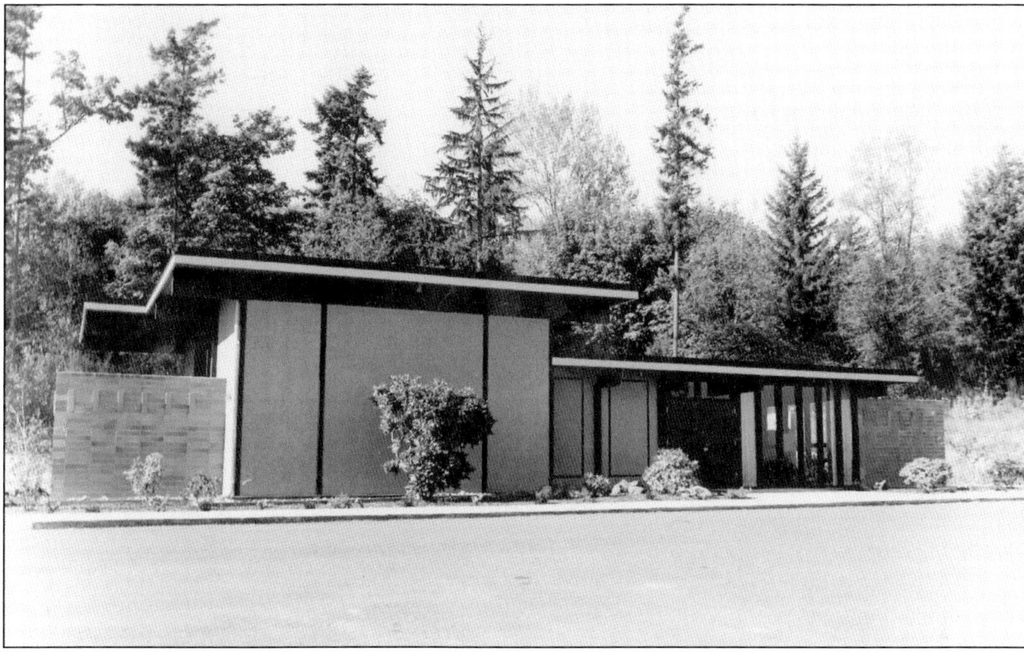

In 1945, Mountain View Cemetery was turned over to the city government. The city cleaned up the cemetery, but few upgrades were added until the early 1970s, after improvement funds were secured from a bond. The new office seen here was built in 1971, and a new mausoleum was added in 1974.

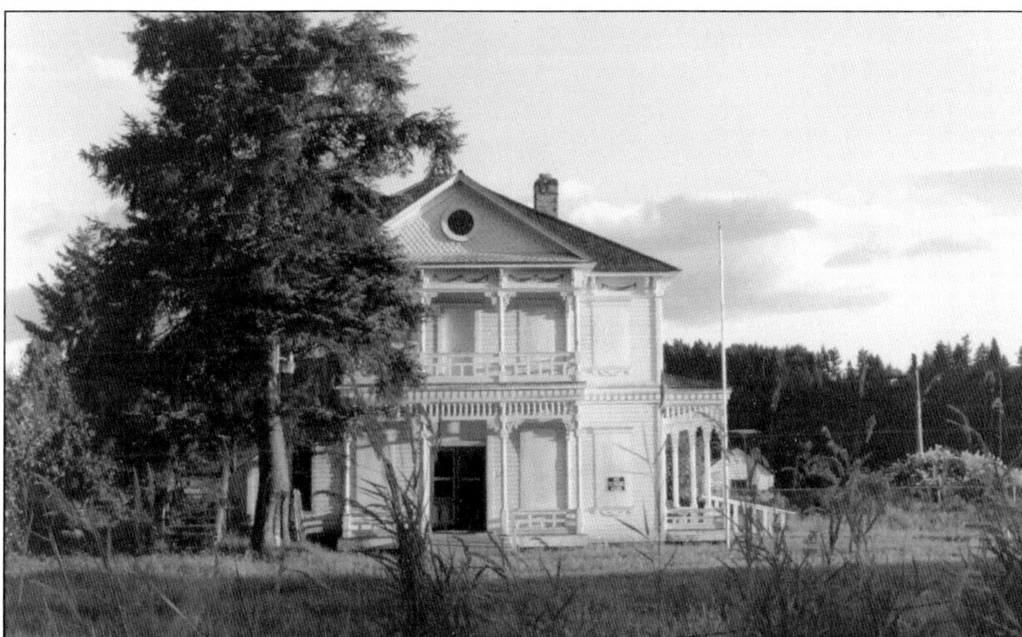

The Neely Mansion, located on the eastern outskirts of Auburn, was one of the largest mansions in the White River Valley when it was built in 1892. Historically minded citizens banded together to get the building listed in the National Register of Historic Places in 1974, and the building and grounds continue to be restored today.

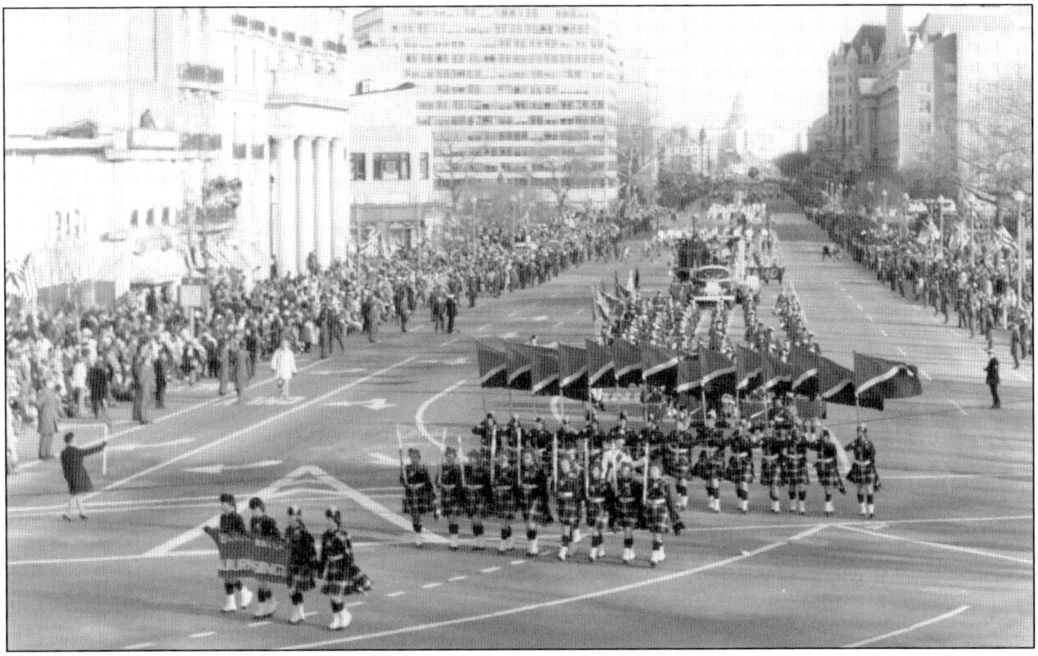

Auburn American Legion Post No. 78 supported many community activities, including the Black Watch Junior Drum & Bugle Corps, seen here around 1976. The band, also known as the Black Watch Highland Regiment, participated in many parades and community events in Auburn, as well as in the 1977 inaugural parade.

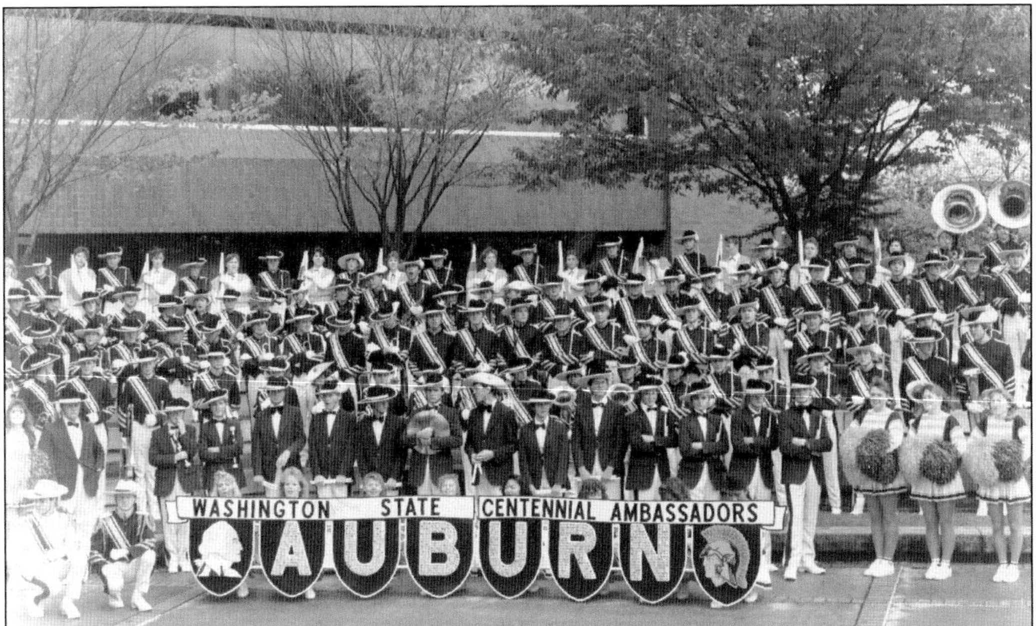

The Washington State Centennial Ambassadors was a marching band made up mostly of students from Auburn High School. Their banner, seen here, shows images of George Washington on the left and a Trojan, the high school's mascot, on the right. The band was part of Auburn's celebration of the Washington State centennial in 1989.

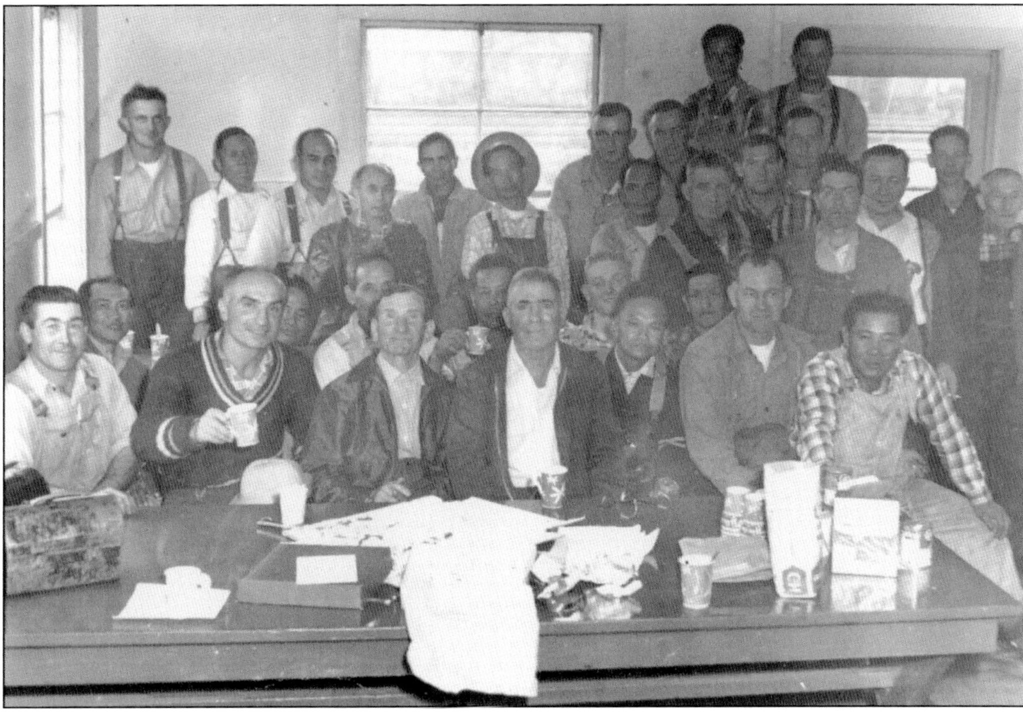

With the expansion of the highway system, trains became less important for moving people in Auburn and became a strictly freight enterprise. Despite these changes, experienced railroad workers were still valuable employees to the railroad companies. In this 1964 image, a section crew at the Auburn Yard poses in their lunchroom.

In 1967, the Auburn Yard office received its first computer. It was quite large, requiring an entire trailer to transport and house it, and it was located near the main yard office. Seen here inside the computer trailer are Northern Pacific railroad employees, from left to right, Robert Ainsworth, Antonio Tamburello, and Rodger Campbell.

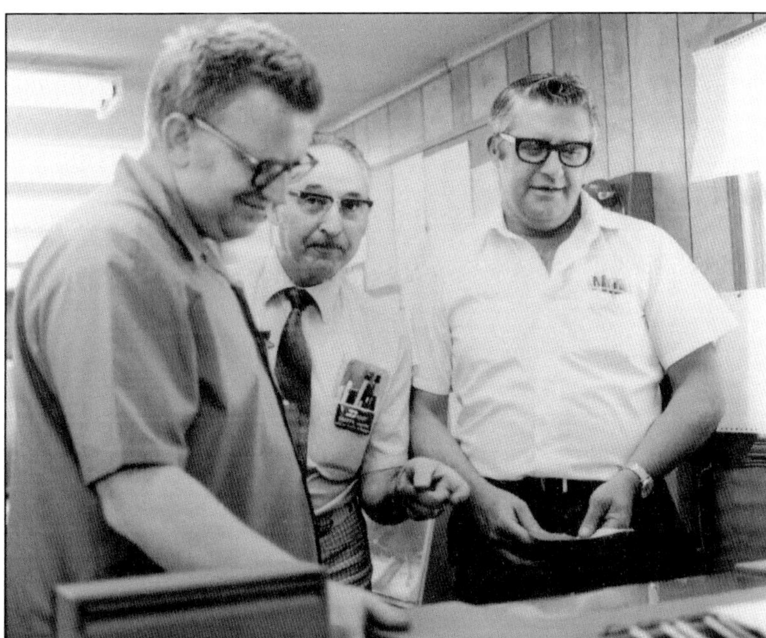

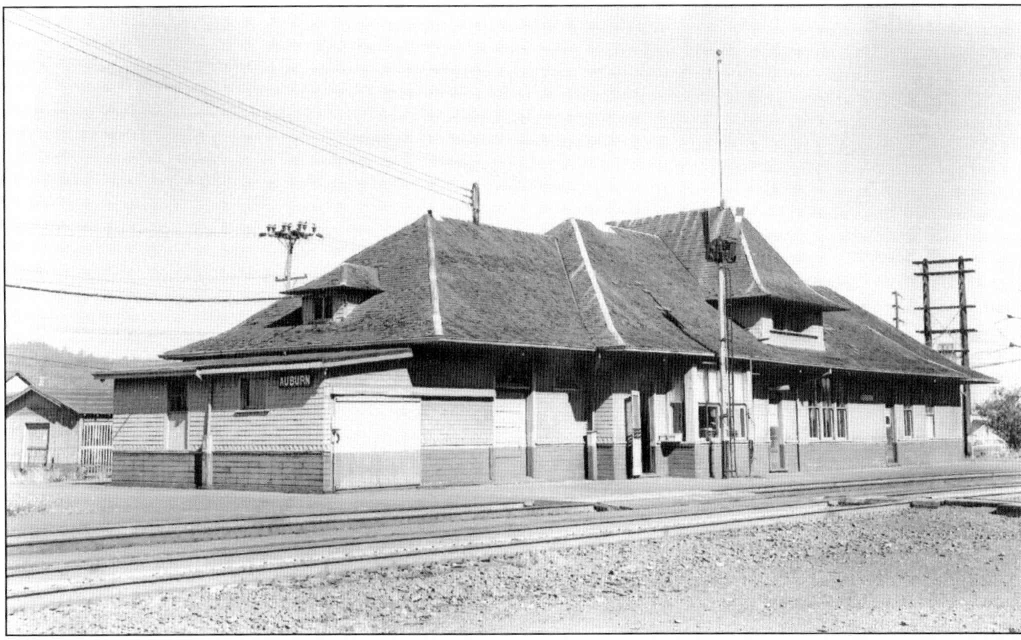

In 1970, the Northern Pacific Railroad merged with three other major railroads to form the Burlington Northern Railroad. The Auburn station, seen here at the time of the merger, continued to be used by the Burlington Northern Railroad as an office, but it was never again the bustling station it had been in a previous era.

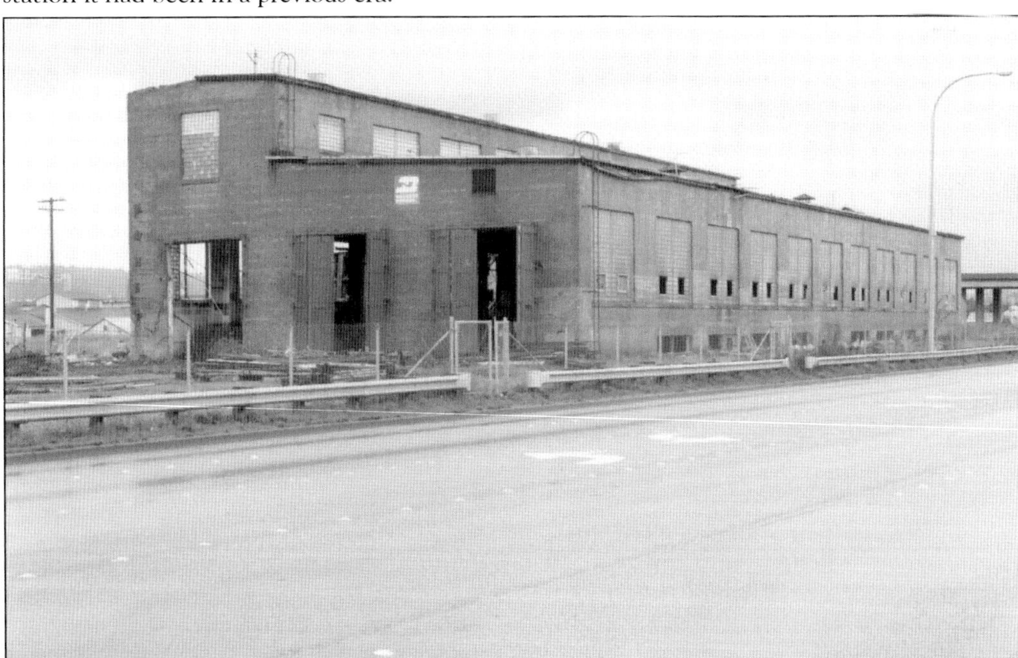

One of the last vestiges of Auburn's earlier generations of railroads disappeared when the Northern Pacific (now the Burlington Northern) diesel house was demolished in 1987. The brick structure was used for 43 years to house and repair diesel locomotives. The Burlington Northern logo can be seen above the right doorways.

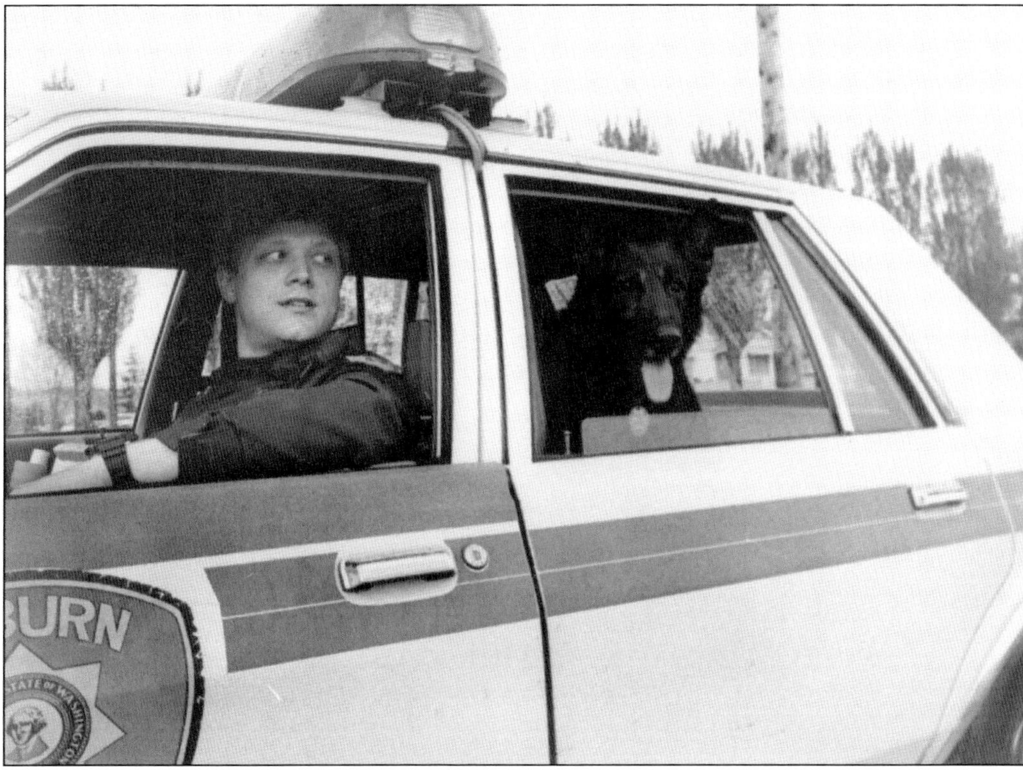

In the 1980s, the Auburn Police Department was able to add specialized units thanks to increases in police budgets and cooperation with neighboring police departments. Above, officer Jim Kelly rides with Auburn's German Shepherd K-9 officer, Judge. Below, city and police officials pose in front of a Drug Abuse Resistance Education (DARE) vehicle. The DARE program began in 1983 and quickly spread throughout the country, encouraging police officers to go into schools and teach a zero-tolerance policy toward drug and alcohol use. Despite its initial popularity, the program was not effective at its goals and faced criticism in the late 1990s and 2000s.

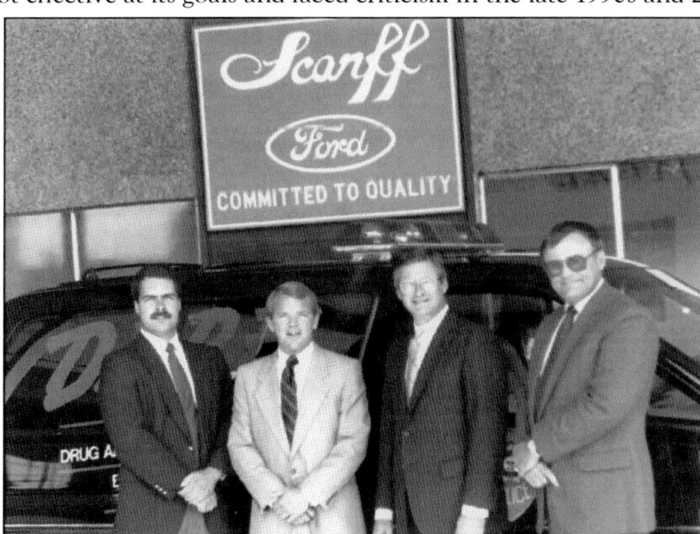

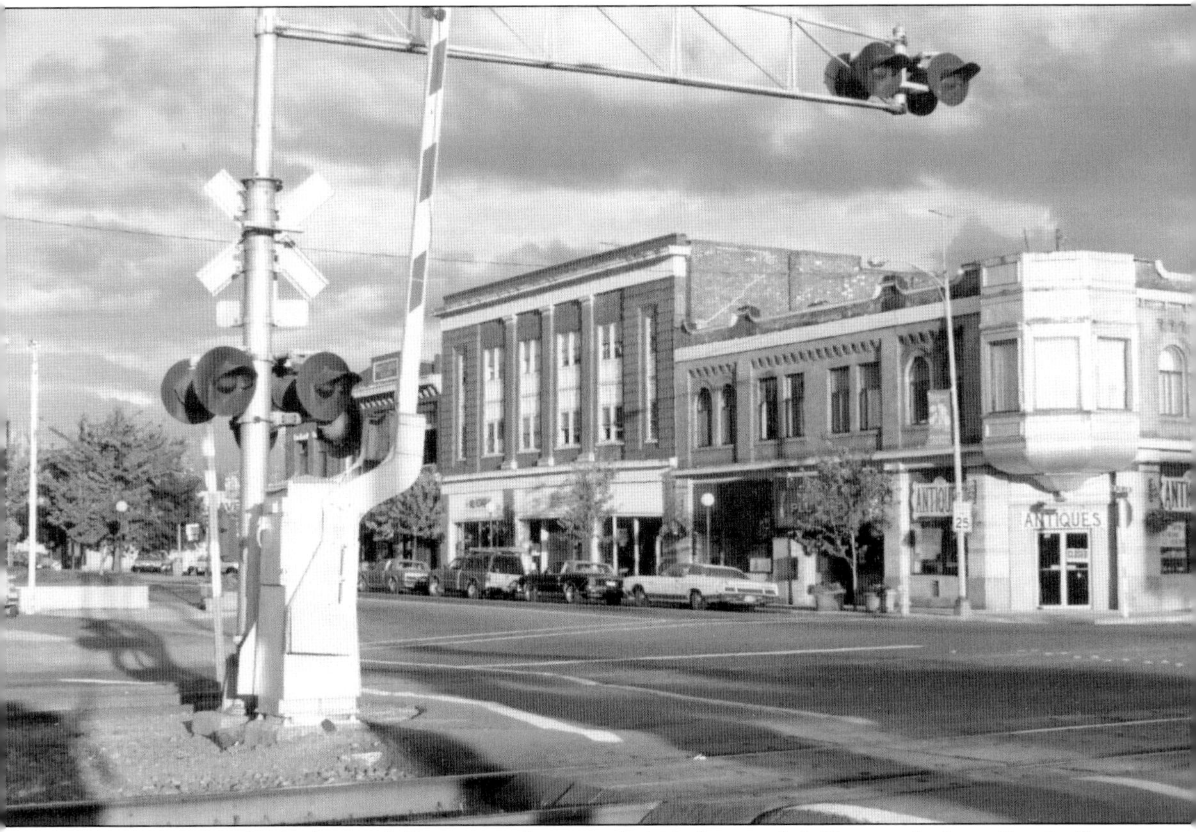

Main Street looked very different on the eve of 1990 than it did 30 years before. City hall was now on its own block of West Main Street, the trains that rolled through downtown carried cargo instead of commuters, and industrial companies had replaced agriculture as the major employer of Auburn's citizens. The electrical lines that once crisscrossed overhead had been completely replaced by underground lines, and new city ordinances regarding business signage created a less crowded downtown image. This 1989 photograph, taken on the corner of B Street Northwest and West Main Street, shows the original facade of the Tourist Hotel on the right, though it had been converted into an antiques store by the 1980s. The coming decades would see more ups and downs for Auburn, but Main Street would remain at the city's heart.

Eight

AUBURN INTO THE 21ST CENTURY 1990–2013

Like most suburban American cities, Auburn's march into the 21st century has been paved with questions about a changing economy, population, and workforce. By the 1990s, Auburn had become somewhat less of an independent city and more of a traditional suburb; many of its residents commuted outside of the city to work, while an increasing number of its workers were commuting into Auburn from cities around the region.

New groups of immigrants began to come to the Auburn area, especially Latino immigrants but also significant populations from the Ukraine and Somalia, with each group opening businesses, churches, and other facilities to serve their communities. As with each previous wave of immigrants, some racist elements have raised concerns over new ethnic groups "stealing jobs" or contributing to crime rates, but in reality, these new immigrants have done what all other immigrants before them have done: established homes, raised families, and contributed to the rich diversity of the King County population.

Downtown Auburn saw a slump in commerce due to the loss of several large anchor stores, but commercial ventures on the outskirts of town began to make up for it. The Supermall of the Great Northwest opened in Auburn with much fanfare in 1995, though the shopping center found it difficult to compete for sales with other regional indoor malls. In 2012, the mall was purchased by a new ownership group that made significant renovations and reopened the mall as The Outlet Collection in 2013.

Other entertainment opportunities came to Auburn in the 1990s and 2000s, bringing with them jobs and prosperity, especially for the Native Americans in the Muckleshoot Indian Tribe. The Muckleshoot Casino opened in 1995, providing a much-needed revenue stream for the tribe. With profits from the casino, the tribe was able to build several new facilities for tribal members, most notably the Muckleshoot Tribal School, where native students could receive a quality education and aid in the resuscitation of their native language, Whulshootseed. Emerald Downs, a horse racing track, opened just east of Auburn in 1996 and was purchased by the tribe in 2002.

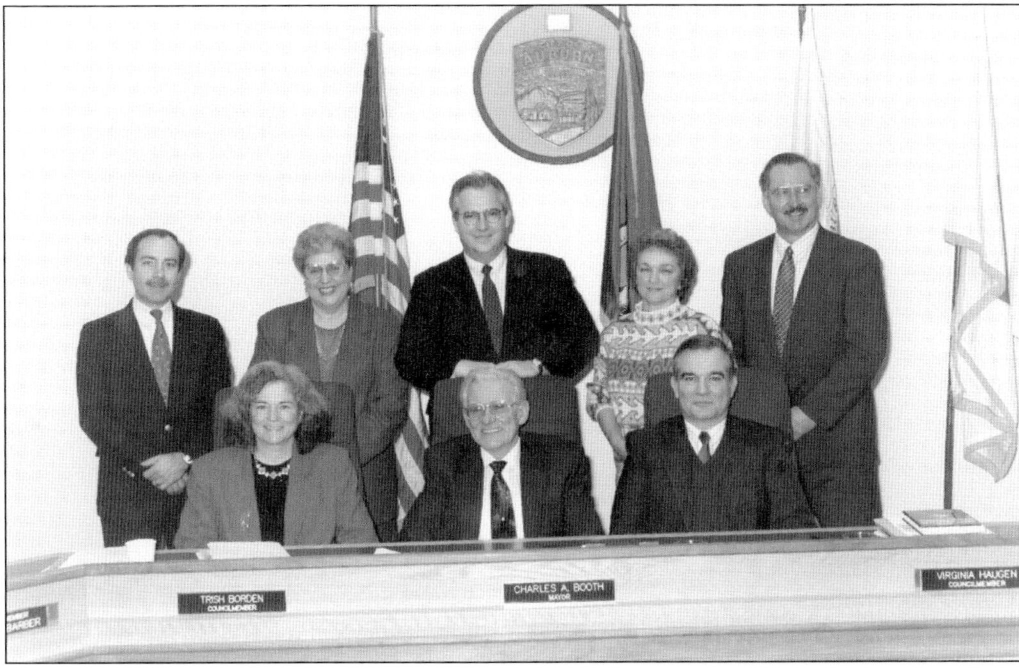

The 1990s saw a significant increase in the number of women working in all departments of Auburn city government. In 1999, three of the seven positions on the city council were held by women. The city council poses here with Auburn mayor Charles A. "Chuck" Booth in the council chambers at city hall.

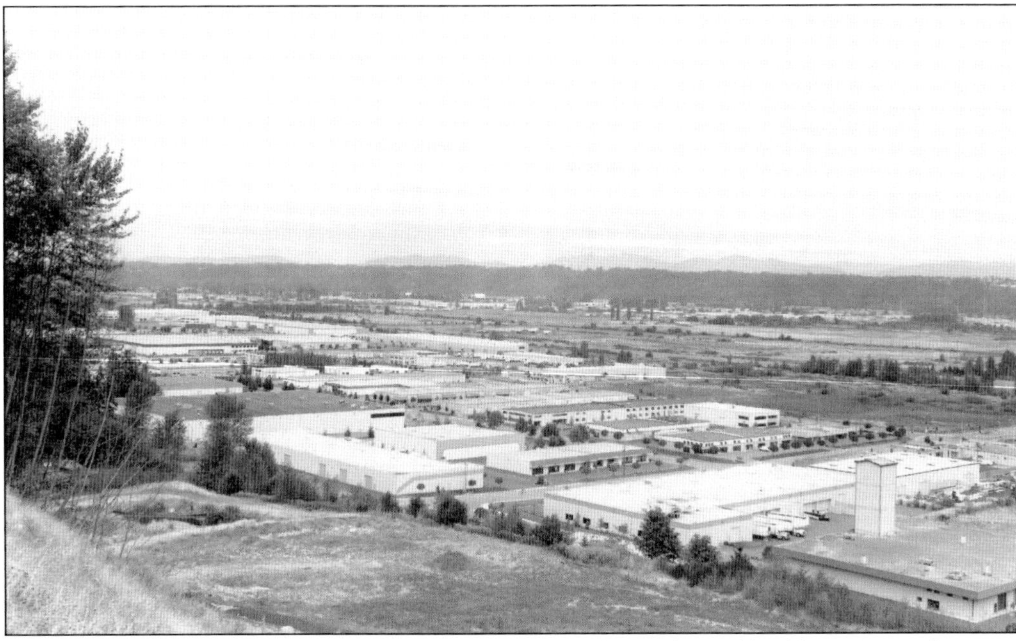

By the 1990s, the west side of Auburn was largely devoted to industrial buildings. Ease of access to several highways combined with affordable land on the valley floor encouraged many manufacturers to expand their operations in Auburn. This 1993 photograph shows a span of warehouses in north Auburn, close to the Emerald Downs racetrack.

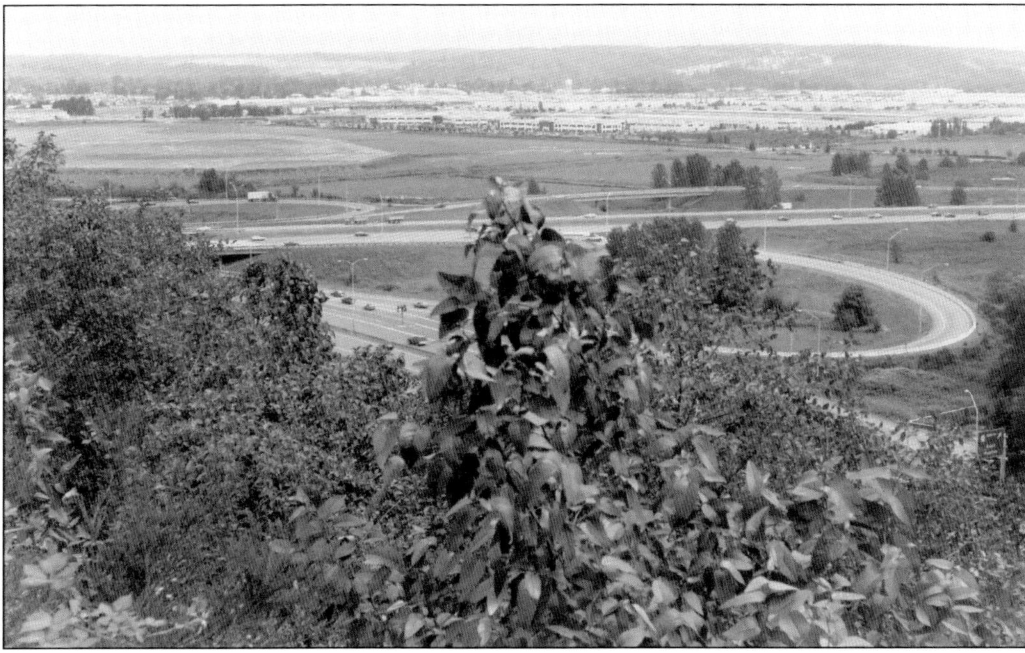

The Supermall of the Great Northwest chose to build on a site between Fifteenth Street and Highway 18 in west Auburn in the early 1990s, seen above before construction. Auburn residents had mixed feelings about the mall; some applauded the new jobs the mall would bring while others worried about the negative impact a mall could have on already struggling downtown retailers. The Supermall opened to great fanfare in the summer of 1995 after several delays and financial problems. One of its flashiest anchor stores, Incredible Universe (below), had lines out the door on opening day. Sadly, the Supermall found it difficult to compete with other area shopping malls. Incredible Universe closed in 1997, and other anchor stores followed suit.

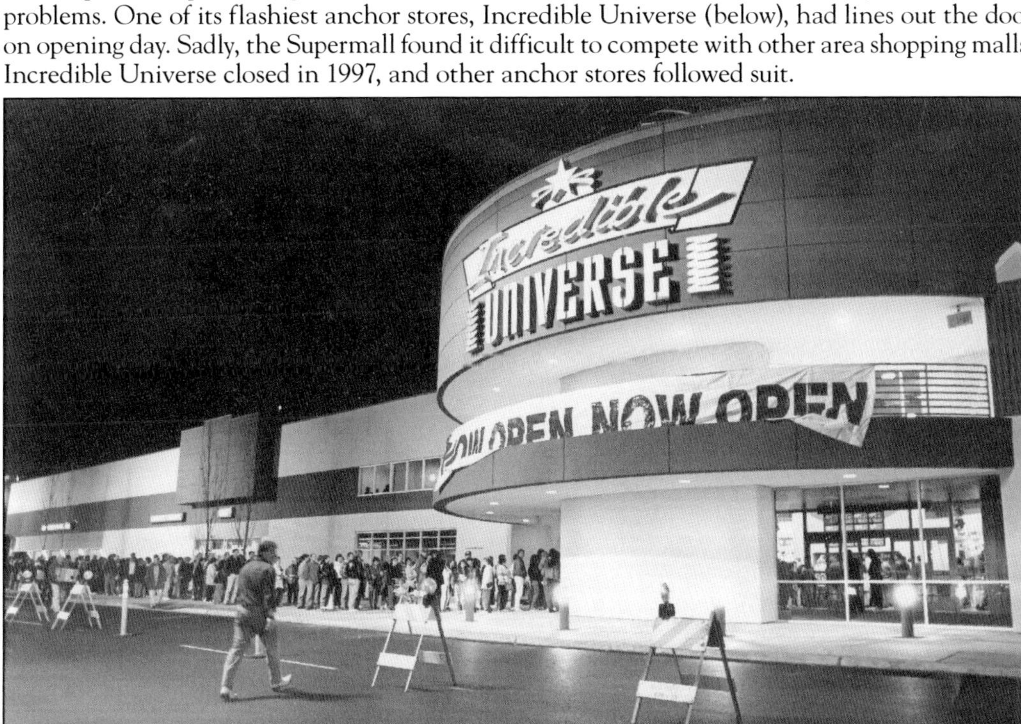

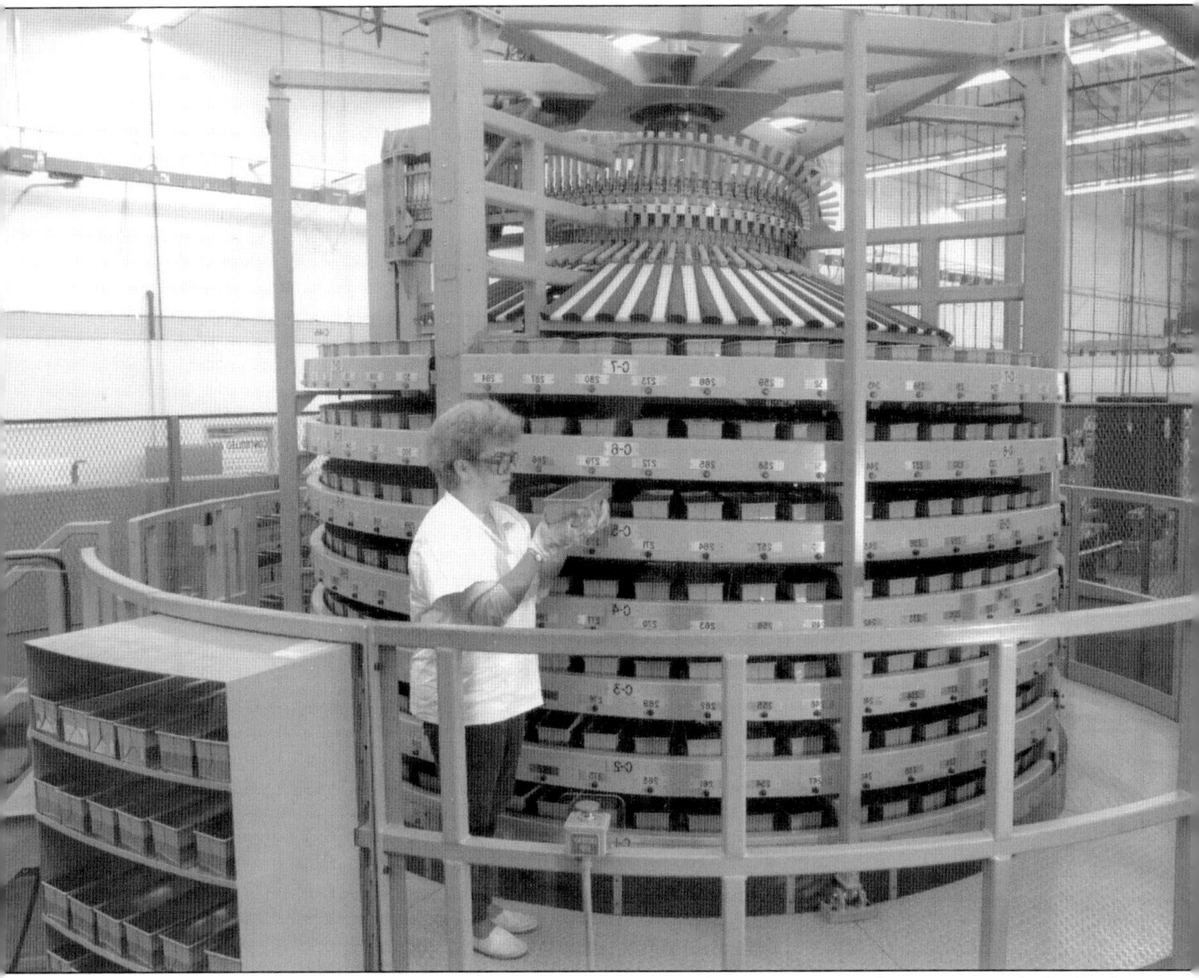

Boeing continued to operate its plant in Auburn, seen here in 1990, where it provided jobs for thousands of Auburn residents. In the fall of 1995, members of the machinists union went on strike for higher wages and better job security. The strike lasted for 69 days, and emotions ran high on all sides. One Auburn man was a victim of retaliatory arson when he crossed the picket line in November. In an unrelated incident, 28 Auburn plant employees were hospitalized after being exposed to a cloud of toxic gas that was accidentally released by inexperienced supervisors while workers walked the picket line outside. Many Auburn retailers also suffered, as striking laborers declined to spend as much money as usual during the holiday season. Everyone in Auburn was happy to see the machinists go back to work in December 1995.

Cavanaugh Hardware was one of the longest-lasting businesses in Auburn. First opened in 1887, the hardware store continued to be family-run until its closing in 2008. Pat Cavanaugh, seen here in 1999, and his wife, Jan, owned the store and maintained a friendly, hometown atmosphere with their customers.

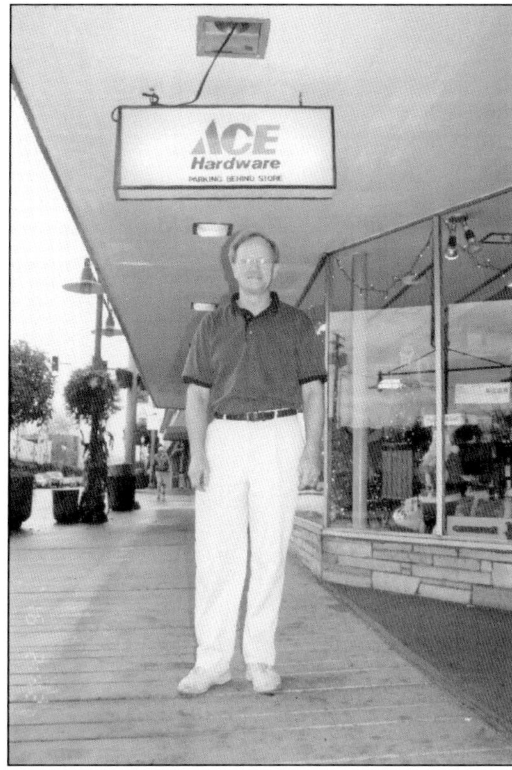

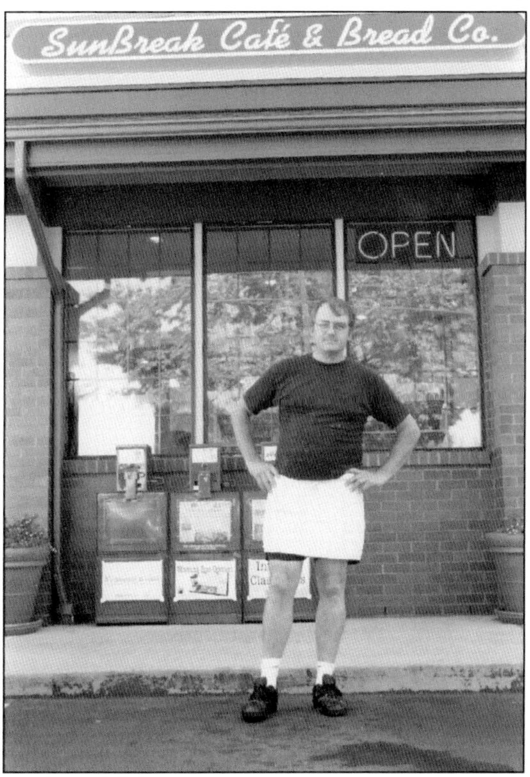

The Sunbreak Café put Auburn on the food map in the 2000s when Seattle food critics began writing reviews of the hardworking bakery and favorite breakfast spot. Opened in 1982 by Bruce Alverson and seen here in 1999, the Sunbreak is best known for its banana breads and generous portions.

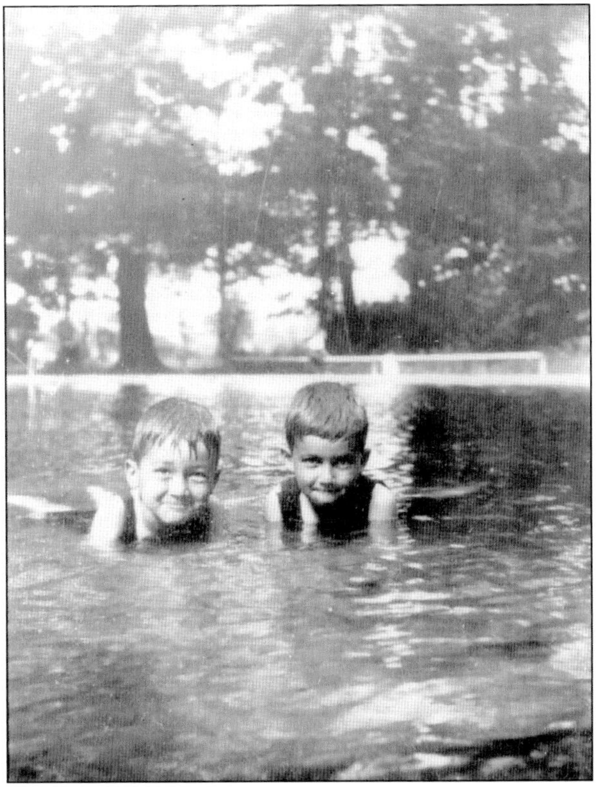

Auburn's City Park, seen to the right being enjoyed in the 1930s, was lauded as one of the most modern parks in King County when it opened in 1926. It was Auburn's second and largest public park, located close to downtown Auburn, city hall, and other city services on E Street. Several large artifacts have been displayed in the park, including a steam engine and a Nike missile. In 2000, the memorial below was erected in the center of the park, and the park was renamed Veteran's Memorial Park. A community center was built in the park in early 2007 to house the Auburn offices of the Department of Veterans Affairs, the American Legion post, and a public hall for rentals and community events.

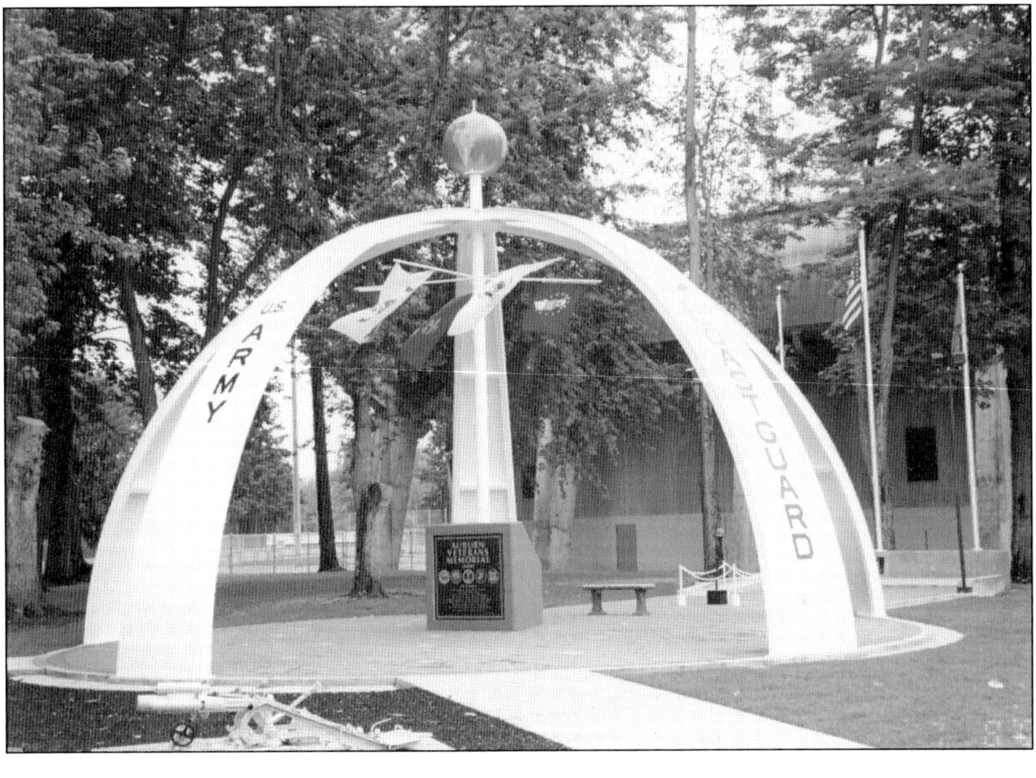

Bibliography

Andrews, Mildred Tanner. *The First 100 Years: Auburn School District*. Auburn, WA: Auburn School District Centennial Committee, 1996.

Bagley, Clarence B. *History of King County, Vol. 1*. Chicago: S.J. Clarke Publishing Co., 1929.

Crowley, Walt. "Interurban Rail Transit in King County and the Puget Sound Region." www.historylink.org. Last modified September 19, 2000.

Densho. "About the Incarceration." www.encyclopedia.densho.org/history. Last modified 2012.

Elliot, James. "Green River Valley Clay Becomes Architectural Terra Cotta: Meade Pottery & the Northern Clay Company 1905 to 1927." *White River Journal*, July 1996.

Flewelling, Stan. *Farmlands: The Story of Thomas, A Small Agricultural Community in King County, Washington*. Auburn, WA: Erick Sanders Historical Society, 1990.

Flewelling, Stan. "Auburn Area Churches." *White River Journal*, October 2002.

Harmon, Alexandra. *Indians in the Making: Ethnic Relations and Indian Identities Around Puget Sound*. Berkeley, CA: University of California Press, 1998.

Koch, Joe. *Lieut. W.A. Slaughter: Frontier Soldier*. Auburn, WA: Joe and Alice Koch, 1991.

Marshman, Michelle. "Go For Broke: The All Japanese 442nd Infantry Regiment." *White River Journal*, January 2006.

Scarff, Bob. "Auburn Our Story: Bob Scarff." YouTube video. Posted by "watchauburn," June 1, 2010. www.youtube.com/watch?v=aDVEamBYc6M

Sprau, David T. "How Auburn Became a Railroading Town, Part I: Featuring the Northern Pacific's Palmer Cutoff." *White River Journal*, January 2002.

Stein, Alan J. "Flood submerges South King County beginning on November 14, 1906." www.historylink.org. Last modified September 23, 2001.

Suttles, Wayne and B. Lane, eds. "Southern Coast Salish." Handbook of North American Indians, Vol. 7. Washington, DC: Smithsonian Institution, 1990.

Vine, Josephine Emmons. *Auburn: A Look Down Main Street*. Auburn, WA: The City of Auburn, 1990.

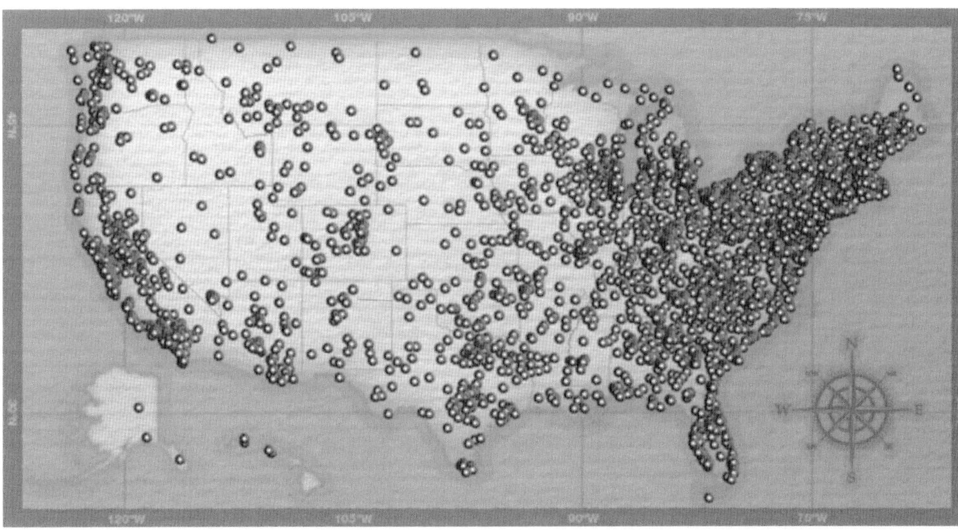